To Make Another World

Studies in protest and collective action

D1474597

Edited by

COLIN BARKER
PAUL KENNEDY

HN
17.5
.T6x
1996
West

Avebury

Aldershot • Brookfield USA • Hong Kong • Singapore • Sydney

© Colin Barker and Paul Kennedy 1996

All rights reserved. No part of this publication may be reproduced, stored in a retrieval system, or transmitted in any form or by any means, electronic, mechanical, photocopying, recording or otherwise without the prior permission of the publisher.

Published by
Avebury
Ashgate Publishing Limited
Gower House
Croft Road
Aldershot
Hants GU11 3HR
England

Ashgate Publishing Company
Old Post Road
Brookfield
Vermont 05036
USA

British Library Cataloguing in Publication Data

To Make Another World: Studies in Protest and
Collective Action
    I. Barker, Colin II. Kennedy, Paul T.
    303.484

ISBN 1 85972 326 8

Library of Congress Catalog Card Number: 95-83279

Printed and bound by Athenaeum Press, Ltd.,
Gateshead, Tyne & Wear.

Contents

vi

About the authors

Paul Bagguley, a Lecturer in sociology at the University of Leeds, is author of *From Protest to Acquiesence? Political Movements of the Unemployed*, Macmillan, 1991, and co-author of *Restructuring: Place Class and Gender*, Sage, 1990. He is joint convenor with Colin Barker of the British Sociological Association study-group on 'Protest and Social Movements'.

Colin Barker, a Senior Lecturer in sociology at Manchester Metropolitan University, is author of *Festival of the Oppressed: Solidarity, Reform and Revolution in Poland, 1980-1981*, 1986 and edited *Revolutionary Rehearsals*, 1987. He is an editor of *A Socialist History of Britain*, a book series produced by the Northern Marxist Historians Group in association with Pluto Press; and is joint convenor, with Paul Bagguley, of the British Sociological Association study-group on 'Protest and Social Movements'.

Sue Clegg is a Principal Lecturer and Research Fellow at Leeds Metropolitan University where she runs a research methodology course for post-graduate research students, and organizes research supervisor training. Her research interests are in feminism and research methodology, and has recently undertaken work on child sexual abuse. She is a member of the editorial group for *A Socialist History of Britain*, produced by the Northern Marxist Historians Group and Pluto Press.

Chik Collins is based at the University of Paisley. He is currently completing a PhD on the way in which working class groups receive and respond to the implementation of significant social changes which affect their lives, and has authored a number of articles, book-chapters and reports on this theme.

Gareth Dale is currently completing a PhD on social movements in East Germany at the University of Manchester. During 1989, as an English literature tutor in Potsdam, he participated in the East German democracy movement. He has published several articles on social movements in East Germany, and on identity politics.

Nick Howard lectures in sociology in the Division of Adult Continuing Education at the University of Sheffield. He has published articles on the impact of the post-Armistice food blockade of Germany in the run-up to the 1919 Peace Treaty, on an oral history of the Weimar years from Wilhelm Necker, revolutionary and later finance director of the Bauhaus, and on the role of the social democratic parties during the German revolution.

Alan Johnson is head of Contemporary Political Studies at Edge Hill College of Higher Education, is co-author of *Growing Old and Needing Care,* Avebury, 1995.

Paul Kennedy is a Senior Lecturer in the Department of Sociology and Interdisciplinary Studies at Manchester Metropolitan University. His research interests are in Third World development studies and issues relating to social change and environmental problems. His publications to date have mostly been in the field of economic change in Sub-Saharan Africa: eg *African Capitalism, the Struggle for Ascendancy,* Cambridge UP, 1988.

Jonathan Purkis is a doctoral student and part-time lecturer in sociology at Manchester Metropolitan University. He is engaged in an ethnographic study of the radical environmental protest group, Earth First! He writes for and is on the editorial board of the journal *Anarchist Studies* and is currently co-editing a book on contemporary anarchist culture and politics. Also a part-time musician, he lives in a Pennine village near Huddersfield.

P.A.J. Waddington, Professor of Sociology at the University of Reading, is author of *The Strong Arm of the Law, Calling the Police,* and *Liberty and Order* as well as numerous articles on policing and police work. In 1992 he led an international inquiry into the policing of the Boipatong massacre in South Africa and advised the Goldstone Commission on the Causes and Prevention of Public Violence and Intimidation on reform of South African public order law and policing policies.

1 Introduction

Colin Barker

The essays in this volume originated as contributions to a lively and multi-stranded conference on 'Alternatives Futures and Popular Protest' at Manchester Metropolitan University in April 1995.

The study of protest and collective action is more established on academic agendas in the United States and in Europe than in Britain. This is perhaps slightly odd, given the extensive contemporary and historical significance of these issues in the making and remaking of British society. For if the academic study of popular protest is relatively underdeveloped, the phenomenon itself is widespread, as a glance at any week's national and local news reveals. Behind, and interwoven with, the formal oppositions of official politics run myriad strands of locally, nationally and internationally focussed protest activities, formal and informal. Neighbours in a street organize a petition or a temporary blockade of a busy road after a child is injured; thousands of people participate in efforts to defend the welfare of veal calves; the testing of atomic weapons on a remote Pacific atoll becomes the occasion for a multitude of protests across the globe.

Processes of social transformation within capitalist society regularly throw existing patterns of life and moral assumptions into confusion, inviting forms of resistance and the elaboration of alternatives. A number of these pressures are registered in the essays here: the impact of workplace closures and de-industrialization on particular workforces (Collins) and also on whole urban regions (Johnson); state attempts to shift the burden of taxation (Bagguley) and to rationalize welfare provision (Barker); growing rifts between popular aspirations and existing political and social systems (Dale

1

and Clegg); the social disasters imposed by imperialist war (Howard); growing perceptions of threat to the environment (Kennedy and Purkis).

The literature on social movements is essentially concerned with the creative responses groups make to the problems that capitalist development generates for them, as they search for means to control the potentially devastating effects on their lives of changes imposed from above and outside, and as they envision alternatives. Its subject-matter is thus central to problems of contemporary social and political practice.

A number of interrelated themes are woven into these essays. One of these is the widespread existence of oppositional ideas within modern society. As Bagguley suggests, perhaps the largest and most effective single protest movement in postwar Britain, the campaign against the poll tax, was underpinned by a 'moral economy' of the kind that Edward Thompson (1971) detected within eighteenth century food riots. This 'complex *bricolage* of individual and collective sentiments and rationalities' is generated and sustained as a shared if often subterranean set of critical popular responses to everyday inequalities of power.

A 'moral economy' may seem to be a relatively fixed set of collectively shared prejudices. But, constructed as it is from shifting daily experience and remade and reinforced through informal networks, a moral economy is subject to continual innovation. Additional themes appear within what Clegg terms 'the common sense of an era'. Among those registered in these essays are the shifting evaluation of the place and rights of women (and men) and the relations between them, and a deepening anxiety about environmental issues which underlies the movements discussed here by Kennedy and Purkis.

At any one time, overt political behaviour may be a poor guide to these structures of evaluation, feeling and aspiration. Often existing as what Scott (1990) terms 'hidden transcripts', they have the capacity, seen clearly in Dale's account of the autumn and winter of 1989 in former East Germany, to erupt into the public arena with devastating power. Or, as in Howard's fascinating historical recovery, they can quietly undermine a whole imperial military machine. The study of social movements tends to throw into question those accounts of social order which treat it as the product of value consensus. Here, submission to authority seems more fragile, resting more on pragmatic judgements of the current risks of open expression of desire, given an awareness of unfavourable power balances and dispositions of forces.

The study of social movements deals with slippery objects. Marwell and Oliver declare, with reason, that defining the term 'social movement' is a 'theoretical nightmare' (1984, pp.4-5). Clegg's discussion of the women's movement in Britain distinguishes between broad and narrow definitions, recognizing that each contains its own partial truth. Too often, we 'know' movements through their public spokespeople and activists; only occasionally, as in Dale's account of the homemade banners and the informal editing of popular slogans within the insurgent crowds in Leipzig, do we get to hear the voices of the 'rank and file' — and thus, also, to estimate the relation between those voices and those of the recognised oppositionists. Nor are the boundaries between 'movements' as neat and tidy as theory might hope: is Earth First!, in Purkis's essay, part of the history of environmental protest, or of anarchism? Questions like these pose practical issues for participants in movements. For they involve dilemmas and arguments about movement meanings and identities, about the relation between specific protests and larger narratives and theories. Within movements, different tendencies contend over such matters as the degree to which issues should be 'isolated' or 'generalized' (as in Barker's discussion of a community protest), and thus about movements' forms, direction and leaderships. Such internal arguments surface in various forms in a number of these essays.

There is a distance between the existence of a 'moral economy' and its actual expression in a practical movement. If the moral economy (a critical aspect of popular commonsense) provides intellectual resources on which people may and do draw, its forms of expression are as diverse as human ingenuity. As Bagguley stresses, most of the time (including those moments when it energises collective action) the public disclosure of popular feeling is constrained by another aspect of common sense, which he terms 'informed fatalism'. This duality of everyday political consciousness sets up tricky problems for those who seek to activate and lead movements. Collins explores the processes by which activists work to capture and transform existing linguistic modes which were not originally designed as containers of protest. Dale offers us one image of this: a portrait of Honecker carried on a demonstration against the regime, only now in a parodic-travestying form (on which see Bakhtin, 1981, ch 2). Collins shows us witty communist shop stewards playing with their opponents' language, mocking and converting it into an offensive weapon. (Consider the passage that climaxes in 'Why aren't you standing on your own two feet?') Purkis shows us EF! protestors seizing mahogany tables, thereby seeking to impart comic, and thus realist, distance to commercial goods on the grounds that they are 'stolen property'.

Everyone, remarked Gramsci, in a notable assault on all elitist thinking, is an intellectual. But, he added, not everyone has the function of an intellectual (1971, p.9). Those who seek — successfully or not — to perform that function within movements haunt these pages. Ratcliff (1984) argued some years ago that social science should pay more attention to the role of the 'cadre of committed grass-roots level "militants"' we find in every movement. There are no movements without ideas, or without those specific people who seek to embody those ideas in practical organization and activity. Activists of various kinds appear in these pages, as protestors, organizers, representatives (actual and would-be), leaders, speakers, academics, agitators, even ethical business people, all performing that 'intellectual function' which is inherent in all protest activity.

We can understand little about social movements if we ignore the always problematic relations between activists and followers within them. If sometimes — as in the anti-poll tax movement, or Howard's 'shirkers' revolt' — movements seem to us to be spontaneous and leaderless, we are probably admitting that we don't know enough about them to grasp their complex internal dynamics (Goodwyn, 1991). Sometimes, as in these two examples, a movement can be effective without any strong central leadership, because the participants hold effective individual sanctions (non-payment, opportunities for desertion) in their hands. In other cases, movement success depends on overt coordination, and immediate individual sanctions are less available. This characterised the situation facing the campaigners against hospital closure in Barker's study. In such circumstances, issues concerning what leading cadres of movements say and do, and how they organize themselves, become more critical. These are themes that appear, variously, in the essays by Clegg, Collins, Dale, Johnson and Purkis. Certainly leaders and their immediate core cadres do more than simply 'represent' movements in an unmediated fashion. Whether successfully or not, they play a creative part in formulating projects, defining goals, responding to antagonists, containing or expanding mobilization. The tasks are always complex, and by no means always adequately achieved, as Johnson's study of Militant's leadership in Liverpool argues. In Dale's account of the East German revolution, the huge crowds in the street demonstrations clearly had aspirations that went well beyond the visions of the middle class New Forum leaders, but never found an adequate leadership and organizational form through which to achieve them. Purkis's study poses a different dilemma: how do those who reject 'leadership' (treating it as embodying the principle of bureaucracy) break out of the relative isolation of 'direct action' politics to reach wider audiences and achieve wider mobilizations?

Most social movements and protests have a clearly defined target and opponents. It is the interaction between movements and the forces they contest that shapes their development. Waddington, in the final essay in this volume, offers a unique study of one element in the structure of movements' opponents: the police. Waddington shows how a theme that appears in Collins' paper on the language of opposition also shapes police responses: they negotiate 'terms' to manage and contain demonstrations and other potential sources of disorder in London, using essentially non-legal means to pursue their own interests in avoiding 'trouble'. Although, as the essays by Howard and Dale also remind us, officialdom is not always so successful.

On one issue in recent debates, that surrounding 'new social movements', the authors here are anything but unified. What is perhaps at issue is what should count as a sign of 'newness': is it the nature of the issues and demands posed by movements, or the character of the surrounding society, or again some characteristic of the movements themselves: their organizational forms, ideas, activities, social compositions, or relations with audiences and antagonists? Some of these essays reveal scepticism about 'newness' claims on many of these dimensions, while others are more inclined to accept and celebrate novelty. In some of the practices of the 'new' movements (witness the essays by Kennedy and Purkis) there are powerful echoes of older traditions, of both the 19th century cooperative and *narodnik* movements.

Social movement theory, like its object of study, is in constant flux and development. We hope that further conferences and publications will extend the theoretical development of some of the themes explored here.

Our particular thanks to Maggy Taylor for her extraordinary assistance in the production of this volume.

References

Bakhtin, M. M. (1981), *The Dialogic Imagination: Four Essays*, University of Texas Press, Austin.

Goodwyn, Lawrence (1991), *Breaking the Barrier: The Rise of Solidarity in Poland*, Oxford University Press, New York.

Gramsci, Antonio (1971), *Selections from the Prison Notebooks*, Lawrence and Wishart, London.

Marwell, Gerald and Oliver, Pamela (1984), 'Collective action theory and social movement research', *Research in Social Movements, Conflict and Change*, Vol.7.

Ratcliff, Richard E. (1984), 'Introduction', *Research on Social Movements, Conflict and Change*, Vol.6.

Scott, James C. (1990), *Domination and the Arts of Resistance: Hidden Transcripts*, Yale University Press, Yale.

Thompson, E. P. (1971), 'The moral economy of the English crowd in the eighteenth century', *Past & Present*, 50, February.

2 The moral economy of anti-poll tax protest

Paul Bagguley

For the first time a government had declared that anyone who could reasonably afford to do so should at least pay something towards the upkeep of the facilities and the provision of the services from which they benefited. A whole class of people — an 'underclass' if you will — had been dragged back into the ranks of responsible society and asked to become not just dependents but citizens ... And the eventual abandonment of the charge represented one of the greatest victories for these people ever conceded by a Conservative Government (Margaret Thatcher, *The Downing Street Years*).

Introduction

Margaret Thatcher's evaluation of the anti-poll tax movement seems remarkably congruent with that of many of those who participated in or have studied the movement in any detail (Burns, 1992; Reynolds, 1992). This is contrary to the major academic assessment of the whole poll tax episode, which largely dismisses the popular mobilization against the tax as having little or no role in its abolition (Butler et al, 1994, pp.297-98). My purpose in this chapter, however, is not to debate the success or otherwise of anti-poll tax protest, as I have argued the point in more detail elsewhere (Bagguley, 1995a and 1995b). What I wish to do here is to examine the mobilization against the poll tax in terms of E. P. Thompson's concept of a moral economy.

The poll tax was proposed by the 1987 Thatcher government as a new form of local tax to replace the rates. The poll tax, or community charge to give it its official name, was a flat rate tax on individual adults. The only concession to the ability to pay was that those on social security benefits, etc. only had to pay a proportion of the standard tax. However, this still meant for many individuals with little or no income that they had to pay local taxes for the first time, and at the same level as those on high incomes. Not surprisingly, with the benefit of hindsight perhaps, the poll tax was actively opposed by millions of people.

In this chapter I shall examine in some detail the underlying moral response to the poll tax that contributed to generating the massive participation in the movement. I shall attempt this through an examination of the political morality of the activists in particular, and through their accounts, that of the participants. The interviews with activists that I draw upon below, were carried out in Leeds in 1990, and further details of these have been published elsewhere (Bagguley, 1995a).[1] Furthermore, much of my argument will go against the grain of many contemporary accounts of class and politics in contemporary societies such as Britain. Briefly, such accounts often suggest that class is no longer a major political issue, that class-based inequalities no longer inform and motivate political action. Often it is asserted on the basis of rather flimsy evidence that class movements have been replaced by 'new social movements', or that consumption now has some kind of priority over production as a politically structuring set of social relations (see for instance Bauman, 1987; Lash and Urry, 1994).

In contrast to some of what is argued in this literature, I find myself in closer affinity with the more empirical Weberian tradition of British sociology, which continually demonstrates the salience of class for voting behaviour and social identities among the working class in Britain (Goldthorpe and Marshall, 1994; Marshall et al 1988). Although largely associated with the Weberian tradition in British sociology the broad concept of 'informed fatalism' also has roots within the Marxian tradition (Abercrombie et al, 1980, pp.165-6). From this kind of analysis I want to develop the idea of 'informed fatalism', where working class protest does not routinely occur due to the perceived immutability of capitalist social relations. This helps to explain the lack of protest prior to, and after the poll tax.

Further, I want to develop some of the themes from this literature in relation to E. P. Thompson's notion of a 'moral economy'. In particular I want to argue that the anti-poll tax movement in part reflects a class consciousness in the form of a moral economy. Broadly my aims are twofold. Firstly, to provide an examination of the moral dimension of opposition to the poll tax, but not one which pretends to be a comprehensive account of what happened and why. Secondly, I want to link together these broader theoretical issues regarding Thompson's moral economy, class consciousness and the possibilities of collective action among the working class in the conditions of contemporary capitalism.

Thompson's moral economy and the poll tax

E. P. Thompson's paper 'The Moral Economy of the English Crowd in the Eighteenth Century' was first published in the journal *Past and Present* in 1971. It has generated much debate among historians, a debate considered in some detail by Thompson himself some twenty years later (Thompson, 1993, pp.259-351). Although apparently widely admired among sociologists, the work has rarely been used and developed by sociologists, and certainly not in relation to contemporary social movements, protest and collective action in the UK. There are many purposes to Thompson's original paper, and I wish to draw upon its arguments selectively for theoretical development. Most of all I want to suggest that the concept of a moral economy is an especially useful way of understanding certain aspects of opposition to and protest against the poll tax. Furthermore, I have a more purely theoretical case to make. In particular I want to begin to open up a theoretical dialogue between Thompson's notion of a moral economy and some wider debates in sociology concerning popular notions of social justice, and the relationship between agency and structure in the explanation of protest and collective action. Although Thompson has warned against extending the concept of the moral economy, he has pointed approvingly to some alternative applications, and has cited the 1984 miners strike as a recent example of a moral economy being mobilized in opposition to 'free market' forces (Thompson, 1993, p.340).

One of Thompson's principal polemical targets in his paper was the economistic explanation of Eighteenth century 'food riots'. He argued, and showed in considerable empirical detail, that crowd action was motivated by something more than economic necessity. Economic factors were a necessary, but insufficient, explanation for the observed patterns of riotous behaviour around food prices. He suggested that:

> ... the men and women in the crowd were informed by the belief that they were defending traditional rights or customs; and, in general, that they were supported by the consensus of the community ... it is true of course that the riots were triggered off by soaring prices, by the malpractices among dealers or hunger. But these grievances operated within a popular consensus as to what were legitimate and what were illegitimate practices in marketing, milling, baking, etc. This in turn was grounded upon a traditional view of social norms and obligations, of the proper economic functions of several parties within the community, which, taken together, can be said to constitute the moral economy of the poor. An outrage to these moral assumptions, quite as much as actual deprivation, was the usual occasion for direct action (Thompson, 1993 p.188).

The moral economy might be said to be the cultural mechanism not only providing an extra-economic motivation for collective action among the poor, but also one that regulated 'the market', and the political relations between the ruling classes and their subordinates. However, I want to suggest that the poll tax violated what is seen in Britain as what is legitimate and what is illegitimate in terms of taxation. What Thatcher described as 'dragging the underclass into citizenship' violated people's notions of what was acceptable, and indeed affordable. What was previously a political market, a regime of taxation regulated by a moral imperative around the economic ability to pay, became a free market where everyone was to be forced to pay. As the activists that I interviewed argued:

> I think basically it was the extra cost that got people up in arms ... and the fact that the rich people were getting off lightly and they were having to pay more, the so called poor people, that was what they objected to strongly and a lot of them said: 'if people are entitled to housing benefit and rates benefit on the basis of ability to pay they should get some sort of poll tax benefit' and they weren't gettin' it. I think that was it and the fact that

everybody who seemed to speak at rallies used to quote the Earl of Harewood, you know, it's going to cost him something like £700 per year for his 4,000 acres of big mansion, and there are people living down here in this two-bedroomed house who are going to have to pay twice as much. I think that got home to a lot of people, because that more or less came out at every meeting that we went to ... the difference between the rich people and their big houses and the poor people in the small houses (Halton Moor).

I think initially it was the high cost for most people, I also think that there was also a very big element of the unfairness of the tax and that the rich and the poor paid basically the same amount ... the unfairness of it was a very big factor ... I think there are still a lot of people who haven't paid who couldn't pay, and there's no question of them being able to pay in a hundred years, and I think in the majority of people who don't pay that is the case (Bramley).

... the majority of people who are involved in our campaign cannot afford to pay it, right, and the need to defend each other against the consequences of not paying. I think moral outrage goes hand in hand with that, it you see that you are worse off, and everyone else in your area is worse off ... Then of course there is a feeling of moral outrage that what is happening is wrong (Leeds Fed. Secretary)

So far I have been concerned to show how opposition to the poll tax was an expression of an underlying moral evaluation of the poll tax's principles, and that this interpretation is roughly congruent with some aspects of Thompson's account of the moral economy. However, Thompson further suggests that the legitimation of a particular mode of collective action was also sanctioned by the moral economy:

... for the popular ethic sanctioned direct action by the crowd, whereas the values of order underpinning the paternalist model emphatically did not (Thompson, 1993, p.212).

There are two aspects of this argument one can examine in relation to the poll tax. Firstly, one can see the response of the Labour Party and the Trades Union leaderships as a paternalist one these terms.

11

They vigorously opposed the poll tax, apparently in concurrence with the values of the moral economy opposed to the poll tax. Yet they equally vigorously opposed the idea of encouraging non-payment, or actively supporting those who did no pay for whatever reason (Bagguley, 1995a, p.11). In some localities Labour-led councils equally vigorously prosecuted people for non-payment (Reynolds, 1992, p.155). Secondly, non-payment was popularly sanctioned, at least in those places where it was widespread:

> ... if you went on that estate and knocked on any door and said 'Have you paid your poll tax?' they'd say 'No, I'm not fuckin' payin' it either'. I mean none of them are paying it ... (Gipton).

> ... people say 'Oh no well the rest of the street aren't going to pay I can afford to pay but stuff it I'm not going to, I'll save some money', but I think the overwhelming majority of people round here who said they weren't going to pay it ... simply could not afford it (Belle Isle).

> ... you thought you were isolated but then you'd be talking to people 'Oh I haven't paid' ... you'd be in a street 'Have you paid it?' and he says 'No course not' ... (Tinshill).

These accounts from activists are supported by both opinion poll data on opposition to the tax, attendance at demonstrations, as well as official figures on the level of non-payment (Bagguley, 1995a, pp.21-5). Non-payment of the poll tax, therefore, has a similar status to the riot in Thompson's formulation. Non-payment, as I shall show below, required minimal organization, and was directly comparable to the food riot in these terms. As Thompson argues:

> In truth the food riot did not require a high degree of organization. It required a consensus of support in the community, and an inherited pattern of action with its own objectives and restraints (Thompson, 1993, p.238).

I should, perhaps, refrain from arguing too directly from Thompson at this juncture. It is difficult to identify a widespread action comparable to that of non-payment of the poll tax that provides the basis for the poll tax to be in a direct lineage of popular protest in the same sense as the food riots examined by Thompson. As a particular tactic food riots occurred time and time again. However, the same cannot be said of non-payment of the poll tax. It simply cannot be seen as a form of routine popular protest in this sense. Rent strikes on council estates perhaps form one obvious comparison. But to push the comparisons any further at this point would be to overemphasize continuity and tradition in forms of protest as against the invention and initiative specific to particular political opportunities. Nevertheless, it is the ease of organization of specific forms of protest action that deserve attention. As the activists that I interviewed suggested:

> ... people would just sit at home and not pay. They didn't come out and be active and do things. So whilst at first it drew a lot of people in, I think eventually people just thought 'well I'm not payin' it, I've done my bit' ... (Burley).

> ... it's all about people sort of feeling 'well there's nothing you can do' ... and then you try to make people think 'well yes there is something you can do', you oppose it. And that's where the poll tax's strength has been as well because it's been very easy, it's very easy not to pay it, I mean ... you know, you can oppose this, you do nothing, you just do nothing, it's so simple isn't it, you haven't got to do anything ... (Gipton).

What these activists are identifying in the instance of the non-payment aspect of opposition to the poll tax is both the ease of a certain kind of significant opposition — non-payment — and a certain reluctance to participate publicly in meetings and demonstrations. Whereas 200,000 people demonstrating in central London in April 1990 and 22,000 people participating in fifty or more local demonstrations in the early months of 1990 (Bagguley, 1995a, pp.21-22) is quite impressive, it was only the tip of the iceberg. The vast majority of opposition was effectively 'private'. Sitting at home and doing nothing.

This illustrates some important issues. Staying at home and doing nothing in not paying was, as we have seen, widely and publicly sanctioned. Yet it demonstrates a clear difference from the phenomena that Thompson was examining, which were very public occasions of protest. They had their material consequences through public collective action. Non-payment of the poll tax demonstrates the potential of what one may paradoxically term 'privatized collective action'. Perhaps the instance of the poll tax shows that the moral economy can have a private as well as a public expression. However, this is not to argue that the protest was entirely 'privatized'. Such 'private' individual protest was only possible on a mass scale because people acted in the knowledge that many other people were not paying. Furthermore, as I have argued elsewhere, in Leeds at least the vast majority of households were effectively informed of their rights, and of the legal risks they faced as non-payers, by the local anti-poll tax unions (Bagguley, 1995b, p.716). This directly contradicts the arguments of Butler et al, who insist on the paradox that whilst the non-payment campaign was ineffective in their view, the 'fact of non-payment in inner-city areas undoubtedly helped undermine the poll tax' (Butler et al, 1994, p.298). Consequently, I believe that these apparently isolated, individual, privatized acts of non-payment really had an organized collective base. Effective political organization made a significant difference.

Thompson further highlights the under-development of the political character of food riots supported by the moral economy. He argues that they were:

> ... a pattern of social protest which derives from a consensus as to the moral economy of the commonweal in times of dearth. It is not usually helpful to examine it for overt, articulate political intentions ... (Thompson, 1993, p.246).

For a core of committed activists in the anti-poll tax movement there clearly were overt political intentions, but for many who participated the intentions may have been more mixed or limited. They may have been limited to outrage at the immorality of the poor having to pay personal taxes, and the immorality of the rich paying the same as those of merely average economic means. Like any social movement the anti-poll tax movement was the expression of a complex *bricolage* of individual and collective sentiments and rationalities. Among activists there were varying degrees and types of political motivation:

> ... it didn't seem fair to me that people who ... could well afford it and were previously paying thousands of pounds would suddenly

14

be subsidized by people who're struggling to live ... and that's what it boiled down to ... It was a totally unfair tax, I mean the whole idea that everybody should contribute something to the services is not, in principle, it's not a bad idea provided it's based on the ability to pay rather than on the basis of everybody pays so much which is all wrong (Halton).

I didn't want to pay the poll tax, I mean crudely speaking it was the notion that somehow this new tax will take from the poor and give to the rich which was quite clearly the intention, and the effect it would have on, you know, loads of friends. Myself in particular, you know, all of a sudden would be expected to pay £350 ... a lot of money was going to be taken from me and given to the rich ... I'm a political person, you know, and I think you get involved in anything that you can see you can potentially mobilize people against what you think is wrong in society. So it's sort of combination of self interest in one sense but also realising that the potential for beating it is there which in the long run I think proved to be the case (Beeston).

Well I suppose it's my Christian faith really, that's the boring answer ... to me the poll tax was like the sort of icing on Thatcher's sort of gruesome cake because ... it takes away people's vote because people will keep off the electoral roll ... it just seems so basically wrong ... it's very easy to talk to people about the poll tax, it's so clear why it's unjust, you know and it just goes against everything I believe in (Gipton).

So even among these politically active individuals, although active for different reasons, there was an underlying sense of moral outrage. Opposition to the poll tax for them was as much a moral issue as one clearly articulated in a political programme.

In his more recent comments on the debate inspired by his original paper, Thompson has expanded somewhat on his earlier discussion. One aspect of this later elaboration of his argument is the way he emphasizes the collective and rational nature of riot as a form of collective action:

... riot is a group, community, or class response to crisis; it is not within the power of a few individuals to riot. Nor need it be the only or the most obvious form of collective action — there may be alternatives such as the mass petitioning of the authorities, fast days, sacrifices and prayer; perambulation of the houses of the rich ... (Thompson, 1993, p.263).

Similarly, with opposition to the poll tax there were many modes of collective action: demonstrations, riots, bill burnings, long distance marches, petitioning, and yes people prayed for an end to the poll tax. Although I do not know of any sacrifices, I would be interested to hear from anyone who happens to know of any! However, what was most effective in my view was simple non-payment, illegal but easy. Thompson further suggests that riot was a rational response to the circumstances he was examining in the eighteenth century, and that riot: '... takes place, not among helpless or hopeless people, but among those groups who sense that they have little power to help themselves ...' (Thompson, 1993, p.265).

In the instance of the poll tax it provided people with an opportunity to 'help themselves'. This is one of the most fundamental things to understand about protest among poor people more generally, they need accessible targets for their actions in order to give them the sense that they can influence events and circumstances in their favour (Bagguley, 1991; Piven and Cloward, 1977). The very nature of the poll tax requiring individuals to positively do something to pay it was precisely its weakness. It set itself up as an easy and realistic target. Whilst it may be rational to do something about one's circumstances, if there is no realistic target that one can reasonably influence then fatalism is the most likely result.

The moral economy as a collective reality

I now wish to examine some more abstract theoretical issues through this consideration of Thompson's work concerning questions of agency and structure in the context of collective action, especially the nature of the moral economy as a collective cultural reality. Thompson has little of direct interest to say about the issue of agency and structure in the texts under discussion here, and he has addressed such questions in more detail in his widely known polemics against structural Marxism and its inheritors (Thompson, 1978).

However, there is one point at which he uses a powerful metaphor to express only one aspect of the structure/agency tension in the context of food riots, where he suggests: '... how ideas presented themselves as actors in the market-place, between producers, middlemen and consumers' (Thompson, 1993, p.275).

The image here is immediately one of ideas acting on people, or acting through them and mediating their relations with others. But this would be to present his argument too simply. Clearly there is a sense in which Thompson is arguing that the moral economy was a collective reality extending across time and space, being reproduced through people's actions and from their collective memories of past events, through their sharing of ideas, arguments, and other every day forms of interaction. There is a sense in which this echoes certain themes in the work of both Durkheim and Giddens. This moral economy was a collective representation, where the relations between producers and consumers, and the level of prices in times of dearth were classified by the poor as in some sense 'sacred'. Thompson seems to imply that the actions of hoarders and sundry other profiteers were seen to pollute that 'sacred idea' through their actions (Thompson, 1993, p.188). This is not to argue that these beliefs are literally religious, but that they act in a similar way to religious beliefs. The moral economy defined clear moral boundaries for acceptable and unacceptable economic actions. Similarly in relation to the poll tax, to tax the poor, as Thatcher attempted to do was a 'profanity' in the popular imagination. As Thompson goes on to argue about the cultural, symbolic and the ethical underpinnings of the moral economy:

Another feature of this culture which is of special interest to me is the priority afforded, in certain areas, to "non economic" over direct monetary sanctions, exchanges and motivations ... Again and again, when examining the behaviour of working people in the eighteenth century one finds it to be necessary to "decode" this behaviour and its symbolic modes of expression and to disclose invisible rules unlike those which a historian of subsequent working-class movements has come to expect (Thompson, 1993, p.11).

No other term seems to offer itself to describe the way in which, in peasant and early industrial communities, many economic relations are regulated according to non-economic norms. These exist as a tissue of customs and usages until they are threatened by monetary rationalizations and are made self-conscious as a "moral economy". In this sense, the moral economy is summoned into being in resistance to the economy of the "free market" ... The rationalizations of "modernizations" of the capitalist market offended against community norms and continually called into being a "moral" antagonist (Thompson, 1993, p.340).

These passages seem both realist and Durkheimian. It seems evidently realist in the reference to disclosing the 'invisible rules' implies a theoretical and analytical labour to describe, resorting to realist language, the underlying structure of the moral economy, and how it generates distinctive effects. That is it has a determinant expression in the behaviour of working people. Similarly the 'tissue of customs' is 'made self-conscious', or the moral economy being 'summoned into being'. All of these ways of thinking seem to me congruent with the British realist tradition of thought (Bhaskar, 1975; Pawson, 1989)

The idea of non-economic regulation of the free market has several Durkheimian resonances. Durkheim wrote of the way in which the modern market is unregulated by social norms, leading to the immorality of anomie in the ceaseless pursuit of insatiable desires, which is only feasible in the apparently limitless field of the free market (Durkheim, 1984, pp.304-5; 1952 pp.246-58). Although it would be rash of me to push such a comparison too far, the similarity between Durkheim's and Thompson's comments regarding the regulation of markets is striking. Finally, the way in which Thompson writes of markets offending 'against community norms' is strikingly similar to Durkheim's analysis of sacred beliefs.

A further implication of this analysis concerns the essential continuity of the 'moral economy' throughout 'modernity'. Although it may change in its particulars, the essential conflict between traditional moral beliefs and the free market morality remains. Thompson, rather like Durkheim's account of the morality of mechanical solidarity, implies a sharp break between the moral economy and the impulses behind subsequent working class movements. Indeed he is sharply critical of attempts to extend his notion of the moral economy to the contemporary working class in some studies (Thompson, 1993, p.341). Further evidence for this view in Thompson's account is the way in which he refers to the moral economy occurring in peasant and early industrial communities (Thompson, 1993, p.340), and the way he distinguishes between the different kinds of analysis required by the historian of food riots compared to the historian of nineteenth century trade unions (Thompson, 1993, p.11). However, as I noted above Thompson did refer to the 1984 miners' strike as an instance of the mobilization of a contemporary moral economy (Thompson, 1993, p.340). Consequently I see the application of the idea of the moral economy to the anti-poll tax movement as a theoretically legitimate development and application of Thompson's ideas.

The poll tax was seen in popular discourse as an issue of distributive inequality. This was most frequently expressed in terms of the language or discourse of class. Of course such distributional inequalities imply aspects and dimensions of inequality and material exclusion wider than class alone: gender, race and ethnicity, age and disability. Issues of hierarchy and power, although initially raised implicitly, quickly came to be confronted materially as the tax was implemented, and legal proceedings commenced against non-payers.

I want to theorize this aspect of opposition to the poll tax in terms of a cultural realism. I want to suggest that this popular discourse constituted a resource that made anti-poll tax protest possible. The literature on class consciousness, social justice and material inequalities comes to the same conclusions time after time, namely that it is not the intensity of material inequalities that gives rise to protest and collective action, but the perception of them. The perception of inequalities can be further broken down for the purposes of analysis. Marshall (1988) for instance has usefully distinguished between the cognitive and evaluative dimensions of perceptions of material inequalities. In the cognitive dimension lies the mere perception of material inequalities, people may or may not see them. Even if they do perceive material inequalities, then they may or may not evaluate them negatively. Even if they were perceived and negatively evaluated this may not lead to collective action to change those material inequalities, due to the perceived immutability of capitalist social relations. It is this last aspect that has been referred to as 'informed fatalism'. This last aspect, can also be related to the concept of the moral economy, in that it involves both a perception of economic inequalities, and a negative moral evaluation of those inequalities. It is this collective moral evaluation which has a distinct cultural reality.

We can think of this moral economy as having a deep and long history in Britain. We can further think of it as a collective phenomenon, a collective representation, a resource which acts as a mechanism of tremendous causal power. A resource that agents may draw upon in order to act in certain ways, and to persuade others to act. Consequently, for the resources of the moral economy to be activated requires the knowledgeable purposeful action of subjects. Further, for this causal power to be realized, in order for agents to draw upon this symbolic resource, a particular context or contexts are required. These contexts enable people to attempt to make this mechanism work. Hence the term cultural resources, which are collectively produced and held symbolic representations that enable certain interpretations to be made, and provide the tools for the production of new symbolic resources. They are drawn upon by agents in particular contexts in this instance the specific contexts of collective action. A collective action context minimally consists of the issue, the perception of opportunities for action on that issue, and the cultural, material and organizational resources that agents can draw upon on in mobilizing collective action. Symbolic resources , when realized in a collective action context become motivations for protest, and collective action. They become sources of social boundary and identity for protesters, defining who is and who is not 'one of us', part of the movement.

This question of identity is a persistent theme of social movement theory from Blumer to contemporary postmodernist writings, and, indeed Thompson's account of the emergence of working class identity (Thompson, 1963). So these theories, classical like Blumer and 'postmodern', such as Melucci, have no particular claim in my view to being privileged theorizations of 'identity politics'. All politics, all social movements, have a moment or aspect concerned with identity in the sense of individuals identifying with the movement, albeit in a variety of ways. Consequently much postmodernist argument about 'identity politics' in contrast to other forms of politics is a theoretical chimera.

The fatalism of a bounded rationality

Marshall et al continuing something of a tradition in British sociology, have argued that the subordinate classes in Britain are marked by their 'informed fatalism'. This is what others have elsewhere variously described as 'pragmatic acceptance' (Mann, 1970), or paraphrasing Marx, the dull compulsion of social life (Abercrombie et al, 1980). Indeed Abercrombie et al propose a synthesis of Marxian, Durkheimian and Weberian insights on this question by arguing that:

> ... the subordinate classes are controlled by ... 'the dull compulsion' of economic relationships, by the integrative effects of the division of labour, by the coercive nature of law and politics (Abercrombie et al 1980, p.6).

This lineage of analysis in British sociology is usually associated with those of a Weberian persuasion. However, I should make clear that its strongest theoretical roots lie within the Marxist tradition, as Abercrombie et al indicate (1980, pp.165-6), yet in more recent years the idea has been given most prominence in Weberian writings. Although often specifically related to working class consciousness in a rather narrow way, the idea of informed fatalism has a number of analytical insights that are of more generic value in understanding the dynamics of popular protest. It sees the subordinate classes are variably informed about their material circumstances, and recognizes that they are not entirely satisfied with them. The notion can be developed to show that the subordinates have a rationality consistent with both their beliefs — their moral economy — and with their social circumstances. This rationality can be seen in a sense as bounded. Not merely bounded in the sense of guided or channelled either institutionally or by values and beliefs. But in some sense held in check by the knowledge of the apparent impossibility of the circumstances. This particular kind of binding of rationality leads to fatalism — Marshall et al's notion of informed fatalism. The analysis of protest now comes to focus on those situations, on that particular context, that mix of institutional and organizational conditions that leads to the **unbinding** of this rationality. This is to put the issue in rather stark abstract theoretical terms. In reality things are often much less clear cut, as some are more fatalistic, or bound, than others, and in circumstances of collective action people are never entirely unbound. These things usually exist as partial tendencies.

This approach also has the advantage of focusing of the intricate inter-relations of agency, power and the structures of domination in a way that stresses their contingency, the essential uncertainty with respect to their permanence. One never knows when some subtle shift of circumstance, some new re-alignment of the institutional matrix will crack open the opportunities for collective action that multiplies its effectivity beyond the wildest dreams of the participants. This is exactly what happened with the poll tax. It was this process of the 'unbinding' of rationality of the poor non-payers. Their routine fatalism was overcome through the opportunities afforded by the poll tax not to pay.

Notes

1. In the extracts from the interviews I have given the location in Leeds of the activist being quoted, rather than their name. The interviews were conducted with activists from as many of the local anti-poll tax unions in Leeds that I could contact. There were around 30 such groups in 1990, and I managed to contact around 20 in 1991 when I carried out the interviews.

References

Abercrombie, N. et al (1980), *The Dominant Ideology Thesis,* George Allen and Unwin, London.

Bagguley, P. (1991), *From Protest to Acquiescence? Political Movements of the Unemployed,* Macmillan, London.

Bagguley, P. (1995a), 'The Mobilization of Anti-Poll Tax Protest in Leeds', *Sociology and Social Policy Research Working Paper 6,* School of Sociology and Social Policy, University of Leeds, Leeds.

Bagguley, P. (1995b), 'Protest, Poverty and Power: A Case Study of the Anti-Poll Tax Movement', in *Sociological Review,* Vol.43, No.4, November.

Bauman, Z. (1987), *Legislators and Interpreters,* Polity Press, Cambridge.

Bhaskar, R. (1975), *The Possibility of Naturalism,* The Harvester Press, Brighton

Burns, D. (1992), *Poll Tax Rebellion,* AK Press, London.

Butler, D. et al, (1994), *Failure In British Government: the politics of the poll tax,* Oxford University Press, Oxford.

Durkheim, E. (1984), *The Division of Labour in Society,* Macmillan, London.

Lash, S. and Urry, J. (1994), *Economies of Signs and Space,* Sage, London.

Mann, M. (1970), 'The social cohesion of liberal democracy', in *American Sociological Review,* Vol.35, No.3.

Marshall, G. (1988), 'Some Remarks on the Study of Working Class Consciousness', in Rose, D. (ed.), *Social Stratification and Economic Change,* Hutchinson, London.

Marshall, G. et al (1988), *Social Class in Modern Britain,* Unwin Hyman, London.

Pawson, R. (1989), *A Measure for Measures*, Routledge, London.

Piven, F. F. and Cloward, R. (1977), *Poor People's Movements: Why The Succeed, How They Fail*, Pantheon Books, New York.

Reynolds, M. (1992), *Uncollectable: The story of the Poll Tax Revolt*, Manchester Anti-Poll Tax Federation, Manchester.

Thatcher, M. (1993), *The Downing Street Years*, Harper Collins, London.

Thompson, E. P. (1963), *The Making of the English Working Class*, Penguin, London.

Thompson, E. P. (1978), *The Poverty of Theory*, Merlin Press Ltd., London.

Thompson, E. P. (1993), *Customs in Common*, Penguin, London.

3 What is to be done? Contrasting activists' visions in community protest

Colin Barker

Introduction

In recent years theorists of popular protest have shifted their interest towards more 'interpretive' themes. New attention has been paid to such matters as ideology and language, social psychology, the making of collective identities, and issues to do with cognition and 'framing' (e.g. Klandermans, 1984; Gamson, 1992; Melucci, 1989; Eyerman and Jamison, 1992; Snow et al, 1986). Some of this work has been cast at a rather high level of generality, with less empirical study of the ways in which actors work to make everyday sense of the world and act effectively within it. What do protestors actually do, how do they construct their visions of change, what dilemmas do they face when trying to put these into effect, how do they change their minds, how do they succeed or fail and what do they learn from their experiences?

This chapter attempts a minor contribution to that discussion. It contrasts the ways that two groups of campaigners, with distinct political perspectives, organized themselves around an effort to prevent the closure of a children's hospital in Manchester. It represents a preliminary report on an ongoing study of grassroots protest.[1] The chapter concludes with a few reflections on the contrasting themes, relating these to larger debates about social movements.

The issue

For several generations, Booth Hall Children's Hospital has been a valued asset in community life in and beyond North Manchester, providing specialist services for children with unusual and dangerous conditions across a broad region, and a more general service for the immediate population of the northern side of Greater Manchester (North Manchester, Middleton, Rochdale, Oldham, Bury, Tameside). In the early 1990s, it treated some 100,000 child patients a year (Booth Hall Appeals Office, 1993).

For some years, the health authorities have been reorganizing hospital provision within Greater Manchester, closing a number of older facilities. A local community group opposed one closure, the Ancoats Hospital, with a long running occupation; they eventually persuaded the health authority to open a community clinic on the old hospital site (Dunne et al., 1993). For some time Booth Hall, which is not the only specialist children's hospital in Manchester, has been slated for closure.

The proposal produced popular disquiet and suspicion, not least because of the wider political context in which it appeared: welfare cuts, the introduction of market principles within health services, and a growth of social deprivation across the region. A local newspaper polled its readers on the question, 'Should Booth Hall stay open or close?' The write-in vote registered 1,004 against closure to just 3 in favour (*Moston Express*). Two informal polls of local GPs also suggested strongly that they too favoured the retention of a children's hospital at Booth Hall.

In 1993, defence of the Hospital became the object of two separate campaigning groups. One, centred on the Labour Party, adopted the name of the Save Booth Hall Campaign (SBHC); the other, initiated by the Socialist Workers Party, called itself the Parents Action Group for Booth Hall (PAG). With only occasional and limited cooperation between these two groups, each largely acted independently of the other. The two groups' trajectories proved very dissimilar.

Labour and the Save Booth Hall Campaign

Labour is a parliamentarist party, its principal focus and rhythm of activity provided by the election cycle. It has been the ruling party in

Manchester local government for many years. In North Manchester especially, local government representation is akin to the 'one party state' systems noted elsewhere (Dunleavy, 1980; Lowe, 1986). It is relatively unusual for the Labour Party itself to be involved in local protest campaigning. Its council policies have themselves provoked local opposition movements in recent years. Had Booth Hall been a council funded facility — a swimming pool, say, or a homeless hostel or special school — it is unlikely that the Party would itself have run an anti-closure campaign, setting members directly against their own councillors. However, the NHS decision making structure, lacking any element of elected representation, opened a space for direct Labour involvement in protest organization. Indeed, recent experience across Manchester suggests that hospital campaigns are electorally good for Labour.

The Labour Party established the SBHC in the spring of 1993, mostly from within its own ranks. It maintained a fairly tight control over its wing of the campaign. The party's ideas and procedures shaped the SBHC, from its relatively slow tempo of work to its ideology and its organizational form.

The SBHC insisted on a strictly 'one issue' protest, aimed solely at preserving the hospital facility at Booth Hall. This, they argued, was necessary to maintain the widest unity behind the campaign. They rejected suggestions for linking the campaign to wider issues, including the defence of the NHS. Hence some potential issues fell outside their campaigning 'frame'. For example, when the hospital, to cut costs, replaced its own cooking facilities with meals brought in from outside, they noted the development as 'bizarre' but did not link it to a wider notion of 'cuts' in welfare provision and in associated workers' jobs, nor did they make it an occasion for protest. Their focus was on preserving the hospital as a community service but not as a significant employer. Questions about jobs were the province of trade unions, operating in their own demarcated sphere of responsibility. They merely noted a TUC national demonstration over the health service in November 1993, as 'something for trade unionists'. They rarely mentioned the hospital workforce in their meetings. Although they knew that criticism of health provision tended to favour Labour and damage the Tories, they mostly refrained from drawing public attention to linkages between the health authority's plans and Tory policies. Their aim was a 'non political' and/ or 'non party political' campaign.

There was a paradox here, for the SBHC was very much a Labour Party campaign. The composition of the SBHC committee mirrored the Party's dominance in local politics. It was in good measure a group of 'local notables'. Those who successively chaired the SBHC were all leading Labour councillors, including the Chairs of Finance and Highways. The treasurer and minutes secretary were magistrates. Other members included further councillors and the deputy principal of the largest local further education college. Members also held offices such as school governor and vice-chair of the Community Health Council. Only a minority of SBHC members did not hold such positions, and they tended to play less leading roles.

SBHC members' status in the city gave them access to significant resources. Effectively, the health authorities recognized them as an 'official opposition'. The SBHC selected those invited to attend a health authority preconsultation meeting, and were given platform speaking rights during the actual public consultation process. The SBHC was able to monitor closely the pattern and tempo of health authority decision making, a form of knowledge which the rival PAG never enjoyed. The same local status and contacts also gave the SBHC access to official resources when campaigning. Since the Labour council backed the campaign, they could get printing, mailing, equipment and other assistance from the Town Hall. In the campaign's later stages, the city council underwrote estimated legal costs of up to £100,000 when it launched a Judicial Review challenge to the health authority. The SBHC also enjoyed easy access to local school heads and governors, and to the Lord Mayor who judged a school based poster competition and presided over the prize giving ceremony. This kind of mobilization of resources, which characterized a quite substantial part of their campaign work, did not require the SBHC to look much outside the world of officialdom, where they moved confidently and knowledgeably. Indeed, for some of them, this was the preferred arena of activity, and the one in which their successes were recalled most warmly. One member told a ward meeting:

> With respect, there are two things. It's what we argue in the street, and what we do where it matters, in the sense of we make it ... The reason that they didn't allow the Trust, regardless of the 2.2 million deficit, was because we told them we would go for

Judicial Review if they allowed it. We had them by the short and curlies.

The SBHC also kept up a flow of press releases and stories to local newspapers, with whose editors and journalists they mostly enjoyed good relations.

The official arena did not provide their only activity, for the SBHC also engaged in 'public mobilization' work. In their first nine months, they produced thousands of posters and car stickers, and across the whole campaign area their requests to display these met with a ready response. Shops, churches and other groups took their petition forms, collected signatures and returned them. Small SBHC groups went out on a number of occasions into shopping centres, usually under a direct Labour Party banner, collecting signatures and giving away balloons printed with the campaign slogan. Over a two year period the SBHC organized three lobbies of the health authorities, held three open meetings, a march and rally attended by 460 people and an 80 strong candlelit vigil, and sent two bus loads of protestors to lobby Parliament. They produced and sold 5,000 postcards addressed to the health authority, using a child's design from their successful school poster competition.

Their public mobilization work tended to take a particular form, which Snow and his colleagues have linked to what they term 'frame bridging' (Snow et al, 1986). Here campaigners assume a shared sentiment in the population, and offer a simple means for supporters to register their agreement. People are asked to sign a petition or display a poster, perhaps to make a small financial donation. The activity requires a low commitment of time, energy and public face from members of the public. The interaction is also largely unidirectional, for the campaigners determine the wording of a petition or poster, or the use of donations. Independent initiative or self mobilization by supporters is neither implied nor required by this form of 'micromobilization'. Involving 'monological' rather than 'dialogical' relations between campaign organizations and their supporters (Offe and Wiesenthal, 1985), frame bridging shares some of the assumptions of market transactions, or of most electoral campaign work. A product is offered to a consumer, who decides to buy or vote for it, without other involvement in its design or character.

The SBHC's open meetings followed a corresponding pattern.

They were typically centred on a platform of expert speakers who reported on current developments. From the floor, people spoke about the campaign's general importance, and asked questions of the platform. The 'public' remained a relatively passive audience. Those attending were not especially encouraged to suggest forms of activity, nor were they urged to attend future planning meetings. At their rally and vigil, the microphone was confined to the SBHC's invited speakers, themselves mostly Labour representatives.

The SBHC met behind closed doors in the MP's office in the local Labour Club. Newcomers did from time to time appear, but no particular effort was made to encourage them to return. They rejected a PAG suggestion for unification of the two campaign groups and subsequently reshaped their constitution to minimize any risk of 'takeover' from outside.

A complex of factors contributed to their adoption of this campaigning format. First, Labour's broader political stance has not, historically, been marked by radical practical and theoretical criticism of the existing institutional order (Miliband, 1961, Coates, 1975), including the 'separation of the political and economic' that critics see as underpinning the structures of capitalism (Wood, 1995). Party philosophy does not tend to question existing modes of democratic participation nor to look to popular mobilization as a means to extend it.

Second, larger political conceptions generate their own political habits. SBHC members' chief experience of campaigning took the form of electoral activity, while as councillors most political and administrative work was achieved through committees with settled memberships. These forms of work did not routinely involve promoting self activity by outsiders. As noted, the specific role of Party activist rarely involved protest campaigning, or the acquisition of the skills and confidence required to mobilize others into collective action. Some SBHC members confessed their relative ignorance of the 'nuts and bolts' of protest organization.

Third, electioneering as a predominant method of political work links activists and others in specific social relations, and promotes among them a specific picture of the population. Labour activists met their supporters as a rather staid aggregate of potential voters, somewhat suspicious of 'politics' and 'politicians'. Taken at large, they saw a population which would sign petitions and display posters, but whose response to calls to join a march or a vigil for the

Hospital proved disappointing. Discussing a lobby of the regional health authority, the SBHC secretary asked dourly:

> Will we be able to fill four coaches on a Tuesday in March? After all, we didn't fill the Boggart Hole Clough car park [for our Saturday rally], despite printing 20,000 leaflets.

Fourth, pessimism about the population's readiness for active participation reinforced a view that large shows of widespread public involvement were of relatively little value. As one put it, 'Having people marching up and down for no purpose has never really been my thing. I've always been a matter of doing something achievable,' adding that 'The days of the mass political meeting, the days of massive marches and massive lobbies are, I think, by and large gone.'

Fifth, the SBHC's self enclosed nature produced a kind of vicious circle. Not involving more people meant that more tasks fell on the few who attended meetings regularly, and they suffered from problems of overload. The secretary explained this dilemma in an interview:

> Sometimes you get to be a bit of a control freak when you're in charge of all of this, and I'm sure that we could have orchestrated greater, allowed other people, because there was certainly willingness on the part of other organizations to become involved. But what sort of militated against that was the fact, it's just the **time** that it would take to actually get everybody, coordinating ... and at the end of the day it was something that I neglected to do. I mean I could have sort of promoted other people to do it, we tried a few things and it didn't quite happen the way... and the people unfortunately sort of lost enthusiasm through that.

Lastly, the SBHC's response to rivalry from the SWP and the PAG was a concern to maintain control over the campaign. There were issues at stake beyond the usual rivalry between competing organizations (discussed in Zald and McCarthy, 1987). Leading SBHC members wished to dissociate the Labour Party from some of the PAG's semi-legal forms of activity: collecting funds in 'open buckets', converting a picket into a march without proper notice to the police, or the 'stunt occupation' of an empty hospital ward. In their view, the SWP would divert the campaign onto extraneous matters, such as other issues to do with cuts (implying potential criticism of the Labour council), hospital jobs, pay and conditions, or unrelated campaigns from anti-racism to sexual politics. The SWP, some suggested, wanted to 'exploit' the campaign for their own purposes, and would 'put people off'. To open the SBHC would introduce unwanted controversy over campaign methods, goals and politics. When planning for their open events they discussed carefully how to handle potential 'trouble' from the SWP, by 'referring back to the committee' any suggestions for activity from the floor at the open meeting, and by stewarding by experienced Party members (if necessary with aid from the police) at their march and rally.

However, aspects of this stance made some SBHC members uneasy. For one thing, given the Party's size and potential resources, their own public mobilization work was not as successful as they had hoped. Attendance at open meetings and other events involved less people than the more successful of the initiatives by the much smaller SWP. One member remarked about the PAG demonstrations:

> That was possibly their greatest success you know, in fairness to the Parents for Booth Hall campaign. They were a damn sight more interesting, the first couple [of marches] they had. They actually took them down to the streets of Manchester, to the centre of Manchester, and they were good fun.

Some attributed disappointing turnouts to their own committee's self closure. One loyal Labour activist spelled out his criticisms at some length in an interview. He was disappointed that even most Party members, especially from neighbouring city constituencies, had not become involved. His party, he felt, had missed the chance to involve and 'politicize' new people, thus expanding the ranks of potential Labour members. Although hostile to the SWP, he expressed admiration for what he saw as their capacity to 'involve ordinary people'. He worried about the implications of the SBHC's form of campaign for democracy in general:

> There was a feeling amongst some people ... that the public meetings in a school hall, the poster campaign and things like that were a waste of time. "They weren't really achieving anything.

What were they for?" I disagree with that totally. What they're for, is to take the campaign out to people. What I didn't appreciate, getting involved in the campaign, was that you could sustain a campaign by not doing that, by writing letters to the appropriate people, by appearing and demanding to speak at meetings of the district and regional health authorities, and create that without any public support. I don't think there's any particular legitimacy in doing that. What I've learned from the campaign is that it's possible to do that. It's possible to run a campaign and really represent no one.

The secretary's pessimism (above) about getting people to join coaches for a lobby did not go unanswered. One councillor, from nearby Middleton, replied immediately that success depended on mobilizing 'core groups' in the population, like pensioners' clubs and others. This councillor, identified with the Party's left wing, had been previously involved in extra-party campaigns against both the Poll Tax and the Gulf War. His remarks revealed a more differentiated sense of the population as containing mobilizable groups with their own forms of self organization. The Middleton Party was noticeably more successful than the main SBHC group in mobilizing numbers for the SBHC's march and rally, despite the fact that the distance they had to walk was several miles greater.

Some felt the Labour Party had been 'paranoid' about the SWP, shutting out the PAG when they should have accepted the proffered unification. The SWP's energy and innovative tactics would have shaken things up a bit. 'It wasn't even', said one, 'as if we had a periphery of new contacts to protect from them. They had the contacts, and we should have gone in and recruited them to the Labour Party.' But, he added, the Labour Party lacked the political self confidence to achieve this.

However, such differences never surfaced into open debate within SBHC meetings. Individuals sometimes expressed dissent, but in 'asides'. When the secretary's proposal for a trainful of demonstrators to lobby the Conservative Party conference in the autumn of 1993 was voted down in an unusually acrimonious debate, he muttered, half aloud, 'They're not doing anything here ... They never do anything anyway.' When a PAG member attacked their closed character in a letter to the local press, one working class member (who later stopped attending) remarked, almost to himself,

'Of course it's all true, isn't it. We are the ghost people, aren't we, really? People don't actually know who we are.'

Those who privately favoured a more outgoing campaign did not directly challenge the SBHC's way of proceeding. One reason was that they were themselves unsure how to put into practice their half formed desire for something different. But there were, anyway, no particular pressures to translate unease within the SBHC into open debate. Any sense of 'failure' was moderated. In its own parliamentarist terms, the local Labour Party was a success. All parliamentary and council seats across the Blackley constituency were 'safe'. If the SBHC was a committee of 'local notables', that was a sign of its achievements. Members did not experience a large gap between hopes and immediate reality, certainly not of a kind that might produce a radical questioning of current procedures. Covert grumbles and disquiet do not, under such circumstances, tend to get translated into alternative programmes. Additionally, when the SBHC compared themselves with the PAG's record, they also had reasons for self satisfaction. The PAG had no lasting power. Perhaps the SBHC had involved less people, and perhaps they had been rather unexciting. But they had kept going for over two years, while the SWP, as one Labour loyalist put it, 'marched people up to the top of the hill and then left them there.' The SBHC kept the hospital issue simmering in public consciousness in periods when nothing much seemed to be happening. They might for whole periods, as one member put it, have been 'just being a talking shop' with low attendance, but experience told them this was a normal characteristic of political life. As another commented sarcastically, 'we Labour Party members are inured to boring meetings.'

The SWP and the Parents Action Group

In contrast with Labour, the SWP is anti-parliamentarist. Marxist in inspiration, it is critical of the limits of 'bourgeois democracy'. Its theory and practice centre on a 'socialism from below', which involves working class self transformation through struggle. The SWP's rhythm of work comes not from the election cycle as much as from the ups and downs of class struggle, especially as expressed in industrial conflict. As against those Labour members who believe the age of mass struggle to be over, the SWP reads the current situation as one of temporary 'downturn', and look to shifts in popular militancy as the key to political change. The largest inheritor of the communist tradition of the 1920s, the SWP is inherently a 'campaigning' party, and its members are regularly involved in efforts at working class mobilization in demonstrations, strikes and other militant events. However, outside anti-racist and anti-fascist activities, the party has accumulated far less experience in 'community campaigns'.

Labour's antagonism to the much smaller SWP is reciprocated. The two parties have clashed locally on a variety of issues, including the Poll Tax and the council's closure or withdrawal of funding of local facilities, while SWP members have been deeply involved in trade union disputes among council employees. On the other hand, both parties share a common opposition to the Tory government, and the SWP has collaborated with the Labour Left in a variety of campaign contexts from anti-fascism and opposition to the Gulf War to strike support. Inter-party relations are thus marked by a complex history of competition, opposition and collaboration, which has produced at an interpersonal level a mixture of antagonism and mutual caricature along with liking and respect, differentially combined in different contexts.

The PAG was a hastily improvised campaign, even a 'happy discovery' for the SWP. In the spring of 1993 the local branch had held a small public meeting about Booth Hall, but decided to call a picket outside the hospital in early July. When party members distributed leaflets and posters for this event at local workplaces and on housing estates, the response was much larger than they had expected. They swiftly converted the picket into a march and rally of some hundreds. Out of this came the PAG, whose initial organizing meeting attracted, in addition to their own members, 67 people drawn from a wide area across and beyond the north of the city. At least half were working class women. The new body organized postering, petitioning and leafleting in local shopping centres, and a second march a month later in the city centre which drew over 500 people.

If the SBHC isolated the Booth Hall question as a 'single issue', the SWP sought to 'generalize' to wider working class issues, focussing especially on opposition to the Tory Government, and connecting the battle to save the Hospital with other matters including health workers' pay and conditions, strikes in other industries, and a local anti-deportation campaign. Their leaflets, posters and speakers all sought to draw these connections.

For the SWP, a key measure was their own success in activating local people into self organized campaigning work, within which they might experience the transformative effects of militant collective action. As a 'battling granny' addressed a rally in the city centre, one member remarked admiringly, 'She's never spoken before — that's what it's all about.' Like some contemporary theorists of social movements (e.g. Fantasia 1988, Klandermans 1992, Barker 1995), they saw direct participation in collective action as possessing a potential for rapid transformation of individuals' and groups' visions of themselves and society.

They thus sought to involve as wide a range of people as possible in the PAG's development, looking to new people to take on responsibilities for activity. Their approach thus expressed both a more differentiated and a more motile vision of local working class individuals and organizations. They distinguished between layers in the population, between a currently rather passive but supportive majority and a minority of individuals and groups who 'wanted to fight', seeking to mobilize the energies of the latter to draw more people into the campaign.

The PAG planning meetings were more open in composition and form than those of the SBHC. Apart from the treasurer, there were no officers. People took on 'jobs' as the occasion seemed to demand. Meetings had a rather chaotic appearance: chairing was loose, agendas were 'discovered' rather than preplanned, and discussion often wandered widely. Often much of the detailed business of a particular plan of action was sorted out between relevant individuals after a meeting had formally ended, in discussant chat. Speakers at PAG rallies were more diverse than at comparable SBHC events, including numbers of women, local nurses and trade unionists, a Nigerian woman resisting her family's deportation, a child in leg callipers, as well as SWP and Labour Party speakers.

PAG members' predominant view of the SBHC was that it was 'not doing anything'. They criticized the Labour Party for its closed character and its failure to mobilize large numbers of people into a more militant local campaign. They made one proposal to the SBHC that the two campaigns be unified, but did not press the issue further when the Labour Party declined. Subsequently, some felt this had been a mistake — as indeed did some of the more critical members of the SBHC itself.

While, in its initial stages, the PAG succeeded in mobilizing numbers of new people into activity, and in generating a livelier and more open campaign atmosphere, its trajectory was very different from that of the SBHC. In the summer and autumn of 1993, there was a burst of public activity: two successful demonstrations, large organizing meetings, two lobbies of visiting Health Ministers, a 'fun day' at a local community centre, a 24 hour 'stunt occupation' of an empty ward at Booth Hall, a public meeting, and two bus loads of demonstrators to the TUC health service demonstration in London. But PAG meetings became smaller, its organizing group shrank in size, and it lost its initial impetus. A week before Christmas, an ill prepared 'Children's March for Booth Hall' attracted just 27 participants. The PAG met once more, sent a small lobbying group to the regional health authority, then folded its tent for some months. There was a brief attempt at revival in the summer of 1994, when a march of 270 was held, but the PAG then disappeared again.

The decline of the PAG reflected several difficulties. They could not keep calling demonstrations, for a law of diminishing returns would set in. The PAG worked quite quickly through a repertoire of both familiar and innovative forms of collective action, but soon became uncertain what to do next. And they ran into the survival problem that Stinchcombe (1965) identifies for new organizations. The PAG represented an effort to develop an effective campaigning body composed largely of people who were strangers to each other. Its support came from a diverse body of individuals from across one whole side of a major metropolitan area. Developing social and political cohesion among this diverse grouping was difficult. The PAG represented less an existing 'network' than an accidental aggregate of initially enthusiastic individuals. Additionally, many of those involved in the initial phases relied on inconvenient public transport to get to meetings, and had child care, shift work and other difficulties to overcome.

This in turn affected the SWP organizing core, a mere handful of people. They sustained a very high level of activity, involving disruption of everyday domestic routine and space, on the basis of the 'buzz' generated by their early and unexpected successes. One couple whose home became the organizing centre both had demanding full time jobs and a young child, and lived for weeks in a permanent and exhausting whirl of telephone calls, leaflet writing, printing, attendance at meetings and other events. So long as the events they organized affirmed their vision of the transformative possibilities of collective action, members could remain on a 'political high'. But a shift of tempo became necessary as they themselves began to run out of new ideas, and as PAG meetings shrank to a smaller group.

They did not succeed in finding a formula by which to adjust to a slower tempo and convert the gains they had made in terms of active contacts into a longer lasting and more cohesive body. Most of the SWP's experience of activism was in trade union settings, and their relative inexperience in 'community campaigning' did not prepare them for the initial decline. Their far-flung new network, in any case, represented little of what is normally meant by a 'community': the PAG itself represented the sole basis of mutual association between its various members.

Reviewing their own history, SWP members were retrospectively self critical. They had not, they suggested, sufficiently thought how to develop the campaign, which in any case had taken them by delighted surprise, beyond its early phases. They were ill prepared for the 'long drawn out' nature of the issue, which the SBHC, with its closer sense of the pulse of official decision making, grasped better. In retrospect, they believed that they should have argued within the PAG for a shift of focus, away from the rather random social links of 'the community' and towards a campaign within local bodies like health workers' committees and the wider trade union movement. There the tempo of work might have altered, but it might have been more securely based.

Such a shift would have fitted with their own political conceptions. But they did not make it, for two reasons, one 'external' and one 'internal'. A key factor in the 'opportunity structure' they faced was that workplace organization within Booth Hall hospital itself was at a low level. Union meetings were infrequent, the local UNISON representative was 'demoralized' and looking forward to retirement. Efforts at direct contact with Booth Hall workers proved disappointing. Inside the hospital, the PAG encountered friendly sympathy, but did not locate strategic individuals who might begin to develop the campaign there. Where they looked for a natural centre for a workplace based campaign they met a partial vacuum, which could not be filled in a short period of time. On the other hand, everyday access to the hospital workforce was much easier than in many workplaces, they did enjoy friendly contact with individuals there, and there were signs that a more patient and longer term approach might have borne fruit.

But additionally, in the autumn of 1993, just at the moment when difficulties within the PAG's development were becoming apparent, the SWP itself began an internal process of reorganization. The party's view of its own forms of organization has been restlessly experimental. The SWP became convinced in 1993, by such events as the Booth Hall campaign and other developments, that its existing system of branches was becoming an impediment to further expansion. Accordingly, it set about developing a larger number of more local but, necessarily, initially smaller branches. New organizational forms take time to mature, as unexpected disadvantages of reorganization only appear with experience. The single North Manchester branch was divided into two. This separated the core group of activists who had till then steered SWP work in the PAG campaign. New mechanisms of coordination were slow to develop. On top of that, members were also preoccupied with other matters. As well as reconstructing their own branches, the activists were heavily involved in campaigning on other fronts, notably in mobilizing for a national anti-fascist demonstration and in campaigning against the imposition of Value Added Tax on domestic fuel. Thus, just at the time when they might have reoriented their work around Booth Hall, they were themselves ill-coordinated and had turned their main attention elsewhere. Since no other grouping had emerged within the PAG with a practical capacity to hold the campaign together, the result was a more or less total collapse.

Looking back, members summed up their dual experience. On one side, they saw their own picture of the world as having been validated. One woman said,

> I suppose the thing I remember is how people of all ages, when they get going, the stuff they come out with, the gutsyness, what they were doing, how people change. I mean everything that we say about people was true. And even though you know it, you need reminding of it. But it's absolutely true. The creativeness, what people can do, all that, is all there — they may not believe they've got but they bloody well have. And it isn't necessarily young people. You talk about a lot of fifty, sixty year old women who were dynamite. And that, a real illustration of how people can do things, and how brilliant they are. And they're what made

the campaign, the successes that we had.

But they also felt they had failed to grasp opportunities. As another woman put it:

> We cocked up ... You can have absolutely overwhelming popular support in working class communities, and you can mobilize that, but after a while you run out of places to take it. And unless it can be given some sort of roots its runs out too. 'Cos for us the obvious thing next would be to have action either called by, or in support, of hospital workers... We should have said, 'Why don't we the people in this room give it a crack, why don't we concentrate all our energy on finding the health workers, badgering the stewards' committee, going down, taking petitions not to the health authority but to the nursing staff to give them the feel of strength of support?' Why don't we **fight** for working class organization rather than say, "Oh well"?' I think that was our downturn mentality that made us do that.

Concluding remarks

Activists, whatever their persuasion, constantly monitor their own actions and their effects, privately or in discussion with others. They reflect on successes and failures, become uncertain how to proceed, and in the process learn and unlearn ways of making history, even on a small scale. Their preceding prejudices and understandings partly shape how they take both the knock-backs and the delights of trying to 'make things happen'. Theory certainly guides their practice, but that practice also feeds back into large or small revaluations of their own ideas. Although in different measure, every activist I spoke to from either group had specific reasons for saying, 'Next time, I'd do things differently.'

The contrasting practices and ideas I have attempted to identify rather crudely in the preceding pages have, finally, a bearing on a larger issue in social movement theory. Two opposed prognostic claims have been made. On one side, Zald and McCarthy detect a trend towards a 'professional' model of social movement organization. In this model, campaigners rely less on 'classical' means of popular mobilization and more on skilled specialists, who use new fund raising and other techniques of resource mobilization and who rely on the manipulation of mass media and other means to affect decision makers. In this view, the distance between 'social movements' and conventional 'pressure groups' will decline. On the other hand, Melucci and other theorists of 'new social movements' suggest a different scenario, in which innovative forms of organization will become more prominent. These will involve 'participatory' notions of democratic action, rooted in the self activation of networks and groups within civil society.

The SBHC and the PAG might seem partially to represent the two alternative possibilities — even if 'new movement' theorists might sniff suspiciously at a 'participatory' movement led by a party like the SWP. But the claims for both trends may be misplaced. On one side, Zald and McCarthy admit that their 'professional' model only works in strictly delimited political settings. On the other, many so called 'new' movements have themselves been internally divided over matters of participation and organization. Perhaps more realistic is the view that arguments about 'professional lobbying' versus 'participatory mobilization' have characterized the inner life of popular movements for at least two centuries. Calhoun (1993) points to the presence, in early 19th century workers' movements in Britain, of many features claimed as distinctive of 'new social movements'. Aminzade's (1995) study of 19th century French Republicanism reveals an ongoing argument which he links to a practical distinction between 'liberal' and 'participatory' visions of democracy and representation. Yeo (1980) uncovers, within the seemingly bureaucratic history of British Friendly Societies, an ideological and practical contest in which similar issues were posed. And movements all through the present century have, likewise, been riven by debates and splits over such matters.

The two rival campaigns over Booth Hall were, in themselves, small beer. But the different visions of politics that the two campaigns embodied, and the dilemmas each faced, represent part of a longer and deeper practical and theoretical debate about the nature of society and its possible transformation. That argument will run and run.

41

Notes

1. No researcher comes neutral to the study of popular protest. As
    a member of the Socialist Workers Party in the south of the city, I
    entered this research with my own biases. These, apparent in
    what follows, may seem more exotic than some, but I have
    sought to control them as much as any other field worker would
    hope to do. In any event, I should place on record my grateful
    appreciation for the friendly welcome I received from all those
    involved in both campaign groups, and for their continuous
    helpfulness throughout the two years of my research.

References

Aminzade, Ronald (1995), 'Between Movement and Party: The
    Transformation of Mid-Nineteenth Century French
    Republicanism' in Jenkins, J. Craig and Klandermans, Bert (ed.)
    *The Politics of Social Protest: Comparative Perspectives on States
    and Social Movements*, UCL Press, London.
Barker, Colin (1995), '"The Muck of Ages": Reflections on Proletarian
    Self-Emancipation', *Studies in Marxism*, Vol.2.
Booth Hall Appeals Office (1993), *Press Release*, Booth Hall
    Children's Hospital, Manchester.
Calhoun, Craig (1993), '"New Social Movements" of the Early
    Nineteenth Century', *Social Science History*, Vol.17, No.3, Fall.
Coates, David (1975), *The Labour Party and the Struggle for
    Socialism*, Cambridge University Press, Cambridge.
Dunleavy, Patrick (1980), *Urban Political Analysis: The Politics of
    Collective Consumption*, Macmillan, London
Dunne, Mary Catherine, et al, (1993), *Stitched Up! Action for Health
    in Ancoats*, Church Action on Poverty, Manchester.
Eyerman Ron and Jamison Andrew (1992), *Social Movements: A
    Cognitive Approach*, Polity, London.
Fantasia, Rick (1988), *Cultures of Solidarity: Consciousness, Action,
    and Contemporary American Workers*, University of California
    Press, Berkeley.

Gamson, William A. (1992), 'The Social Psychology of Collective Action', in Morris, Aldon D. and Mueller, Carol McClurg (eds.) *Frontiers in Social Movement Theory*, Yale University Press, New Haven.

Klandermans, Bert (1984), 'Mobilization and Participation: Social-Psychological Expansions of Resource Mobilization Theory', *American Sociological Review*, Vol.49, pp.583-600.

Klandermans, Bert (1992), 'The Social Construction of Protest and Multiorganizational Fields, in Morris, Aldon D. and Mueller, Carol McClurg (ed.) *Frontiers in Social Movement Theory*, Yale University Press, New Haven.

Lowe, Stuart (1986), *Urban Social Movements: The City After Castells*, Macmillan, London.

Melucci, Alberto (1989), *Nomads of the Present: Social Movements and Individual Needs in Contemporary Society*, Temple University Press, Philadelphia.

Miliband, Ralph (1961), *Parliamentary Socialism: A Study in the Politics of Labour*, Allen & Unwin, London.

Moston Express (11 August 1994), 'Your Verdict: Keep Open 1,004, Close It 3'.

Offe, Claus and Wiesenthal, Helmut, (1985) 'Two Logics of Collective Action', in Offe, Claus, *Disorganized Capitalism: Contemporary Transformations of Work and Politics*, Polity, London.

Snow, David A., Rochford, E. Burke, Worden, Steven K., and Benford, Robert D., 'Frame Alignment Process, Micromobilization and Movement Participation', *American Sociological Review*, Vol. 51, pp.464-481.

Stinchcombe, A. L. (1965), 'Social Structure and Organizations', in March, James (ed.), *Handbook of Organizations*, Rand McNally, Chicago.

Wood, Ellen Meiksins (1995), *Democracy Against Capitalism: Renewing Historical Materialism*, Cambridge University Press, Cambridge.

Yeo, Stephen (1980), 'State and Anti-State: Reflections on Social Forms and Struggles from 1850', in Corrigan, Philip (ed.) *Capitalism, State Formation and Marxist Theory: Historical Investigations*, Quartet, London.

Zald, Mayer N. and McCarthy, John D. (1987), *Social Movements in an Organizational Society: Collected Essays*, Transaction Books, New Brunswick.

4 From the women's movement to feminisms

Sue Clegg

Introduction

This chapter has grown out of a series of personal and political reflections on the development of the 'women's movement' and an academic engagement with feminist literature over the last twenty five years.[1] Many women activists and academics have been provoked into similar revaluations and I make no particular claims to originality. Personal originality is valued in academia; in political movements shared knowledge is often of greater significance.[2] Accordingly I have tried to make sense of the diverse and complex set of social activities and political practices captured by the term 'women's movement'. I also locate contemporary feminisms socially and politically in order to assess their relation to the political goal of 'women's liberation'. The term 'women's liberation' now carries a nostalgic resonance and, as should become clear, the reasons for this also form part of the enquiry.

The chapter is structured as follows. Firstly, I describe the development of the women's movement, its purposes and social composition, and attempt some analysis of its historical development in relation to its achievements and limitations. In particular I want to draw attention to how amorphous and ambiguous the concept of movement is, and to demonstrate that competing histories are possible. There are major gaps in our knowledge in terms of systematic study of movement activists and their participation in other social movements, and we are forced to rely on retrospective accounts of activists and the patchwork of surviving documents and leaflets. These problems, however, are not unique to studying the women's movement.

Secondly, I trace, however cursorily, some of the developments in feminist theories and relate these to the history above. Feminism, like any other set of theories which purports to serve and connect to a particular social movement, claims a specific relationship to praxis. There is a double linkage: a sociology of knowledge which looks at links between the movement and the development of ideas, and an epistemology which looks at the knowledge claims made by the movement. My aim is to make connections between the production of feminist theories and the historical decline in the activities of the women's movement. The difficulty, as will become clear, is how to judge the latter. The consolidation of academic feminism however does seem to have occurred in a period of relatively low political activism.

It is no longer possible to speak in the singular of a women's movement; in its place are multiple feminisms. Fierce disputes tore the movement apart as groups of women asserted the particularity of their oppression: as lesbian women, black women, Jewish women etc. New insights about the differences between women produced doubts about the validity of theories based on the commonality of women's oppression. The phenomenological discovery of lived difference supplied one of the bases for a turn to post-modernism in feminist literature. This theoretical move is usually presented as an advance on previously naive and grandiose attempts to theorize women's oppression. I will suggest that this shift is a sign of theoretical and political weakness. New forms of theorizing which seem to embrace racial and other oppressions have not resulted in new levels of theoretical integration or expanded praxis. Meanwhile in the popular media there have been signs of a 'post-feminist' backlash against women's limited gains (Faludi, 1992). It is claimed that feminism has damaged women as well as men, women are again advised to attend to their fertility before it is too late, while men rediscover their true 'wild man' identity. The backlash has served as an ideological denial of widened class, racial and gender inequalities, while attacking the very limited measures that have been taken to eliminate such inequalities (Molyneux, 1993). Despite this, many of the ideas feminists fought for now represent a new common sense. In the context of both real gains and new attacks, the need for theoretical understanding and political intervention remain as compelling as they were 25 years ago.

The women's movement

History

The following sketch of the development of the women's movement is pieced together from contemporary documents: leaflets, manifestos, feminist magazines; and the many retrospective reconstructions which combine political analysis, personal recollection and reflection, as well as sociological theorizing. Histories of the women's movement have been written mostly by women participants and they have a polemical as well as analytical purpose (hooks, 1982). My account, too, is based on personal history and is polemical. Studying protest movements engages the value commitments of authors in a particularly powerful way when they have also been participants. This is true for all study of popular protests, the proper constraints of objectivity notwithstanding. But from its outset the women's movement placed particular stress on the personal and on shared experience as validating knowledge. Therefore much of the writing that emerged took the form of personal political testament (Rowbotham, 1989). Early writing is striking in its heady mix of analysis, personal commentary, and political demands. As one of the defining features of the women's movement, this writing laid the basis for one area of undoubted feminist success, namely, publishing.

The women's movement was born of the radical struggles of the 1960s and shared many of their characteristics. The North American movement was particularly influential internationally, though of course women's movements in different countries were also influenced by distinctive national political and intellectual traditions. The women's movement in the USA took many ideas from the civil rights, anti-war and student movements and applied them to their own understanding of women's oppression. The idea of self-organization was taken from developments in the black struggle, as was the slogan 'sisterhood is powerful'. Consciousness raising had many parallels; in black churches where many of the demands for civil rights were articulated, in the organizational practices of the Student Non-Violent Co-ordinating Committee (SNCC), in western

Maoist ideas about 'speaking bitterness', and so on. The concept of chauvinism was derived from the anti-war and anti-imperialist critique of America's stance towards the rest of the world. Many of the women who were to form the women's movement shared the same social milieu as SNCC activists and the American New Left. But they felt marginalized and felt that their ideas were not taken seriously by their male peers. The macho social style of many young male radicals was based on an image of the streetwise mode of black community activists. As a new generation of young women became politically involved and were more sexually active and confident, they continued to experience sexism and their own oppression. The contradictions between real gains and still present constraints exploded.

The movement also drew on a broader sense of women's oppression and the writing of women like Betty Friedan (Friedan, 1965). Friedan identified the hidden discontents of women, who were often materially privileged, but who nonetheless experienced the frustration and emptiness of lives dominated by the domestic routines of child care. One way of understanding this is in terms of James Scott's analysis of 'hidden transcripts'[3] (Scott, 1990). Women's complaints were already rehearsed in the kitchen, at coffee mornings, in giggly bonding in girls' bedrooms. Hidden transcripts became public as women shared their experiences and drew political conclusions. Complaints about men's behaviour, the trials of child care and housework became the stuff of consciousness raising. By generalizing from experience, women began to theorize the causes of their oppression and demand redress. The excitement is still captured by women reminiscing twenty years after.[4] Scott notes the apparent suddenness of hidden transcripts becoming public, and also the joy, the sense of authenticity and agency. Both these were characteristic of the women's movement which appeared to come from nowhere and delighted and amazed its early participants. Other writers analyzing revolutionary struggles have also noted this mood of 'festivals of the oppressed' when people move to take action to right long experienced wrongs (Barker, 1987).

In Britain, unlike in the USA, there was a close connection with the Labour movement. The first national conference in 1970 was held at Ruskin and there was a strong identification with the 1968 Ford women's equal pay strike (Coote and Campbell, 1987). The original four demands of the movement formulated at Ruskin were: equal pay, equal education and opportunity, twenty-four hour nurseries, free contraception and abortion on demand. In America the National Organization of Women, formed in 1966, had adopted a 'bill of rights' which listed action on employment, education, maternity and child care, as well as the control of women's reproductive lives (although not specifically abortion). More emblematically, in 1968 a group of women protested at the Miss America pageant in Atlantic City and dumped restrictive clothing in a 'freedom trash bucket'. The much quoted and resented comment by Stokely Carmichael that the proper position of women in SNCC was 'prone' has become part of the history of the women's movement, as has the equally quoted although not necessarily read *The Myth of the Vaginal Orgasm* by Anne Koedt. In France the term 'Mouvement de Liberation des Femmes' (MLF) was used by the media to describe the women who placed a wreath on the Tomb of the Unknown Soldier inscribed to an even more unknown person: his wife (Duchen, 1986). In 1971 a manifesto was signed by 343 women who had had illegal abortions, including Simone de Beauvoir. These movements primarily developed in the advanced industrial countries. The range of demands, strategy and activities was broad. From the beginning they were marked by a theoretical eclecticism and difference of views which would later come to be over-simplistically categorized under the headings of radical or revolutionary feminism, socialist feminism, and bourgeois feminism. All feminisms shared a recognition of the need to challenge male privilege (although not necessarily men) and the idea that male power was a root cause of women's oppression.

Broad and narrow definitions

Identifying the social characteristics of the women's movement is problematic. Delineation rests on a definition of the parameters of the movement and who participated. Ideals of women's equality were generated by women's increased social participation in the public sphere at the same time as smaller numbers of women created the women's movement. Broad social and economic secular trends within capitalism brought increasing numbers of women into the work force and into higher education. Access to contraception and falling family size had liberated women from lifetimes of childbearing or celibacy. Yet, women still had the experience of being second class citizens: economically through the denial of equal pay, in remaining legal barriers, sexually in the continuation of double standards of sexual morality, in politics and in the workplace through the denial of office in trade unions and political parties. These contradictions, which impelled some women into the specifically feminist forms of political activism already described, affected a much broader layer of women. Women were active participants sometimes (although not always) raising their own demands alongside and inside the broader struggles for national liberation, better wages and conditions, against racist laws, in solidarity with movements elsewhere (Harman, 1988).

Understanding the contradictions of this complex history makes sense of two seemingly contradictory claims: one is that the women's movement was small, white and middle class, and the other is that many, many more women took part in struggles to advance their cause. Both are true. Women who were not directly involved in the movement in the narrow sense, were involved in re-making their lives through strikes and demonstrations, through the refusal to do housework or have sex on demand. Some of the ideas of the early women's movement such as equal pay and equal rights to education became the common sense of an era. It was the narrower women's movement that black writers like Ida Lewis have attacked: 'The women's liberation movement is basically a family quarrel between white women and white men' (hooks, 1984). Black women have identified themselves as having a commitment to their own emancipation as women and yet reject feminism. Many younger women now take equal pay and equal access to education as self-evident rights without any specifically feminist content. The specific content of the movement is defined by its activists, and the existence of the movement as an independent political form depends on their activities. Feminism was always narrower than its general impact. The broader ideals of the movement, because they reflected real contradictions and changes in women's lives, could function in helping to sustain a more diffuse commitment to women's equality.

Because the women's movement validated the importance of the personal, many of the changes it heralded took place in the 'private' domain. However these changes have frequently been robbed of any specifically feminist content. For example the right for a women to define her own sexual pleasure was an important element in early feminism but has been largely stripped of this specific content in popular women's magazines. Similarly, many women use the prefix

'I'm not a feminist but' before acting in ways that confront sexism. Women (and some men) take action against particular examples of oppression in contexts where old ways of behaving have become open to challenge. The meaning of 'feminist' in popular consciousness has often been shaped by people who are antagonistic to feminism as well as by those who are sympathetic, but its prevalence indicates that the idea of feminism acts as a broad conduit for a whole range of social actions involving women's defiance of traditional roles.

The term, the women's movement, captures both the real, if under-documented, sets of activities aimed at challenging women's oppression by feminists, and also the broader movement of women involved in the social changes in women's lives over the last three decades. This characteristic of the movement as being a combination of 'narrow' and 'broad' layers is, I believe, a characteristic of all movements. Social movements, particularly the new social movements: peace, green, gay, often have a nebulous organizational existence. In the case of feminism this was an issue of political principle involving a commitment to non-hierarchical forms of organization, rejection of official leaders, a stress on the local and the autonomy of individual groups from any central organization. This meant that from the beginning there was no internal theoretical or tactical coherence, rather a commitment to women finding their own voice.

The impact of social movements is also diffuse, ideas overlap with those from the other movements and may become part of popular consciousness in ways which are far removed from the original intentions of movement activists. Movements can and do supply the vocabulary of resistance along with crucial networks of communication and organization. Movements also shape the consciousness of participants about what is possible and this may act to limit aspirations as well as extend them. Parallel understandings are always present when people struggle to change their conditions. In the case of the women's movement this history is especially complex as its history is intertwined with the histories of other, often competing, political traditions.[5]

The movement reconsidered

At this point I will illustrate my argument with some examples from the British women's movement. In terms of attendance at conferences and consciousness raising groups, running specifically feminist campaigns, the overall characterization of the movement as white and middle class is fair. However, it would be inaccurate about most women engaged in struggle and articulating demands for equality. The Ford machinists' strike which marked a critical moment in raising political awareness of women's oppression took place outside the context of a specific feminist input. It could equally be described as part of the history of the labour movement or the women's movement, or both. That strike and others like it had a major influence on women and many men who throughout the following decades, but particularly in the 1970s, set out to challenge male domination in trade unions. They worked to ensure that women's demands for equal pay, for workplace nurseries, for maternity and paternity leave, for the defence of legal abortion, against sexual and racial harassment etc. were part of the trade union agenda. These demands were fought for by activists who at the time defined themselves as feminists, as socialists, as trade union militants, as all three and none.

Differences in political analysis also led to fierce disagreements about the focus of campaigns. The National Abortion Campaign provides a good example, there were bitter disagreements about a trade union focus, between socialists who emphasised abortion as a class issue and feminists who saw it primarily in gendered terms. The official TUC demonstration in 1979 against the Corrie amendment was supported by an estimated 80,000 women and men. This massive protest was an example of the generalized influence of feminist demands. The defence of legal abortion, however, was also independently supported by those parts of the liberal establishment who were responsible for the 1967 Act. Women's reproductive rights also formed an integral part of the socialist tradition and much of the mobilization was due to socialist influence in unions and workplaces. Most importantly, as anyone who petitioned at the time discovered, knowledge of the effects of illegal abortion was deeply embedded in the hidden transcripts of working class black and white women.

Another important example of how different but overlapping groups mobilize was the Grunwick strike 1976-77. Led by Asian women, it became a focus for mass pickets and anti-government anger. It was, and has been subsequently analyzed as, a trade union dispute about the fundamental right to organize, and it inspired a massive labour movement mobilization. It was also a struggle which 'feminists' actively supported. It was a struggle for Asian women and an example of the 'black' community's capacity to organize. It became a pivotal focus for socialists, black activists, and feminists who challenged the inadequate support of trade union officials as well as the perfidy of the government and the activities of sweat shop anti-union bosses (Rogaly, 1977, and Ramdin, 1987, Chapter 9). Above all, of course, it involved the struggle of the striking Asian women to assert their right to organization and protection. All these accounts are correct in so far as there can be no history of the women's movement which does not overlap and intersect with other oppositional currents of the time. A valid explanation must be able to make sense of how different actors understood their activities in the ways they did. A full analysis also requires a careful assessment of the objective possibilities and constraints. There are important differences of analysis about what was necessary to win, whether the strike was winnable, and what organizational and political lessons should be drawn for the future. Feminism as a specific form of analysis which focuses on gender offers only one vantage point. Moreover, disputes like Grunwick's increasingly ceased to be a major theoretical concern for feminists who instead preferred to concentrate on male violence or on a post-modernist denial of the possibility of making objective judgements.

The ideas of the women's movement found an audience among large numbers of women in the late 1960s and 1970s as part of a broader process of radicalization. The women's movement was successful in setting up publications, spreading its influence by developing women's studies courses and study groups both formally inside the universities and more informally in women's groups. The women's movement was also undoubtedly successful in initiating self-help groups which made real progress in a number of areas particularly Women's Aid, Rape Crisis and in relation to women's health with initiatives that were later to become state supported women's health centres and clinics.

However, it also became clear that there were deep divisions within the movement (German, 1989). National conferences were marked by bitter dissension and the final conference was held in 1978; the last national meeting of socialist feminists in 1979 was equally split. There were splits over whether male violence, rape and pornography should become the central focus. There were also divisions between heterosexual women and political lesbianism, not as a matter of particular sexual orientation but as questions of allegiance and political commitment. Black women both in Britain and the USA launched devastating attacks on feminism for its ignorance of racial and class oppression. In France there was an extraordinary spectacle as feminists fought legal battles over the rights to use the name MLF. In Italy the women's movement was the subject of disputes which destroyed the revolutionary left (Harman, 1988). This fissuring cannot be understood as irrational outbursts of internecine warfare; it reflected a series of shifts in political mood into the 1980s when the overall level of social protest declined. The activities around Greenham Common tended to obscure this reality in Britain, but the combination of failed industrial disputes, a growing disillusion with social democratic parties in and out of power, and a decrease in student radicalism, suggests that overall the period was characterized by a sense of defeat and social conservatism.

The adverse political climate reinforced the problem of the social composition of the women's movement. Forms of feminism continued to flourish and there were indeed real gains for some women. Individual women did very well in the professions and business, and feminist ideas formed an influential current in the British Labour Party and the Democratic Party in the USA. However, the social divisions between these women and the mass of their 'sisters' widened in the 1980s. This phenomenon was not unique to feminism. Manning Marable documents the same phenomenon among the black middle class beneficiaries of the black struggle (Marable, 1985). He documents the differences between black middle class and working class politics and experience as the gap between middle class black and working class black incomes grew. Class inequalities grew in both Britain and the USA and that deepened inequalities within gender and ethnic groups. Feminist ideas found fertile ground predominantly among middle class women: among academics, in publishing, and increasingly in areas such as therapy and in social work. This is not to deny that these women faced real struggles inside their own institutions or that acceptance was easy. On the contrary feminists had to fight for their gains, but increasingly the social content was middle class. There were of course feminist interventions — for example against Clause 28 — but many campaigns remained small and internally divided, and much of the joy which characterized the early movement was lacking. Fighting for a common cause no longer united different political tendencies even in action. Bitterness and factionalism was evident even when participating in a common event. I was once told to leave part of a Clause 28 demonstration on the grounds that it was for 'women only' — because as I was holding an SWP placard I clearly no longer qualified! Being a 'woman', like being a feminist, became a matter of particular political identification, an identity which inevitably excluded other women. The campaign over pornography split feminists, and alliances were formed which accommodated social and sexual conservatism particularly in the USA (Chester and Dickey, 1988, and Segal and McIntosh, 1992). In Britain 'reclaim the night' marches on occasion were routed through black areas despite the fact that for black women and men, higher levels of policing would mean increased harassment. As Lynne Segal has so ably demonstrated, the shifting focus of feminist action had major consequences for feminist ideas. She argues that the issues which became popular among feminists idealized the virtues of women while demonizing men, and that socialist feminist ideas were sidelined (Segal, 1987).

Feminist knowledges

The title of this chapter identifies feminisms in the plural. Feminist theory, as the term 'feminisms' implies, involves multiple, fractured and contested knowledges. In the early days of the women's movement there was a sense of a broad unity of purpose generated by joint action which transcended divisions. A generalised commitment to some sort of liberation could temporarily erase the differences between movement activists and broader participants, and between competing analyses within the movement. This has been replaced by at worst bitter wrangling, and at best a deepened appreciation of competing theoretical approaches. Faced with the evident disagreement between feminists, and a clearer appreciation of the real differences in women's lives, some authors have correctly argued for the importance of studying lived experience. They recognise that 'woman' is not a Cartesian essence but forms the basis for a political strategy founded on an understanding of women's historically subordinate role (Stanley and Wise, 1993). However, despite real analytical advances, I want to argue that two major tendencies in feminist theorizing have proved destructive to a politics which could address the problem of women's oppression. The first, is the tendency in the work of some radical feminist authors to focus exclusively on male violence. The second, is the way in which the recognition of diversity and difference has led other feminists to adopt post-mordernism as the feminist paradigm (Nicholson, 1990). There appears to be an 'elective affinity' between post-modernism and feminism. Post-modernism rejects any notion of scientificity or objectivity, and its radically relativist conclusions seem more attuned to the fractured identities of feminism than Enlightenment certainties. While the first group of radical feminist theorists have adopted a polemical, sometimes lurid popular style; the latter 'post-modern' work is often characterized by its academic tone and inaccessibility. Despite these obvious differences both analyzes involve forms of idealism which vitiate political activism.

In the 1960s and early 1970s feminist attempts to grapple with the theoretical problems of explaining women's oppression shared in the sense of discovery which was characteristic of the women's movement. Academics surveying their subject areas found that women were ignored, left out, subsumed under mankind, or presented in stereotyped and sexist terms. Female physiology, for example, was treated as a deviation from the male norm! In work aimed at redressing the balance, metaphors of the hidden and invisibility abound, and feminist writing stressed recovery, finding a voice, putting women back into the picture, and latterly re-gendering men as part of taking gender seriously. This work provided a major corrective and lasting contribution in many disciplines. Alongside this expanded and richly empirical base both 'radical' and 'socialist' feminist theorists sought to provide general explanations of oppression. Unsurprisingly, given the radical milieu of which the women's movement was part, there was a major theoretical engagement with Marxism. Some radical feminists utilized the idea of a separate domestic mode of production while many socialist feminists attempted to remould Marxist categories to include women's oppression. Many theorists tried to marry the historically invariant dimension of unequal power relations between men and women — patriarchy — with a view of history which stressed discontinuity and qualitative change (Sargent, 1981). Radical feminists insisted on the primacy of gender oppression.

The search for a general theory was part of the women's movement's attempt to mobilize women across class, race and other social differences. This was a logical outcome for a movement which has split from the left and from black politics by asserting the political priority of fighting women's oppression. The concept of patriarchal power, even in its most convoluted socialist feminist guise, had as its central problematic the power of all men over all women. The aspiration to a universalistic analysis moblizing the concept of patriarchy was undermined by the critique of black feminists who pointed out that not only had white upper class women shared class privilege with men in exploiting black women and men, but also that bourgeois feminists had sacrificed the interests of black working class women in the suffrage struggle. Feminist theory which focused on the family as the source of women's oppression had ignored the struggles of black men and women to establish the right to unite in families (*Feminist Review*, 1986). Historical work on the constitution of the working class family identified the family as a defence mechanism as well as a site of oppression (Brenner and Ramas, 1984). There were theoretical strands within socialist feminism which were ambivalent about patriarchy theory and which emphasized the importance of class differences and racism. Together with black feminism these might have enabled an enriched understanding of women's oppression not marred by false universalism. This possibility is clearly signalled in the work of bell hooks who argues that sisterhood and solidarity are accomplishments of struggle, rather than an identity arising automatically out of an assumed common oppression. However, socialist feminists and black feminists found themselves largely overtaken by forms of feminism which did exactly what bell hooks had criticized. This was a political defeat as well as a theoretical reorientation. Socialist feminist and anti-racist struggles declined in importance inside the movement. The radical feminism of Andrea Dworkin and Mary Daly focused on the common oppression and victimization of women, with men as all-powerful violators (Daly, 1979 and Dworkin, 1981, 1984).

In the 1980s there was a marked shift in agenda, both theoretically towards concentrating on violence and pornography, and practically to organizing against them. Partly this was because the creation of a 'lesbian identity' led to a re-evaluation of all heterosexual acts as violence. Political lesbianism was a way of becoming women-identified. In Mary Daly's version 'female befriending' involved a commitment to a life of contemplation as the only true sisterhood. Both Andre Lorde and Lynne Segal have pointed out that this vision depended on a privileged social and economic position which allowed some women to withdraw completely from men. The implications are elitist, sisterhood can only be practically achieved by the middle class few, and ignored the impact of racism in structuring black women's lives. Radical feminist versions of political lesbianism were not an inevitable outcome of the recognition of the significance of different sexualities. Many lesbians found that confronting the realities of discriminatory custody rulings and prejudice at work bore little relation to a women-identified utopia. Equally, some lesbians were critical of the ideal of political lesbianism because it obscured the significance of lesbianism as a specifically sexual orientation.

The focus on pornography took up the theme of the representation of women's bodies which has been a major focus of feminist theorizing from the early days of the women's movement. The commodification of women's bodies has given a particular predominance to the male gaze in objectifying women as 'sex'. Andrea Dworkin's emphasis on pornography, however, erased the gap between the representational and the act; pornography itself comes to stand for rape. The idea becomes the fact. Dworkin's work has been criticized for its essentialism in accepting fixed biologically bounded male and female characteristics, and its identification of women as victim. The political strategies that flowed from the emphasis on pornography and the alliance with sexual conservatives of the New Right in the USA split both British and American feminists. However, the similarities between anti-pornography feminism and more academic work on representation have received less attention. The move towards a focus on representation and language, found in both Dworkin and Daly, was shared by much feminist work within cultural studies. Here the adoption of Saussurean analysis led to the assertion that language could be understood only as a system of signification. This involved a denial of the possibility of any relationship between representation and any referent outside the language.[6] There are, of course major theoretical divergences between Dworkin's heavy handed and lurid generalizations, Daly's elaborate punning, and the obscurity of much deconstructivist writing. However underlying these differences there is a common concern with cultural artefacts and their centrality in analyzing 'woman'. This general shift has sometimes been described as cultural feminism to distinguish it from the more robust materialist feminisms, both socialist and radical, which preceded it.

The impact of post-modernist ideas on feminism has been immense. This is not surprising given their general acceptance within academia. In feminist theorizing the self-sufficient truths of philosophy which post-modernism rejects were associated historically with particularly male forms of speech and self-presence. Feminism formed part of the general deconstruction of Enlightenment philosophy. In post-modern analysis, Enlightenment subjecthood was theorized as being achieved through a series of binary oppositions: man/women, active/passive, culture/nature. The Enlightenment subject was male in opposition to its female other. The same form of analysis has been employed in relation to race. Enlightenment 'self' was defined in relation to the other; and the other of Western culture has been racialized and exoticized.[7] Post-modernism with its emphasis on local knowledges and on the discursively achieved self appealed to feminist sensibilities as the women's movement fractured into feminisms based on different identities. Groups of women — disabled, Jewish, lesbian — asserted their right to self-definition and their unique capacity to articulate their own oppression. This created irresolvable dilemmas as one group's reality clashed with another's, for example in the debates in Spare Rib between 'Palestinian' and 'Jewish' women. At a theoretical level post-modernism can accommodate this diversity through its insistence that there can be no basis for adjudicating truth claims. One of the reasons for post-modernism's acceptance within feminism was that it resonated with the increasingly messy state of the movement. I am not convinced by suggestions that post-modernism also allowed feminists a critical position in relationship to knowledge produced in the academy. On the contrary, post-modernism has become hegemonic in many areas, so that rather then swimming against the academic mainstream, feminism has become part of the dominant current. A more cynical interpretation is that the post-modern rejection of emancipatory narratives frees academics to pursue the less politically challenging task of producing local knowledges.

Some feminists have been critical of the rush to embrace post-modernism. They have pointed, for example, to the problem of relativism for a political movement which wants to use its knowledge to challenge the dominant framework. They have also noted the difficulties of theorizing political agency: how do 'women' become capable of resisting their oppression? (McNay, 1992). Post-modernism may be fine for men who have had the chance to stamp their imprint on knowledge — they can enjoy the luxury of letting go — but it may prove a dangerous strategy for women whose subjecthood historically has been denied. Most of these debates, however, have taken place within the parameters defined by post-modernism. Michele Barrett has gone so far as to assert that were she rewriting *Women's Oppression Today* she would begin with post-modernism (Barrett, 1988). Post-modernity is presented as both an existential and philosophical fait accompli. One of the most compelling arguments against post-modernism is that its denial of any criteria for judging truth claims renders it unfalsifiable. Post-modernism is the unfalsifiable foundation to anti-foundationalism! Alex Callinicos, among others, has provided an immanent critique of post-modernist claims to internal coherence and cogency, demonstrating the aporias and contradictions within particular authors as well as between them (Callinicos, 1989 and Norris, 1990). Post-modernism is a mishmash of philosophical claims, a peculiar debate within art and architecture, and a series of often facile claims about late capitalism. Callinicos has also hypothesized about the connections between these ideas and the growing social isolation of a generation of radicals from broader struggles. Feminism represents a particular instance of this broader argument. Academics were able to embrace the idea of new social movements and a plurality of struggles as a move towards greater radicalism rather than a move away from a politics which attempted to challenge real power.

Why then should post-modern feminism not be taken as the theoretical advance it claims to be? Firstly, the arguments about the lack of cogency are compelling; post-modernism cannot be mended or adjusted and the anti-realism at its core makes it incapable of being pressed into the service of a movement committed to acting against oppression. Its failure to theorize personal and political agency is not merely an omission. Agency becomes an essentially arbitrary and illusory product of discourse. This has been cleverly satirized by Ellen Meiskin Wood:

The ultimate conclusion of this argument must be that a caveman is as likely to become a socialist as a proletarian - provided only that he becomes within hailing distance of the.appropriate discourse (Wood, 1986, p.61).

Post-modernist theory denies any possibility of relating politically constituted subjects to the objective conditions in which such subjects come to act. There are real theoretical problems about how objective interests are to be assessed. However, it is necessary to insist on the legitimacy of forms of reasoning which tie the objective circumstances of oppression to an interest in and capacity to act in resisting that oppression. This requires establishing causal connections between circumstances and resistance, but also counter-factual ideology-critique which can explain why people do not resist, as well as explaining why they do. One of my criticisms of patriarchy theory is that it fails to do this.

Political arguments depend on having criteria for judging the truth claims and hence the fallibility of (all) theory. Post-modernism in contrast portrays claims to truth as power knowledges to be preferred on aesthetic or pragmatic grounds. Sexist knowledges have the same status as feminist knowledges. This parallels the radical relativism of thinkers like Dale Spender and Mary Daly and their apparent willingness to let men get on with their own truths while women get on with theirs (Daly, 1985). The impulse to change, and an emancipatory interest in knowledge, is undermined. Finally, post-modernism fails to deal with the particular objective circumstances in which agents come to act. James Scott in his study of peasant and pre-modern revolts notes the frequency with which people fight even when the objective circumstances are not auspicious. He argues for the need to theorize the impulse to revolt and the resources that people draw on. People constantly make judgements about what is possible. One of the functions of an emancipatory theory produced in and through social movements is this constant assessment of objective circumstances.[8] The conditions in which people find themselves provide both the resources and powers for opposition, as well as circumscribing their limits. Both post-modernism and popular anti-pornography feminisms failed to provide a political theory that could contribute to such an analysis. My argument is that this was largely because they were developed in the context of a fractured and failing movement which had lost its liberatory impulse.

Conclusions

I have suggested that the two major theoretical shifts within feminism in the 1980s were influenced by the broader political climate, and by the confusions and divisions within feminism itself. Despite its populist appeal the emphasis on rape and pornography could not provide the basis for generalized political action. If men are so fundamentally different and dangerous to women then a strategy of withdrawal becomes the only possible solution. Separation from men is neither a practical possibility nor is it seen as desirable by many women who believe that the defence of their communities and rights is a shared interest and not exclusively female (e.g. Women Against Pit Closures). It is clear that the political consequences of an emphasis on pornography led to anti-liberal conclusions. Anti-porn anti-men feminism meshes with the fears of the conservative right in blaming working class black and white youth for a multitude of social fears and ills. In a curious twist of theory, those men who exercise least social power in society are blamed, while men with greater social power like the police and courts are regarded as the potential protectors of women's interests. Furthermore, the picture of women as victims and as naturally more peaceable, and in some ecological and anti-war versions as closer to nature, recreates sexual stereotypes that the women's movement rejected. Nor can post-modernist theory provide a mobilizing alternative. Lodged in academia, much of this theory has only the most tangential relationship to any practice outside its walls.

In the 1990s it is not clear what will engender new levels of protest and whether these will focus on grievances that particularly affect women. But there can be no doubt that these grievances are still there. Proportionately many more women live in poverty, and the gap between ideas of women's equality and opportunities still presents contradictions that create the possibility for protest. An interesting new example of social protest is opposition to the Child Support Agency. The demand for men to support their children appealed to many feminists, but its punitive consequences are clear; most men cannot afford to maintain two households. Men's wages rarely now even support one. The crude political reality is that the

Child Support Agency is being used to channel money back into the Treasury, not to women or children. This has created pockets of surprisingly militant resistance on the part of women as well as men.

My belief is that what will prove to be enduring about contemporary feminist knowledge is the rich histories and insights it has given into women's lives. Much work has also rightly exposed the wrongs of women and their strategies of opposition. The women's movement contributed to a language of resistance that can still be drawn on. Although feminism may have splintered, sexist behaviour is now much more often seen as unacceptable, domestic violence is seen as crime, women assume that they have rights to sexual pleasure and that No means No, and despite the efforts of the Christian Right, the defence of safe legal abortion is remarkably resilient. The pattern of women's struggles in the 1990s is not at all clear, nor is it clear whether women will choose to.organize separately. Groups of women in the professions and academia continue to ensure that feminist ideas have a place alongside and sometimes superseding partial and biased knowledges. Whether these are the resources new generations of women will draw on in the fight to combat oppression remains to be seen. Of two things I remain convinced. One is that women's oppression remains a feature of all contemporary societies, as do racism and exploitation. The other is that there will be struggles, covert and open, against forms of oppression and that women will continue to be part of these.

Notes

1. My own relation to the events analyzed is pertinent to the reflexive methodology in the paper, so I will offer some auto-biographical pointers. I was one of the generation of working class girls 'made good' who went to University in 1967 and was caught up in the revolutionary socialist and anti-war politics of the time. In the 1970s the women's movement meant endless campaigns around nurseries, on women's issues in trade unions, on abortion rights etc. For most of that time I was active as a socialist at work, in anti-cuts and anti-racist campaigns and the like. A group of us also met socially as women and discussed sex, work, men, sexual fantasies; all the topics of kitchen and bedroom which came into the open as part of 'consciousness raising'. Towards the end of the 1970s I was involved in a Women and Ireland Group and generally in the socialist feminist debates about anti-imperialism and anti-racism. I collapsed into relative inactivity and political confusion at the end of the decade. The miners strike 1984-85 revitalized me and I have remained active as a member of the Socialist Workers Party ever since. One story out of a generation of political women, except that many joined the Labour Party or remained as independent feminists in the 1980s and 1990s.

2. Academia works on competition, promotion is based on publication and managerial responsibility, research funds are competitively awarded, students are normally assessed individually. Many feminists have debated the contradictions this presents for a feminism based on sisterhood and shared experience. Angela McRobbie has also noted that male definitions of research stress newness and originality at the expense of participation and affirmation (McRobbie, 1982). Others, however, have been critical of feminism as an academic discourse for adopting these supposedly male attributes. bell hooks for example, argues that 'excessive trashing' of other women has become a feature of feminist debate (hooks, 1984).

3. Scott appears more confident that his analysis fits pre-industrial pre-democratic contexts where there is a greater necessity for oppositional speech and practices remaining hidden. He does, however, make some footnoted references to the women's movement. Women's talk prior to its emergence on the political

scene seems to provide a particularly good example of his concept. One interesting avenue to pursue in this regard might be the relationship between hidden/public and private/public; slaves were forced to hide their talk whereas in many ways women's talk was not hidden but rather not heeded because it belonged to the private.

4. Colin Barker suggested adding 'and some men' here. I think it is interesting to note that many men found the ideas of the women's movement exciting, and many early participants were convinced that men would also benefit from greater equality in relationships. The reason we do not have more of these reminiscences in print is because much subsequent feminist theory has popularized the idea that men were really only interested in women's sexual liberation for their own sexist purposes. I think this rewriting is unfortunate. A much better approach is elaborated in two books by Lynne Segal (Segal, 1990, 1992).

5. Overlaps and conflicts between socialists and the women's movement are not new. The classic debates inside the German SPD are a good example (Foner, 1984) as are the debates within suffrage movement (Liddington and Norris, 1978)

6. I am making only a glancing reference to a hugely complicated set of arguments. Suffice it to say that the alternatives are not either a crude reflectionist theory or Saussurean linguistics. There are quite sophisticated materialist attempts to theorize the relationship between language and meaning (Callincos, 1987, Chapter 3).

7. For an elaboration of this type of analysis see the journal *Third Text*.

8. I have drawn heavily on the work of Roy Bhaskar in my thinking about the concept of an emancipatory social theory (Bhaskar, 1986).

References

Barker, C. (ed.), (1987), *Revolutionary Rehearsals*, Bookmarks, London.

Barrett, M. (1988), *Women's Oppression Today: The Marxist Feminist Encounter*, Verso, London.

Bhasker, R. (1986), *Scientific Realism and Human Emancipation*, Verso, London.

Brenner, J., Ramas, M. (1984), 'Rethinking Women's Oppression', *New Left Review*, March/April, pp.33-71.

Callincos, A. (1987), *Making History, Polity*, Cambridge.

Callincos, A. (1989), *Against Postmodernism*, Polity, Cambridge.

Chester, G., Dickey, J. (1988), *Feminism and Censorship: The Current Debate, Prism Press*, Birdport.

Coote, A., Campbell, B. (1987), *Sweet Freedom*, Blackwell, Oxford.

Daly, M. (1979), *Gyn/Ecology*, Women's Press, London.

Daly, M. (1984), *Pure Lust*, Women's Press, London.

Duchen, C. (1986), *Feminism in France*, Routledge Kegan Paul, London.

Dworkin, A. (1981), *Pornography: Men Possessing Women*, Women's Press, London.

Faludi, S. (1992), *Backlash: The Undeclared War Against Women*, Chatto and Windus, London.

Foner, P. (ed.), (1984), *Clara Zetkin Selected Writings*, International Publishers, New York.

Friedan, B. (1965), *The Feminine Mystique*, Penguin, Middlesex.

German, L. (1989), *Sex, Class, and Socialism*, Bookmarks, London.

Harman, C. (1988), *The Fire Last Time: 1968 and After*, Bookmarks, London.

hooks, bell (1982), *Ain't I A Woman? Black Women and Feminism*, Pluto, London.

hooks, bell (1984), *Feminist Theory: From Margin to Centre*, South End Press, Boston.

Liddington, J. and Norris, J. (1978), *One Hand Tied Behind Us*, Virago, London.

Marable, M. (1985), *Black American Politics: From the Washington Marches to Jesse Jackson*, Verso, London.

McNay, L. (1992), *Foucault and Feminist*, Polity, Cambridge.

McRobbie, A. (1982), 'The Politics of Feminist Research: Between Talk, Text and Action', *Feminist Review* No. 12, pp.12-57.

Molyneux, J. (1993), 'The 'Politically Correct' Controversy', *International Socialism Journal* No. 61, pp.43-74.

Nicholson, L. (ed.), (1990), *Feminism/Postmodernism*, Routledge, London.

Norris, C. (1990), *What's Wrong with Postmodernism? Critical Theory and the Ends of Philosophy*, Harvester Wheatsheaf,

London.

Ramdin, R. (1987), *The Making of the Black Working Class in Britain*, Gower, Aldershot.

Rogaly, J. (1977), *Grunwick*, Penguin, Middlesex.

Rowbotham, S. (1989), *The Past is Before Us. Feminism in Action since the 1960s*, Pandora Press, London.

Sargent, L. (ed.), (1981), *Women and Revolution: The Unhappy Marriage between Marxism and Feminism: A Debate On Class and Patriarchy*, Pluto, London.

Scott, J. C. (1990), *Domination and the Arts of Resistance: Hidden Transcripts*, Yale University Press, New Haven.

Segal, L. (1990), *Slow Motion: Changing Masculinities Changing Men*, Virago, London.

Segal, L. (1994), *Straight Sex: The Politics of Pleasure*, Virago, London.

Segal, L., McIntosh, M. (1992), *Sex Exposed: Sexuality and the Pornography Debate*, Virago, London.

Spender, D. (1985), *For the Record: The Making and.Meaning of Feminist Knowledge*, Women's Press, London.

Stanley, L., Wise, S. (1993), *Breaking Out Again*, Routledge, London.

Wood, E. (1986), *The Retreat From Class: A New 'True' Socialism*, Verso, London.

5 To concede or to contest?
Language and class struggle

Chik Collins

The word in language is half someone else's. It becomes 'one's own' only when the speaker populates it with his own intention, his own accent, when he appropriates the word, adapting it to his own semantic and expressive intention ... And not all words for just anyone submit equally easily to this appropriation ... Language is not a neutral medium that passes freely and easily into the private property of the speaker's intentions; it is populated — overpopulated — with the intentions of others. Expropriating it, forcing it to submit to one's own intentions and accents, is a difficult and complicated process (Bakhtin, 1981, pp.293-294).

Introduction

Critical reflection on language and its relation to power and ideology is increasingly central to contemporary social theory. Indeed, a concern with 'discourse' progressively colonizes the social sciences as a whole. For those whose primary interest is around questions of class and class struggle this development might appear as a double-edged sword.

On the one hand the newer trajectory might offer more insights into the processes of subjectivity and consciousness which existing approaches to class and class struggle have clearly found problematic. On the other hand, it has seemed that the orientation towards discourse has often developed at the expense of a concern with questions of class (e.g. see Foster, 1985; Palmer, 1990). Indeed, more than this, for some writers it has precipitated a 'fashionable cult of absolute relativism', or threatened to undermine what they see as 'the kinds of coherent thought that can actually lead to the emancipation of humanity' (see Palmer, 1990, pp.xiii-xiv).

Unsurprisingly, debates have been highly polarised, and amidst the polarisation there is a clear danger. The danger is that those chiefly interested in questions of class and class struggle might neglect to explore fully the ways in which a focus on language or 'discourse' might complement, rather than undermine, their own project. There are, of course, writers who have worked to avoid this danger, and who have been conducting these explorations for some time (Fairclough, 1989, 1993; Foster, 1974, 1985; Foster and Woolfson, 1986; Huspek, 1986, 1988a, 1988b, 1989, 1991a, 1991b, 1993, 1994; Huspek and Kendall, 1991; Mey, 1985; Scott, 1990; Woolfson, 1976, 1977; Woolfson and Foster, 1988). Yet, all would agree that very substantial work remains to be done. The aim of this paper is to offer some results from one case study as a contribution to this work.

The case study is of the struggle surrounding the Upper Clyde Shipbuilders' 'work-in' of 1971-72. This struggle saw the emergence and development of a broad industrial and political movement for the defence of jobs and industry as the post-war boom came to a halt and recession began to bite deep into the Scottish economy. This movement, albeit temporarily, managed to sustain and politically defend a vision of a future without the monetarism and rampant de-industrialization which subsequently blighted Clydeside's working class communities.

My aim here is to draw on the account of the work-in provided by Foster and Woolfson (1986), and some of the archive materials on which their work is based, to look in detail at one particularly interesting episode during the work-in.[1] In a period of nine days during late September and early October 1971 the work-in and the vision of the future which it sustained were subjected to an acute political onslaught. An examination of this episode, then, will tell us something concrete about the dynamics of a contest between competing visions of the future, and about what is involved in the task of sustaining and politically defending a progressive vision. This involves paying particular attention to the language which was mobilised by the two sides in the contest. Using a theoretical framework derived from Volosinov (1986), the following analysis charts the development of the contest over this period. It will show

70

how the leading stewards first rebuffed and then 'expropriated' the social democratic language of 'co-operation' and 'negotiation' which was mobilised against them by the Government, the trades unions and the media in an attempt to bring the work-in to an end. For a period they actually succeeded in harnessing this language to the task of politically defending the work-in and the vision of an alternative future which it sustained.

The Upper Clyde Shipbuilders work-in[2]

The shipbuilding industry on the river Clyde in Scotland has historically been beset by problems of rivalry between a myriad of craft-based sectional groupings blocking wider resistance to dominant power. The consortium of four yards known as the Upper Clyde Shipbuilders (UCS) employing 8,000 workers was no exception. However in the later 1960s and early 1970s a left-wing leadership was consolidated within the trade union shop stewards committees in the four yards. These committees built their authority by redirecting the activity of craft groupings away from sectional inter-craft conflicts and into successful collective battles with management over pay and conditions.[3] In turn the yards became a focus for working class action in the west of Scotland as a whole. One of the region's big business strategists described the yards in 1969 as 'a cancer eating into the whole of Clydeside industrial life' (Foster and Woolfson, 1986, p.164).

In June of 1971 Edward Heath's Conservative Government moved to enforce a policy of closure and mass redundancies on the yards by allowing UCS to go into liquidation. A Government appointed committee of 'experts' reported that a rescue would be unwarranted. Instead a much smaller two-yard company (involving Govan and Linthouse to the exclusion of John Brown's and Connel's) employing some 2,500 was proposed. Their recommendation was expressed in a language which reflected the nascent monetarist agenda developed by the Conservatives in the late 1960s.[4] The UCS was a 'lame duck' which must be sacrificed as part of larger project to make Britain's economy lean and competitive. The media were generally quite willing to follow this line. For instance, in August 1971 *The Observer* reported that:

71

The slimming down of the Upper Clyde is not a case of correcting over ambition, but of phasing out a group of unviable declining shipyards which it was not sensible to modernise where they stood ... It's no use making any bones about it. The fact is that the Connel and John Brown yards must slip painfully into history (8/8/71).

The work force responded with a work-in for 'the right to work' led by the left wing stewards heading the Shop Stewards Co-ordinating Committee. The most prominent of these were Jimmy Reid, James Airlie and Sam Barr. All were then members of the Communist Party of Great Britain. Their demands were a non-negotiable defence of All four yards, the entire labour force, no redundancies.' This strategy proved highly successful.

However more alarming for the Government was the way in which the work-in served to focus an underlying cleavage between monopoly capital and the interests of small and medium businesses which had been developing in Scotland in preceding years (see Foster and Woolfson, 1986, pp.15-131, and 380-433). While monopoly profits would benefit from the reduction of capacity and the smashing of union militancy within the yards, small and medium businesses, would be major losers from a policy of industrial closure. The political space created by this cleavage within the pro-Conservative forces was exploited by the stewards, and the work-in rapidly gained widespread support throughout Scottish society. It served to crystallize and focus a broad opposition to an economic strategy geared overwhelmingly to the interests of monopoly capital. The workers' protest became a popular protest. The durability of this protest can be seen very clearly in the inability of the Government and the media to undermine (or even seriously challenge) the legitimacy of the protest and the authority of the leading stewards in the early stages of the work-in. The work-in began on 30 June, but it was only in the later part of September that the pro-closure forces managed to mount a coherent and sustained attack.

This came in the form of an announcement on 23 September 1971 that a new company — Govan Shipbuilders Limited — would be formed on the basis of the Linthouse and Govan yards 'saving' some 2,500 jobs. Though trumpeted as a new initiative, this was an attempt to implement the existing policy announced in June. The aim was to secure the compliance of the work force with the new company. This would, in turn, depend on undermining the authority of the stewards with their non-negotiable demands, and restoring the orthodox, sectionally based leadership and practices of the official trade unions. Thus, we find a contested future for the work force, with a broad popular unity to defend jobs and industry being posed against sectional conflict, mass redundancy, and de-industrialization.

Of course, the latter option was not expressed in these terms. It was framed in an ideological and moral discourse which attempted to present the policy as being in the best interests of society as a whole. However, the specific form in which the case was made was now changed. The discourse of social democratic consensualism (Beharrel and Philo, 1977; Glasgow University Media Group, 1976, 1982) replaced the earlier monetaristic formulation. The Government would seek 'co-operation' from, and 'negotiation' with, the work force in order to provide 'a real hope for the survival of jobs on the Clyde and shipbuilding on the Clyde' (John Davies, Secretary of State for Industry, BBC TV News, 22/9/71). A failure to comply would put more jobs in jeopardy and so would be 'inflexible' and 'unreasonable'.

From the point of view of sustaining popular protest, and politically defending an alternative to the Government's vision of the future, this was a moment of crisis. The danger lay in the potential appeal of the proposal to the sectional identities which had only recently been overcome within the work force, and which could easily re-emerge. As Foster and Woolfson note: 'It would have been only too easy for the workers of Govan and Linthouse to call for 'realism' and go for their own sectional interests' (1986, p.272). This would have meant the end of the work-in and the popular protest which it had mobilised. In what follows we will examine how the stewards worked to avert this danger, and instead took the opportunity to turn the ideological and moral artillery mobilised by the Government back on the Government itself. Theoretically, the analysis is based on V. N. Volosinov's dialectical and dialogical conception of language, and it is necessary to summarize briefly how that informs what follows.

Volosinov: Marxism and the philosophy of language[5]

Volosinov approaches the studies of ideology, consciousness and social psychology simultaneously as a philosophy of language'. His main contribution, published in Russian in 1929, remains a distinctive one. Two closely linked aspects of this distinctiveness are of importance here.

Firstly Volosinov's object of study is not the word or the sentence, but the utterance which he regards as 'the real unit of speech communication'. The utterance is the unit which contains the essential relationship between the abstract system of language (Saussure's *langue*), and its active deployment in the task of making meanings adequate to the historical moment in which they are deployed (Saussure's parole). It is the unit which contains the relationship between system and performance which is at the heart of 'the problem of the actual mode of existence of language' (Volosinov, 1986, p.45). The utterance, for Volosinov, is always a concrete speech act spoken by a living subject from a specific social and historical location and addressed to the utterances of others. Moreover, in the generative flow of speech communication utterances not only refer to one another, but also embody and 'interanimate' each other. Utterances are not only part of a dialogue, they are dialogical in their very nature. Like dialogue, utterances presuppose more than one voice. The voice of one speaker can be heard 'speaking through' the words of another speaker. As this happens a specific type of relationship will be established within individual utterances between the status and authority of the meanings and evaluations created by the two voices.

Secondly, the distinctiveness of Volosinov's approach lies in his treatment of the relationship between language and social change. He rejects outright the admissibility of 'the category of mechanical causality' which reduces language, ideology and consciousness to some reflection of an ontologically prior and separate 'material base'. Rather, his central theme is the refutation of mechanical determinism and its failure to account 'for the process of the actual dialectical generation of society' from its 'socioeconomic premises'. His own dialectical solution is to see language as determined by 'the living interaction of social forces' (p.41) in existence, while simultaneously seeing it as 'a tremendous social force' which plays a crucial, creative role in determining social development.

From this perspective the study of language gains a central position in relation to social change. Firstly, language helps us to pinpoint key moments in the process of change. Countless ideological threads running through all areas of social intercourse register effects in the word. It stands to reason then, that the word is the most sensitive index of social changes, and what is more, of changes still in the process of growth, still without definitive shape and not as yet accommodated into already regularized and fully defined ideological systems. The word has the capacity to register all the transitory, delicate, momentary phases of social change (1986, p.19).

Secondly, language is seen as a site of struggle where the legitimacy of competing orientations to social change are contested. This contest is seen to have profound sociopolitical significance. Here Volosinov highlights the way in which language is deployed by powerful minorities with the intention of marginalizing subordinate communicative forms and meanings, and motivating subordinate groups to defer to the minority's authority in the management of society and its processes of social change. At the same time he also highlights the way in which the everyday discourses of subordinate groups provide symbolic and cultural resources more appropriate to their own social location ('social purview'). Subordinate groups draw on these resources to generate meanings which are antagonistic to those promulgated by authoritative groups, and which reflect their own perspective on processes of social change. This is why taking the utterance as the unit of analysis, and the focus on its dialogical nature, are so important. For together they direct our attention to the mutable and essentially contestable nature of language.

Having directed our attention to the contestable nature of language, Volosinov also offers us a simple, yet powerful way of grasping the dynamics of this contest. Here the question of evaluation comes to the fore. Anything which is really significant to the life of a social group is subjected to their evaluation. Whether explicitly or implicitly, whenever they speak about it they evaluate it from the point of view of their own 'social purview'. Because of this their utterances carry distinctive 'evaluative accents'. In actuality, we never hear or say words, we hear and say what is true or false, good or bad, important or unimportant, pleasant or unpleasant and so on (1986, p.70).

Volosinov refers us to the importance of changing evaluations within words and the role which they play within the 'dialectics of theme and meaning'. Here the term meaning is used to refer to the stable and fixed aspects of the symbolic resources which are available to speakers in the generation of concrete utterances. Meaning in this sense is a 'received' meaning. When these resources are deployed generatively in the utterance they are thematized — tailored by the speaker to create meanings adequate to the demands of their precise social and historical location. And here: it is precisely evaluation that plays the creative role. A change in meaning is, essentially, always a re-evaluation: the transposition of one particular word from one evaluative context to another (Volosinov, 1986, p.105).

The rub is that different groups with radically different points of view share a single language. Yet when they speak, their characteristic evaluations produce quite different meanings within the same words. The result is that the singular nature of the language can serve to mask the competing meanings which different groups realise when they speak. Powerful groups will seek to reinforce this masking of diversity and conflict — by inhibiting the development of meanings antagonistic to their own, and by devaluing, ridiculing and marginalizing hostile meanings where they do develop. However, at other times we find a polarization within language, as different groups realize antagonistic evaluations of the vital processes of social and economic change which are affecting their lives. The same words are mobilized in different ways, with different meanings and intentions, by different speakers. Words come to embody 'the clash of live social accents'.

> Class does not coincide with the sign community, i.e. with the community which is the totality of users of the same set of signs for ideological communication. Thus various different classes will use one and the same language. As a result, differently oriented accents intersect in every ruling class strives to impart a supra-class, eternal character to the ideological sign, to extinguish or drive inward the struggle between social value judgements which occurs in it, to make the sign uniaccentual. ... In actual fact, each living ideological sign has two faces, like Janus. Any current curse word can become a word of praise, any current truth must inevitably sound to many other people as the greatest lie (Volosinov, 1986. p.23).

At the same time Volosinov maintains that it is only in the context of the more significant social crises that this 'inner dialectic quality' of meanings becomes really visible. And so we return to our case study of such a situation.

Contesting alternative futures: (i) the attack

When the renewed attack by the pro-closure forces (outlined earlier) came in late September the biggest selling Scottish tabloid, The Daily Record, and the main broadsheet,the Glasgow Herald, both provided clear support for it. The *Glasgow Herald* argued:

> (T)he time for demonstrations and non-cooperation which might destroy all chances of ever getting Govan Shipbuilders off the ground is past. The full time union officials now have a duty to take over from the shop stewards and work with the management to ensure that the maximum number of jobs is preserved (23/9/71).

The same day's *Daily Record* carried separate photographs of John Davies (Secretary of State for Industry) and Dan McGarvey (leader of the Confederation of Shipbuilding and Engineering Unions) which were constructed to appear like a face to face dialogue between the two. The headline urged: 'SPEAK UP BROTHER DAN'. The editorial added:

> You have been remarkably silent during the current Clyde crisis. Now is the time to speak out. You have left brothers Jimmy Reid and James Airlie to lead the workers' fight from the shop floor. But now is the crunch (23/9/71).

This attack was sustained over the coming days. For instance the next day's Daily Record led on the theme of 'NO TALKS! NO CASH!' — Government assistance to the new company would not be forthcoming unless work force co-operation was secured. A further article on an inner page rammed home this same message (24/9/71, p.1, p.5). The same day's Glasgow Herald carried three UCS articles on the front page. One of these was the full text of a Commons statement made by John Davies the previous day, in which he argued that it was in the 'interests of all concerned' that negotiations begin as 'continued uncertainty can only prejudice the future' of the new company (24/9/71, p.1).

(ii) Negation

The stewards responded to the Government's attack by calling a mass meeting for the 24 September. Here they would put their reply to the work force. In developing their reply, and in putting their case more generally, they capitalized on the wording of a letter written in 1969 by the Conservative neo-liberal, Nicholas Ridley. The letter, drafted while the Conservatives were still in opposition and later leaked, proposed to 'butcher' shipbuilding on the upper Clyde.

> We could put in a government 'butcher' to cut up UCS and to sell (cheaply) to the Lower Clyde, and others the assets of UCS to minimise upheaval and dislocation. I am having further views on the practicability of such an operation, which I will report. After liquidation or reconstruction as above, we should sell the government holding in UCS even for a pittance (quoted in Foster and Woolfson, 1986, p.179-80).

The following is an extract from the speech made by Jimmy Reid to the mass meeting:

> And so we are saying to you workers the unreasonableness in the whole position is that of the Government, despite the exposure, despite the mass condemnation, they have pushed through their policy to butcher our industry and don't let any leader writer talk to us about reasonableness and inflexibility. The unreasonableness and the inflexibility is that of the Government. For our part we'll go and see Davies, Heath, anybody ... on the basis ... that we'll discuss any proposals ...that deals with the four yards and gives guarantees to the labour force in these yards. [We'll] talk to anybody ... but all the time they come back to the butchery of our industry. And I want to say here and now, don't let there be division in our ranks, I'll tell you this much, and I'm speaking personally here, if the Government succeeded in the butchery of our industry I'd rather be on the dole than be amongst the two and a half thousand that would be left to grovel, accept wages reductions and all sorts of other things, and I'm telling you it would be a short term solution because their objective would take place in a year or so, and it would be the end of our industry in the Clyde, and its like a murderer who wants to murder us, we've

found out, we've defended ourselves against the murder and people say 'please negotiate with the murderer, you might stop him from piercing your heart, but he can cut off your legs and arms and there's a sensible compromise'. And when you're lying bleeding they will tell you in a year or two, wi' you minus the legs, why aren't you standing on your own two feet ? And brothers our proposals therefore spring from a sense of responsibility to ourselves and to our families and our community and in the last resort to the British working class. It's impossible for us to accept this ... we are not capitulating to the butchery ... There will be no co-operation, and this is what we're putting to you with this board, no co-operation, that we close the ranks as a united labour force and tell them that they are not on ... So, we are appealing to you, its a simple proposal, there will be no co-operation, because that's the butchery we all reacted to on the 29th of July.... I know that despite how certain papers will play up, the mass media, that we can get through to our fellow workers and say 'Why should we co-operate with proposals and plans, that are butchery, that were butchery eight weeks ago, they are butchery today, and we are having no truck with butchers?' (UCS Transcripts, Vol.1).

Here we see the transposition of words between evaluative contexts very clearly — from the Government's attempt to generate a social democratic solution, to that of a militant shop steward who has won a position of authority in leading a united work force at the centre of a popular protest. It is not only the proposals which are contested, but simultaneously — through the force of thematization — the meanings of the terms in which they are framed. And here, indeed, it is evaluation which plays the crucial role. The use of the term butcher, the significance of which is already known to the workers, allows an instant re-evaluation of the terms reasonable and flexible as deployed by the Government. At the same time Reid refuses to concede entirely the positive content of such terms to the Government side. The workers are reasonable and flexible within the bounds of what they themselves define as a legitimate solution. This is the platform on which Reid constructs his plea for the unity of the work force which would be needed to hold out against the Government and maintain the work-in. Here the indignity of accepting butchery, and the prospect of further humiliations for a weakened labour force add to the moral authority of the utterance.

In turn this provides the basis for the transposition of the terms co-operation and negotiation. The image of the murderer hacking at the limbs of his victim articulates powerfully with the notion of butchery. This clears the path for Reid to call on the workers' responsibility to themselves as a united work force, and to their class, and to state emphatically, and with almost immediate repetition, that 'there will be no co-operation'. The received meanings of the terms negotiation and co-operation have been thematized and transposed to another evaluative context. They now take on predominantly negative meanings in direct opposition to those of the Government. Negotiation now means negotiation of the terms of defeat at the hands of the butcher. Co-operation means co-operating with the butchery of the shipbuilding industry.

The stewards clearly carried the work force at this stage. Their language, expressing the wider progressive unity on which the work-in was based, was preferred to the social democratic formulations of the pro-closure forces which could have led to the re-emergence of sectional conflict and undermined the whole popular protest. Reporting on the mass meeting the *Sunday Times* observed that:

> ... the men were sticking solidly to their theme that all jobs should be saved; the only man to speak against was heartily booed before completing his third sentence (26/9/71).

Yet, as the *Sunday Times* also observed, the danger of an unholy compromise remained:

> ... neither Reid nor Airlie is under any illusions about the danger of a split in solidarity. The hard fact is that for the first time since the work-in started, concrete offers of jobs have been made, admittedly totalling less than a third of what the men want. But the pressure to grab this albeit meagre carrot is there for all to see ... National union leaders would doubtless like to settle for the [Govan/Linthouse - CC] jobs, then talk about saving others later. This sort of compromise will not commend itself to Airlie and Reid ... Any compromise will break their grip, so releasing the dissident elements they have so far been able to check (26/9/71).

Continuing events served to emphasize this. Dan McGarvey's response to the developments of the 23 and 24 September was that:

Members elect leaders to lead them [i.e. official leaders - CC].
And leaders don't have the luxury of taking a dogmatic stand in a
serious situation (quoted in *Daily Record* 28 September 1971).

In short, McGarvey singularly failed to contest the meanings of the
terms co-operation and negotiation as they were deployed by those
in favour of closure. At the same time the media continued to
hammer the pro-closure line.

The way forward lies with making a success of what is left of
Upper Clyde Shipbuilding. That may not be grasped by the shop
stewards nor by most of the workers. It is grasped by the more
orthodox union leaders who are seeking to reassert themselves
and save what they can (*Glasgow Herald*, 28/9/71).

Yet, in the coming days the stewards were able not only to sustain
their case, but to force the pro-closure forces onto the retreat, and
ultimately to defeat the Government's line of attack. Here, indeed,
the strategic deployment of language in a heated political contest
was showing itself to be 'a tremendous social force'.

(iii) From negation to 'expropriation'

The crucial factor at this stage was that the Government still needed
the 'co-operation' of the work force to end the work-in and the
broader sociopolitical crisis which it was serving to focus. If the shop
stewards could hold their ground then the Government were going
to have to cede some of theirs.

In 'discussions' — 'discussions' being distinguished carefully from
'negotiations' — the chairman of the new company admitted that a
solution which avoided closures and redundancies altogether might
be possible. On the 29th he indicated that he was prepared to
consider the inclusion of the Connel yard in the new company. At the
same time he acknowledged that 'co-operation' would not be secured
unless there was a solution which included the John Brown yard in
Clydebank. On the 30 he indicated that he would also be prepared to
consider the case of Clydebank seriously. He attached two conditions
— Government backing and work force co-operation. Sam Barr
reported to a meeting of the shop stewards.

I couldn't tell you the way that Stenhouse is leading us or anything else like that but all I know is that this Government is in the worst position now because what they tried to do in the press yesterday has boomeranged. And he's made that public brothers, he's made it public and it'll be in the press tonight and television also that he's prepared to consider Clydebank (Report to the Co-ordinating Committee, 30/9/71, UCS Transcripts, Vol.1).

On that night's BBC TV news Stenhouse was asked about the prospects for saving the John Brown yard. He replied in the following terms:

If I was asked by the Government, the question, is the work force ... going to fully co-operate, and I mean jackets off, none of this bloody nonsense, and really getting down to it, and that the Government was going to make the finance available to it, then of course I would have to give this very serious consideration (BBC TV News Transcripts).

This retreat meant a change in the context of speaking, and led to a further development in the linguistic contest. The following is an excerpt from the oration given by Reid at a further mass meeting of the work force on 1 October 1971.

We have said from the outset; anyone, the Government or anyone else, will be guaranteed full co-operation — and I will come to that in a minute — based on the recognition of the four divisions and the entire work force. ... When Mr. Stenhouse indicated that he was for the four yards given these two conditions [Government backing and work force co-operation - CC], we right away said well one of them is met. We will co-operate. We will co-operate by unleashing the creative ability, and in some instances it would be genius, of the entire labour force. That is the co-operation that we are talking about ... We will co-operate with anyone on that basis. ... So we say the first condition is met, Mr Stenhouse, and next Tuesday the Minister of Trade and Industry, in our opinion must heed the new situation. Scottish industrialists now say yes, they are prepared to consider and take over the four divisions. The work force and the trade unions say yes. We will co-operate. We will co-operate in making this industry one of the most developed and advanced shipbuilding complexes in the world. There is one party yet to make its contribution and that is the Government and we are appealing here this morning for the unanimous vote, the unanimous vote of every worker in UCS to say yes. We will honour our commitment, and the Scottish community must say now and before next Tuesday that if the Government refuses to make its contribution then it is committing one of the greatest crimes against the Scottish people that has been perpetrated this year, and they are on their own. And the leader writers of the Scottish and British press can start getting their pencils and pens out and rewriting editorials as to the pig-heads, the obstinates, the dogmatists, because they will be in London and not the Clydeside ... with the attitude now adopted by the new company, or the new board, the ball is right back in the Government's court and we believe that if there is any sanity or humanity in this Government, then on Tuesday faced with almost the unanimity of the Scottish community they have got no alternative but to make their contribution and their investment, and their commitment.

And given that on Tuesday, the real negotiations will start; because we have been prepared on every occasion and we have stated it, we will go anywhere, we will see anyone given that there is a principled basis to the negotiations; the principled basis being that of ... the conditions laid down right from the outset by the co-ordinating committee on behalf of the united labour force of these yards (Mass Meeting, Clydebank, 1/10/71, UCS Transcripts, Vol.1).

This utterance takes the meanings generated in the earlier situation and addresses them to the new situation to generate quite new meanings. These not only negate the Government's case, but appropriate the positive moral content of the Government's language for the workers' case. Co-operation is now to mean co-operation to preserve all the yards with no job losses: 'That is the co-operation that we are talking about'. Negotiation also takes on a positive inflection because it is to be on a 'principled', as opposed to an immoral, basis: 'the real negotiations will start'. Thus the terms which had originally been mobilised in an attempt to bolster social democracy and sectionalism were expropriated by the stewards and hurled back at the Government who were now on the receiving end.

The pro-closure forces had lost the initiative in the deployment of some of their own chosen linguistic weapons. In the space of nine days, the moral force of the language of social democracy was, albeit temporarily, appropriated for the purposes of sustaining class unity within the work-in as the basis for a wider popular protest against the vision of de-industrialization and mass unemployment in the west of Scotland.[6] This is why the Government, 'which could orchestrate the reporting of events on a mass scale and rapidly change the principal focus of its case' (Foster and Woolfson, 1986, p.412) promptly did so in early October.

Discussion

The value of this episode, and of the materials which exist to allow us to study it in such detail, is, as outlined earlier, that it allows us to examine the concrete dynamics of a contest between competing visions of the future. This also means that the episode is particularly amenable to analysis within the framework of concepts provided by Volosinov. The conjunction of the episode and the analytical framework then allows us to begin to draw out some points for discussion regarding what is involved in the task of sustaining and politically defending a progressive vision. For the purposes of this discussion I would like to address three main points.

The first point regards the nature of the critique which the stewards mobilized against the pro-closure forces. This was, above all, an immanent critique. That is, it did not involve a simple counter-position of opposed value systems expressed in mutually exclusive conceptual categories. Instead it involved challenging the vision of the pro-closure forces on their own grounds. Those grounds were not that closure represented the narrow interests of monopoly capital on Clydeside, but that it was in the best interests `of all concerned'. The whole vitality of the stewards' case seems to have derived from their ability to undermine and expose the real agenda behind the Government's formulations on the basis of the latter's own claims to the moral high ground. Indeed it was only on this basis that the stewards could, when the opportunity presented itself on 30 September and 1 October, complete the 'difficult and complicated process' of expropriating the pro-closure language of universal interests and harnessing it to their own agenda. From this perspective, the ability of the ruling capitalist minority to propagate their claim to govern in the name of universal interests is their key legitimatory strength, but also a central political weakness. For these claims provide opposing forces with the criteria of evaluation according to which their own mendacity can be demonstrated (cf. Scott 1990; Hoffman 1990). The task of political leadership is to be able to respond strategically in those moments when the ruling minority is politically exposed to this type of critique, and to capitalize on the opportunities which the situation offers.

The second point follows directly from this. The UCS episode also demonstrates the utter dependence of the 'tremendous social force' of language on the specificities of the context in which it is mobilized (cf. Collins, in press). At one level this is obvious enough. The idea of 'the right to work', and of a 'work-in' to defend jobs and industry will clearly have an appeal in a society which is moving from an expectation of relatively full employment to a situation where chronic unemployment is becoming the norm. At another level it is less obvious, and it is here that the mutability of the terms 'co-operation' and 'negotiation' within the contest are so important. They demonstrate that those formulations which are emancipatory and progressive, and those which are subjugating and reactionary are not subject to prescription on an a priori basis. Instead, what is important, it seems, is not the ability to censor language, but the ability to contest and redefine received meanings creatively in response to shifting contexts of life and struggle.

This leads to our third point. The ability to contest and redefine received meanings is not a special gift delivered only to militant shop stewards and political activists. Volosinov argues that this is ever present in linguistic exchange in a society marked by systematic inequalities of power and wealth. However what Bakhtin seems to be stressing in the quotation at the beginning of the chapter is just how 'difficult and complicated' this task can be for working class subjects immersed in the immediacy of survival and existence at the sharp end of the powerful minority's restructuring of British society (cf. Collins, 1991; Collins and Lister, in press). So it is here that the task of leadership is crucially important, and the UCS episode seems to demonstrate this. That task is not one of dictating other people's interests, or of presuming to know other people's interests better than they know them themselves. It is one of responding strategically and creatively to the problems which these other people pose for themselves in the contest over alternative futures, and of helping to provide and develop the symbolic, cultural and organizational resources with which they themselves can provide answers.

Conclusion

The aim of this chapter was to contribute to the work of exploring how a focus on language or 'discourse' can continue to complement and enhance the approach(es) of social scientists whose primary interest remains focused on questions of class and class struggle. Drawing on Volosinov, it has pointed to the crucial importance of the contestation of key ideological meanings which takes place in moments of social crisis, highlighting the role which the outcome of such contests plays in helping to shape the subsequent path of development. This is not to suggest that discourse itself determines the path of social development (cf. Collins, 1995). Rather it is to suggest, as Fairclough has argued, that:

> ... language is both a site of and a stake in class struggle, and those who exercise power through language must constantly be involved in struggle with others to defend (or lose) their position (Fairclough, 1989, p.35).

Something of this same logic applies to the orientation of the social sciences towards language itself. The danger remains that a distaste for the specific directions taken by some writers focusing on language or discourse, might lead others, with different concerns, away from the type of engagement with language which its manifest importance in the politics of social development demands. To some this might seem analogous to leaving the observation of the empirical facts to the empiricists. The point is not to concede, but to contest.

Notes

1. Tape recordings of the proceedings of the shop stewards' Co-ordinating Committee and of the mass meetings of the work force during the work-in were made by one of the shop stewards. These were subsequently transcribed by Charles Woolfson of Glasgow University. The transcripts are stored, in three volumes, in Glasgow University Archives together with other relevant materials — including transcripts of British Broadcasting Corporation news coverage.
2. This section draws heavily on Foster and Woolfson (1986).
3. See Foster and Woolfson, 1986, Ch.3.
4. See Foster and Woolfson (1986, p.120) for a summary outline of this agenda.
5. There has been a protracted debate about the authorship of this text. Volosinov was a member of a study circle in the 1920s led by Mikhail Bakhtin, and also involving P. N. Medvedev. The debate surrounds whether Bakhtin was in fact the sole, or the main author of a number of texts attributed to his collaborators (e.g. Volosinov, 1986, 1976; Medvedev, 1985. See Gardiner, 1992, pp.196-197 for some discussion and further references. Also see Matejka and Titunik, 1986; Shukman, 1988).
6. Foster and Woolfson trace the beginnings of the infamous 'u-turn' of the Heath government to the steps which it was forced to take at this point. The problem for the government was not so much the work-in and of itself, as the way in which it crystallized the chasm within the Government's own political base and left its broader economic strategy politically exposed to a popular protest lead by left wing shop stewards. (Foster and Woolfson, 1986. For a brief summary of the main argument see pp.15-19, and 273-281.)

References

Bakhtin, Mikhail M. (1981), 'Discourse in the Novel' in *The Dialogic Imagination: Four Essays by M. M. Bakhtin*, Michael Holquist (ed.), Trans. Caryl Emerson and Michael Holquist, University of Texas Press, Austin.

Beharrel, P. and Philo, G. (1977), *Trade Unions and the Media*, The

Macmillan Press, London.

Collins, Chik (1991), *Community Participation in the Ferguslie Park 'Partnership': A Report to the Ferguslie League of Action Groups*, FLAG, Paisley.

Collins, Chik (1995), 'The Dialogics of "Community": struggle and identity in a Scottish working class housing scheme'. Paper presented to conference on 'Ideas of Community', University of West of England, 13-14 September 1995.

Collins, Chik (in press), 'The Pragmatics of Emancipation: a critical review of the work of Michael Huspek', *Journal of Pragmatics*.

Collins, Chik and Lister, Jim (in press), 'Hands Up or Heads Up: Questions on Community Work and Campaigning', in Shaw, M. and Cooke, I. (forthcoming, 1996), *Community Work Practice: re-asserting a radical agenda*, Moray House, Edinburgh.

Fairclough, Norman (1989), *Language and Power*, Longman, London.

Fairclough, Norman (1993), *Discourse and Social Change*, Polity Press, London.

Foster, John (1974), *Class Struggle and the Industrial Revolution*, Methuen, London.

Foster, John (1985), 'The De-classing of Language', *New Left Review*, No.150, pp.29-45.

Foster, John and Woolfson, Charles (1986), *The Politics of the UCS Work-In*, Lawrence and Wishart, London.

Gardiner, Michael (1991), *The Dialogics of Critique: M. M. Bakhtin and the Theory of Ideology*, Routledge, London.

Glasgow University Media Group (1976), *Bad News*, Routledge and Kegan Paul, London.

Glasgow University Media Group (1982), *Really Bad News*, Readers and Writers, London.

Hoffman, John (1990), 'Has Marxism a Future', *Communist Review*, No.7, pp.14-21.

Huspek, Michael (1986), 'Linguistic Variation, Context and Meaning: A Case of -ing/in' Variation in North American Workers' Speech' *Language in Society*, Vol.15, No.2, pp.149-163.

Huspek, Michael (1988a), 'The Politics of the UCS Work-In', *Journal of Pragmatics*, Vol.12, 1, pp.136-142.

Huspek, Michael (1988b), 'Language Analysis and Power', *Semiotica*, Vol.72, No.3/4, pp.341-359.

Huspek, Michael (1989), 'Linguistic Variability and Power: An analysis of YOU KNOW/I Think variation in working class speech', *Journal of Pragmatics*, Vol.13, No.5, pp.661-683.

Huspek, Michael (1991a), 'Taking Aim on Habermas's Critical Theory: On the road toward a critical hermeneutics' *Communication Monographs*, Vol.58, No.2, pp.225-233.

Huspek, Michael (1991b), Language and Power', *Language in Society*, Vol.20, No.1, pp.131-137.

Huspek, Michael (1993), 'Duelling Structures: the theory of resistance in discourse', *Communication Theory*, Vol.3, No.1, pp.1-25.

Huspek, Michael (1994), 'Oppositional Codes and Social Class Relations', *British Journal of Sociology*, Vol.45, No.1, pp.79-102.

Huspek, Michael and Kendall, Katherine (1991), 'On Withholding Political Voice: An analysis of the political vocabulary of a 'nonpolitical' speech community', *The Quarterly Journal of Speech*, Vol.77, No.1, pp.1-19.

Marx, K. and Engels, F. (1976), 'The German Ideology', in *Collected Works, Volume 5*, Lawrence and Wishart, London.

Matejka, Ladislav and Titunik, I. R. (1986), 'Translators' Preface', in Volosinov (1986).

Medvedev, Pavel N. (1985), *The Formal Method in Literary Scholarship: A Critical Introduction to Sociological Poetics*, The MIT Press, Cambridge, Massachussetts.

Mey, Jacob (1985), *Whose Language: A Study in Linguistic Pragmatics*, John Benjamins, Amsterdam.

Palmer, Bryan, D. (1990), *Descent into Discourse: The reification of language and the writing of social history*, Temple University Press, Philadelphia.

Shukman, Ann (1988), 'Introduction' in Shukman, Ann, ed. (1988), 'Bakhtin School Papers', *Russian Poetics in Translation*, No.10, Department of Linguistics, University of Essex.

Scott, James C. (1990), *Domination and the Arts of Resistance: Hidden Transcripts*, Yale University Press, New Haven and London.

UCS Shop Stewards Committee (n.d.), UCS Shop Stewards Committee. Transcripts of Tape Recordings, in 3 Volumes, Glasgow University Archives, UGD 181.

Volosinov, V. N. (1976), *Freudianism: A Marxist Critique*, Academic Press, New York and London.

Volosinov, V. N. (1986), *Marxism and the Philosophy of Language*,

Harvard University Press, London.

Woolfson, Charles (1976), 'The Semiotics of Working Class Speech', Working Papers in Cultural Studies, No.9.

Woolfson, Charles (1977), 'Culture, Language and the Human Personality', *Marxism Today*, August,pp.229-240.

Woolfson, Charles and Foster, John (1988), *Track Record: The Story of the Caterpillar Occupation*, Verso, London.

News sources

BBC TV News, BBC TV News UCS Transcripts, Glasgow University Archives, UGD 180.

Daily Record, June-October 1971.

The Glasgow Herald, June-October 1971.

The Observer, 8/8/71.

Sunday Times, 26/9/71.

6 The East German revolution of 1989

Gareth Dale

Until 1989, Communist rule in East Germany seemed perdurable, buttressed by a Wall which SED leader Erich Honecker promised would still be standing a century later. Popular revolt seemed doomed to fail. From June 1953 — the date of a workers' uprising — until 1989, the GDR suffered a dearth of collective protest. To many this seemed entirely natural. Scores of western scholars — such as Samuel Huntington and Zygmunt Bauman — predicted Communism would enjoy a lasting stability based on its structural immunity against revolution. Nor were East Germans themselves much wiser. The state had always been able to crush collective action, it seemed omnipotent. Even the toughest dissidents could sink into resignation: Baerbel Bohley, only weeks before becoming a prominent spokesperson of the 'Citizens' Movement' (CM), could lament that 'change from below is out of the question' (in Hirschman p.185).

So when a mass protest movement arose in the autumn of 1989 — in the teeth of the fiercest repression — all were taken by surprise. Almost overnight public life was transformed. For decades ordinary East Germans had been denied any say in public life, any influence on political power. Suddenly all that changed. Over five million people — from an adult population of some twelve million — came together in an enormous and sustained protest movement. Demonstrations of over a hundred thousand people occurred every week for more than three months — and that was just in Leipzig. Political meetings attracted mass audiences: the first week of November alone saw 230 reported meetings, attended by over 300,000 (Mitter/Wolle, p.248). Mass collective action began in September, peaked in November and again in January, and did not ebb until February.

The movement transformed society — not only its political institutions but whole spectra of behaviour and consciousness. For collective protest was a novelty, its forms and norms had to be invented anew, its aims deliberated, and tactics put to the test of practice. Even the initial small triumphs over the state's ban on collective action turned a host of convictions on their heads. People who had for years vented grievances and criticisms in closed circles of trusted friends and colleagues now turned on their televisions to see vast crowds giving voice to similar grievances and demands. The recognition of belonging to a powerful alliance forming around shared goals elicited strong emotions. Thus, one participant recalls his first demonstration, which he experienced as fundamentally liberating:

> At last the great community which I and my friends had been longing for was discovering collective action, at last we had begun to overcome that feeling of impotence (Bahr, p.101).

This forging of an alliance of the powerless found expression in the rallying cry of the early demonstrations: 'We are the people!' The slogan asserted the broadness of the movement's base — uniting young and old, worker and intellectual, Communist and anti-Communist.[1] It embodied, further, the desire for democratic change — not merely in its formal meaning of free elections and parliament, but in the deeper sense of ordinary people seizing the political agenda and insisting upon their right to have a say in the transformation of society.

One after another, previously fenced-off areas of state control were prised open to popular intervention. Each day seemed to bring news of impossible developments actually occurring, from the dethronement of Honecker to the fall of the Wall. The democratic space forced open by the mass protests was filled with a tumult of desires and demands. Meetings were called in workplaces and colleges where myriad long-suppressed grievances were aired, and redress demanded. I recall a meeting of students where discussion raged for hours around a riot of issues and demands: for student input to university policy, for better heating; a five-day week; exchanges with western universities; more pianos; an end to obligatory courses in Marxism and in military training; and for the rewriting of history textbooks. A huge thirst for politcal discussion and education arose. Channels of communication sprang up and deepened: between neighbours and colleagues, between strangers on street corners and in bars. Opposition groups set up 'contact centres' which became hives of activity and debate. One activist recalls one such, where visitors 'engaged in inflamed discussion, forty people and more often filled all the rooms, cigarette smoke hung in the air, the doors were still swinging long after midnight. It was euphoric.' (*Anstiftung*, p.337) A visiting scholar described the wall-newspapers at his college: "It takes half an hour to go down the corridor and look at just the new additions that were pinned up the previous day" (Marcuse, p.54). The effervescence of pent-up desires and the breathtaking array of ideas coming up for discussion was especially visible on demonstrations. Slogans branched out to cover every conceivable issue: freedom for political prisoners; opposition to nuclear power; for the legalization of busking; for an independent Saxony; for disabled rights; against fascism; for an end to school on Saturdays; for fewer police; for pollution controls; for solidarity with the Romanian revolution and the victims of Czech police violence, ... and many more besides. Demands like these were purposive, while others — such as 'Stasi pigs!' — were 'consummatory' (Rule, p.198): they expressed rage, the cry against past oppressions and the desire for justice.

The slogans on demonstrations were not simple reflections of aggregated individual demands, but were collectively contested and elaborated. Broad areas of agreement notwithstanding, different groups within the movement pursued different ideas and strategies; demonstrations were sites of disagreement and contest over aims and strategies. Some slogans caught on more than others. As one witness recalls,

Individuals shouted many different things. But clear choices were made. By no means all chants were taken up by the crowd ... the various chants were discussed. Someone might shout something which was then countered with 'Don't shout that here! You're on the wrong demonstration!' or suchlike ... [T]here was this intuitive understanding of what was suitable, or representative of majority opinion (Bahr p.97).

The demonstrations were scenes of great drama and creativity, they came alive with songs and chants. The culture of political humour that had previously been encoded and concealed within 'hidden transcripts' of resistance (Scott, 1990) now emerged in the guise of satirical slogans emblazoned on countless home-made banners. Communist propaganda was impudently rescripted; for example, one banner replaced the word 'toil' in 'As we toil today, so shall we live tomorrow' by 'demonstrate' (Lang, p.12). An image of Honecker was carried aloft, as on official May Day parades, except now as a photomontage, clothed in prisoner's gear. In workplaces, noticeboards were plastered with leaflets and petitions. In short, society was electrified by the clash of political forces and a Promethean culture of protest.

Exodus

Recalling how the spirit of protest stormed the streets of East Germany, the questions invariably arise as to why revolt occurred at that particular juncture and took that particular form. The rest of this article addresses these issues.

At the most fundamental level the revolution was, of course, bound up with the terminal crisis of the Soviet system. From the mid-1970s onwards, East Germany suffered almost permanent and intractable economic stagnation. The failure of the Honecker regime to cope with this — except through desperate measures of enforcing austerity and expanding borrowing — nourished frustrations and discontent throughout society. So when Gorbachev's regime began to undertake major reforms in Moscow, its efforts were followed intently by millions of East Germans. Ever larger numbers felt confident to voice discontent, as indicated by a rising flood of petitions over individual and local grievances sent to the authorities. And although no organized reform wing emerged within the nomenclatura, the changes propounded by the Kremlin (which was to Communists as the Vatican is to Catholics) nourished burgeoning disaffection amongst *apparatchiks*.

Gorbachev's reforms unintentionally ensnared the SED leadership in an inextricable dilemma. Copying the Kremlin would risk not only revolt, but also direct subordination to western capital — as already evinced in Hungary. On the other hand, confronted with the tide of reform sweeping Eastern Europe Honecker's stance was irremediably Canutian, as became clear in the summer of 1989.

Hungary's reorientation westwards led it to dismantle the 'Iron Curtain', with Moscow's blessing. Before long, East Germans began to use the opportunity to emigrate. When in August the trickle became a flood, the East German regime was forced to react. Powerless to affect Hungary's decision, it relied — in vain — on a media campaign which condemned the emigrants as traitors. The ineffectuality of their propaganda drove SED leaders mad with frustration: one of them, after watching West German coverage of the exodus, screamed 'I just want to smash the television.' (Stephan, p.104). Any hopes they nurtured that full-scale repression would be assisted by Soviet troops — as had occurred in 1953 — wilted when Moscow signalled it would abstain. This filled GDR leaders, according to one of them, with 'a growing insecurity as to whether to give the order to shoot, ... [O]ur self-confidence crumbled.' (Kuhn, p.32).

The impotence of the state leadership reverberated downwards, sending lower functionaries into confusion. Even the Stasi was affected. One officer confessed, 'We didn't know what we should do. No signals came from above.' (Riecker, p.238). This was, according to one journalist, a ubiquitous phenomenon: 'For all *Stasi* officers ... the failure of the top leadership to act in response to the exodus of mid-1989 led above all to demoralization' (Pond, p.125).

The regime was beginning to fragment. Its inability to suppress the emergent threat to its power galvanized society from top to bottom. Political questions flooded popular discussion: Would all borders be closed? Would repression be intensified? Were the emigrants right to leave? Should we emigrate too? The Stasi's informants reported 'open, massive and critical discussion' sweeping the workplaces (Meinel/Wernicke, p.133). Protest letters and resolutions began to pour in to the authorities and the media. Everyone knew that something dramatic would happen. But an awareness of the depth of crisis did not necessarily imply a realization of the potential for collective protest. For that to happen, individuals had to be sensitive to the widening political opportunities resulting from the faltering of the regime and the politicization of the masses, and to act upon their intuition by organizing protest. This was no automatic process. For in order to organize at all, the state's ban on oppositional activity had to be successfully challenged. Furthermore, potential participants had to be sufficiently persuaded of the urgency and viability of protest as to trump their fears of police violence and other sanctions.

Demonstrations

Despite the incipient fracturing of regime unity, most state leaders were confident that repression would work, as it always had done in the past. Thus on August 31st, when Stasi chief Mielke asked a colonel 'will a 17 June [the 1953 uprising] occur tomorrow?', the reply came firmly: 'It won't happen tomorrow, it won't happen at all; that's our job after all.' (Mitter/Wolle, p.125).

But Mielke and cohorts did not reckon with the commitment displayed by several groups of demonstrators in the following weeks. The pioneers of organized resistance were would-be emigrants who protested in order to provoke the authorities into expatriating them. For many months emigrants had gathered each Monday at a Leipzig church, before marching out to chant their demand: 'We want out!' Though small, their action was significant. For simply by demonstrating, they undermined the prevalent myth of the state's omnipotence. Moreover, their actions provoked an organized response from 'political' oppositionists. These rejected emigration as a negative solution to problems that required domestic political change. They joined the emigrants' demonstrations, but raised slogans criticizing both government and emigrants, such as 'Freedom of travel, not mass exodus!'

Each Monday demonstration and each report in the West German media boosted numbers on subsequent protests. Even the early demonstrations of only a few thousand people revealed the vincibility of the security forces. By late September demonstrators in Leipzig were able to make fools of the police, breaking through police lines and drumming on police cars (with the occupants inside!) One report describes how eight stolen 'police hats flew through the air, to the cheers of the demonstrators'. (Doehnert/Rummel, p.151)

In early October a second major contest occurred, in Dresden. 15,000 would-be emigrants besieged the station in an attempt to board westward-bound trains. The police managed to thwart them in this aim, but failed to stop them regrouping to form a permanent demonstration (of fluctuating size) which wound through the city, periodically scuffling with police, for a marathon eighty hours.

Episodes like this illuminated the state's weakness and spurred the confidence of new layers to demonstrate. Confidence was also generated within the process of mobilization itself. Individuals usually attended protests alongside friends or colleagues (See Opp and Voß). At political meetings in churches, fears would subside as thousands united in song and political prayer before marching together out onto the streets. Uniting in action around shared aims imparted to individuals powerful feelings of strength. In almost all accounts of the period, empowerment through solidarity emerges as a *leitmotif*. One observer was impressed 'how people in a crowd demanding justice gain the ability to mount resistance, overcome fear and muster the courage to meet force with force' (Zwahr, p.45). Another pointed to the inverse power relation between state and protestors, where the latter, 'in coming together for collective action experienced their own power and simultaneously the impotence of the powerful' (Baule, p.43).

Solidarity was not miraculously born on demonstrations but was created, often consciously. Activists distributed leaflets and spread information of forthcoming events via 'whisper propaganda'. Protestors persuaded acquaintances to come along. Demonstrators called on bystanders to join in. Protest norms were created, with crowds chanting 'We'll be back again next Monday!' and 'Bring others along too!' In ways such as these, 'cultures of solidarity' (Fantasia) were fashioned; individuals were encouraged to align their interests and identities with those of the movement as a whole.

By the second week of October the fracturing of the regime was proceeding apace. The strength of the protests prompted some state leaders to (cautiously) indicate disagreement with the prevailing hard-line strategy. Signs of variegation at the top exacerbated the doubts circulating amongst lower ranks; middle-level officials were especially prone to vacillation due to their proximity to the demoralized SED grassroots and the inflamed general public. As protests spread, these officials were pummelled by popular anger; one confessed to her diary that 'accusations are hailing down on me' (Liebsch, p.50). Keenly aware that their superiors were offering no solutions to the crisis, many functionaries became vociferous advocates of reform.

Of even greater concern to the regime were growing signs of unreliability in the security forces. Least reliable were the conscript police and members of the 'factory battalions' (a voluntary workers militia), with both forces suffering significant desertion in October. Mutiny was provoked in part, according to a Stasi investigation, by the direct influence of demonstrators, or, in Stasi-speak,'the effect of negative-enemy influence, such as solidarity with demands of the oppositional movement New Forum'. Moreover, the report continued:

> At times of security force deployment, many factory battalions were influenced by the frequently massive curses of demonstrators and passers-by, such as: 'shame on you — workers against workers' (Mitter/Wolle p.222).

The infection even spread to the army, with dozens of soldiers (including SED members) disobeying orders. One military official described the situation in early October — when troops were ordered to prevent demonstrations — as close to mutiny: 'when their battalions were assembled, resistance broke out, especially amongst the soldiers. They spoke out openly, saying 'we won't beat them up' (Opp et al., p.290).

In Leipzig on 9 October the contending forces met in a decisive battle. In the preceding week the state had made it clear that any attempt to demonstrate would be crushed. Despite the presence of thousands of soldiers and police, many of whom were armed, an astonishing 80,000 people demonstrated. Local leaders faced a dilemma. Honecker had insisted the demonstration be suppressed 'by any means necessary', but another SED leader, Krenz, was sounding somewhat less martial. Caught between a variegating politburo and a vast demonstration, the local chiefs countermanded Honecker's orders and instructed the army to hold back. It was this moment — determined by the size of the demonstration — that established the (relatively) peaceful character of the revolution. 'Erich, we can't beat up hundreds of thousands of people' said Mielke to Honecker (Przeworski, p.64). These words may be apocryphal, but nonetheless express an important truth. A similar conclusion was drawn by participants. One woman described the scene as she and her friends made their way to the demonstration and witnessed:

> ... an endless river of people, and from it we suddenly felt courage and strength, '[...] an incredible feeling of solidarity, that they couldn't shoot us all, they couldn't imprison us all, they couldn't

set their dogs on us all' (Kuhn, p.128).

Shortly afterwards the crowd broke through police lines, upon which 'a delirious cry filled the air, a cry of liberation.' (Lindner/Grüneberger, p.214).

Radicalization

The movement had won its first major victory. The regime was forced to make concessions, beginning with the replacement of Honecker by Egon Krenz. However, the ensuing attempts to placate protest through personnel reshuffles and liberal reforms tossed the regime onto the horns of a dilemma. On the one hand, each concession and each functionary's resignation proclaimed the efficacy of the protests. Each success — particularly the defeat of the regime's repressive strategy — attracted new recruits to the movement; each triumph boosted their confidence to make furthergoing demands. Each turn of events brought new horizons into view, goals that only weeks before had seemed utterly impossible. Upon each announcement of reforms, questions arose on the streets: Is this enough? Can we trust these people? If not, what must be done to ensure that reform continues? What institutional changes could cement our success? On the other hand, the government refused to submit to all the movement's demands. Inevitably, it attempted to brake the process of change, to stall reform, to shore up the state's fracturing structures. But every such move ignited anger on the streets and stimulated calls for more radical opposition to the regime.

This contradiction was axial to the revolution's next phase. No sooner had Honecker been ousted than the prolific banner designers got to work, pointing to the inanity of dressing wolfish Krenz — who only months earlier had been flattering the butchers of Tiananmen Square — in benevolent garb. 'Egon, what big teeth you have!' read one witty banner, (referring to Krenz's gross dentures.)

The government's conciliatory gestures were petrol on the flames of revolt. Aiming to channel protest into arenas controlled by the state, 'dialogues' were organized — for a where officials could face questions from the public, and debate with academics or, occasionally, oppositionists. However, only a small minority attended, many more saw them as a diversion, a ploy to conceal immobility on substantive questions behind a facade of conciliation. Soon frustration was being vented on the streets through slogans such as 'Dialogue's alright, but deeds are better!'

By the end of October the temperature on demonstrations was rising. Hitherto, hopes had generally been invested in government-inspired reform. Slogans berating the regime had usually been playful and punning. But now they became sharper, attacking the SED's power monopoly and calling for the abolition of the Stasi. 'Work down the pits, Stasi gits!' went the chants, 'Lock the Stasi in their prisons!' A new mood gained ground, demands became more radical. Not halting at the call for Krenz to abdicate, a growing minority now sought the destruction of the old regime, demanding that the entire government resign, with its replacement to be determined through free elections. But of all such demands which were attacking the very walls of state power the one which rang out the loudest was the call for the freedom to travel West. Krenz's government, increasingly desperate in the face of the movement's accelerating radicalism, was forced to make substantive reforms. In early November it promised that opportunities for travel to the 'non-socialist abroad' would be greatly enlarged, although with specified restrictions. Only a couple of weeks earlier such a major concession had been barely thinkable. But so rapid was the crescendo in self-assertiveness on the streets that the announcement was met not with gratitude, but with a clamour of indignation which focused in particular on the government's failure to promise adequate provision of the hard currency that visiting the West required. In panic, the government announced the decision which at once symbolized the irrevocability of reform and the movement's greatest triumph: opening the Berlin Wall.

For a time, this monumental concession really did take the wind from the sails of protest, giving breathing space to the regime. For some weeks many East Germans were more occupied in revelling in the novelty of visiting West Germany than in tracking the course of domestic events. But before long demonstrations had reached and surpassed previous levels. Travel and protest were not incompatible — as one banner put it: 'Last night in Munich for a beer — then back again for the demo here.' Indeed, with Munich beer priced in D-Marks (scarce as gold for most East Germans), another need began to fuel protest: the demand for hard currency. By a delightful twist of fate it was at precisely this juncture — dominated by a growing chorus of material desires — that the findings of a government committee investigating ruling class corruption began to be publicized by the (now uncensored) media. The SED regime had relentlessly preached equality and austerity to its subjects. Now, it was revealed, its leaders themselves lived in gluttonous luxury. Honecker owned a fleet of fourteen cars, including a Mercedes, while presiding over a system that made workers queue for fourteen years to buy even a Trabant — that fibreglass symbol of Eastern inferiority. Most galling of all, it was revealed that each year millions of D-Marks were diverted from the hard-pressed economy to buy western commodities for bureaucrats who, in public, had always smugly championed the superiority of 'their' economy.

These scandals inflamed popular opinion and sparked a further radicalization of protest. Banners proliferated with slogans such as 'Manual labour for bureaucrats!', 'Minimum wage for the Politburo!', and 'Privileged of the world — abolish yourselves!' Demands could be heard, especially in the workplaces, for state leaders to be brought to justice. By early December the movement was steering away from moderate demands for institutional reforms and towards confrontation with the regime. Demonstrations became more militant. Stasi informants reported that 'there is always a hard core of demonstrators who try to prolong the demonstrations and to redirect them towards buildings of the SED, state apparatus and MfS [Stasi]' (Mitter/Wolle p.250).

In early December, news of file-shredding by the Stasi catalysed a new wave of demonstrations calling for its abolition. In many cases protestors surrounded and occupied Stasi headquarters. In Dresden, demonstrators forced entry and interrogated the officers inside. In Erfurt, a crowd led by 'Women for Change' broke in, confiscated machine guns and pistols, and locked the guards in a cupboard. Throughout the land 'Citizens Committees' were formed to monitor the activities of the Stasi, with the intention of preventing further destruction of files.

Meanwhile, new layers were joining the movement. Prisons erupted in revolt. In one, Bautzen, all two thousand prisoners struck, and most went on hunger strike. They demanded an immediate amnesty, the reform of the criminal code, and better conditions. Elsewhere, prisoners struck to demand input into prison decisions.

The movement began to enter the workplaces. There had been

activity here in previous months, but only of a low-key and barely publicized sort. For example, workers would threaten industrial action if management removed a 'subversive' leaflet from the noticeboard, or they would collectively write resolutions criticizing the SED leadership. In one factory, workers had threatened to strike if the leader of the state-run trade union did not appear in person to answer their demands. Not long afterwards, the same workers had elected a committee to investigate management corruption in their factory (Simon, p.134). But drama on this scale had been exceptional.

In December, however, the picture changed. A wave of industrial action swept through over a hundred workplaces, involving tens of thousands of workers. Aims were often limited to workplace issues, but invariably with a political slant. Demands included the sacking of managers, the dissolution of 'factory battalions' and of SED factory-organizations, or expressed opposition to the hiring of former Stasi officers. Militants began to agitate for new elections to trade union bodies, and for new, independent union organization. Some of the newly elected works councils insisted that they be granted access to the company's accounts or be empowered to elect the firm's directors. Strikes were frequently threatened over demands for workers' codetermination in enterprise decisions, or at least for their right to veto 'excessive impositions' by management. (*Spiegel*, 11.12.89, p.104). National political issues were also addressed, most commonly in the demand for the unconditional dissolution of the Stasi, while the zenith of December's wave of workplace militancy was a general strike in Plauen which called for a referendum on the question of German unification.

Winter Palace betrayed

By early December, then, the movement's trajectory had clearly shifted. Having begun with rather diffuse calls for political reform, the bulk of protestors were now mobilizing around demands that struck at the heart of state power. The revolution seemed to be shifting from Girondin moderation to Jacobin radicalism. But, as is well known, such a progression did not occur; 'the masses,' writes Klaus Hartung (p.72), 'were deprived of their storm of the Winter Palace.' The SED elite clung on to power right through to the spring of 1990, giving the ruling class as a whole sufficient time to rearrange its structures of rule. As one banner put it: 'A snake sheds its skin, but stays a snake'. This process initially entailed promoting 'second row' functionaries and displacing control over the main levers of power from the SED to the state executive, but later focused on the transmutation of bureaucratic power into private capital, and the removal of incriminating documents from archives so as to assist elites in conserving their power and status during the transition from Communism.[2]

Hartung's thesis of betrayal does not imply that revolutions inevitably march towards the seizure of power by organized radicals. It does, however, suggest that inherent in the revolutionary situation were potentialities which, if realized, could have led to a somewhat different outcome. In particular, the ousting of the SED from power was, between early December and mid January, distinctly possible. The two chief prerequisites were present. Firstly, the mass movement had gained enormous momentum both in terms of numbers involved and the radicalism of demands. A large proportion of the populace would undoubtedly have supported any attempt to unseat the Krenz or Modrow regimes. Secondly, from late October onwards the regime was simultaneously in acute disarray and committed to democratic reform; it was thus in a poor position to meet insurrection with violence. Government documents reveal a picture of panic in the Politburo.[3] The SED leadership was guided by one overriding goal: to regain control of society by weakening the mass movement and preventing it from radicalizing further. The sheer unpredictability of events, together with constant policy changes, disagreements over strategy, and personnel reshuffles at every layer of the state and SED had thrown the regime into confusion. Central Committee meetings were drowned in clamour as functionaries tried to blame one another for the crisis. Many bureaucrats fled the sinking ship through resignation or, less frequently, suicide. All that SED leaders could hope for was that some semblance of order be maintained within the ranks. As one politburo member insisted to SED officials who were contemplating resignation: 'No, that's not on, we must ensure an orderly transfer [of power], we're not deserters!' (in Zimmermann/Scütt, p.61).

The security forces had also been critically weakened. Various sections were being dissolved (the factory battalions) or reduced in size (the Stasi). Internal splits arose, with hard-line officers resisting reforms which their superiors instituted to appease protest.

Mutinies shook the army, with conscript soldiers taking command of their barracks. Police joined the demonstrations, bearing their own banners opposing corruption in the force and the destruction of documents. Even the Stasi was not exempt: five hundred of the elite 'Dzierzynski' regiment blockaded the national headquarters to prevent the removal of files.

By mid November the state leadership was clearly in a very tight corner indeed. No amount of concessions, it seemed, would appease the movement — even opening the Wall had not been enough. On 21 November Hans Modrow, the prime minister, met General Schwanitz, the Stasi's new chief, to discuss tactics. 'Time is pressing, like a hand on our throats' said Schwanitz, 'we must get this pressure [the protests] off us, ... our power is at stake, let's not kid ourselves about that.'[4] But Modrow had thought of a ruse. 'By no means all those on the streets are our enemy' he said, then proposed an ingenious 'game', namely that the 'friendlier' sections of the movement — i.e. the Citizens' Movement organizations such as New Forum — be offered a sufficient taste of power to cement their allegiance to the state, whilst leaving the key centres of authority untouched. Schwanitz agreed, and added: 'We must talk with these forces, persuade them to accept us as partners, that they feel engaged in a common responsibility to uphold state security.'

At first glance, this conversation seems absurd: how could Modrow possibly envisage cooperating with the opposition? Only weeks before, the CM organizations had been among the pioneers of protest; only thirteen days earlier they were still illegal. The clue to this puzzle lies in the refraction of the movement into divergent factions. Essentially, CM supporters — and particularly its leaderships — had undergone a lesser degree of radicalization than the 'unorganized' masses. This had become apparent at an early stage. Even before the watershed of 9 October, the New Forum leadership had begun to distance itself from the demonstrations, warning of the dangers of 'actionism'. One spokesperson insisted that

New Forum did not set out to organize demonstrations and march through the cities at the head of thousands of people. New Forum's aim is to get dialogue underway, ... negotiation is the decisive factor, and I believe that will take time (*Die Tageszeitung*, 5.10.89).

A week later, Rainer Eppelmann — leader of 'Democratic Awakening' (and future CDU government minister) — called on people to stay away from demonstrations (Reuth/Boente, p.110). Other CM leaders confessed to fearing the 'force of the population', and warned that 'one may no longer be able to restrain the demonstrations' (Rein, p.24). Indeed, the CM groups generally sought to restrain rather than arouse mass activity. Even on 4 November in Berlin, when up to a million people demonstrated, 'none of the speakers tried to mobilize, to send out battle orders' (*Die Tageszeitung*, 6.11.89). Such faint-heartedness was not a product of inexperience but expressed a wider political strategy. CM leaders saw their role primarily as a think-tank of reform policies, which would be implemented through inter-elite negotiation with the government. Accordingly, demonstrations were seen as a 'revocable force with which to pressurize the government.' (*Die Tageszeitung* 17.1.90).

However, if the CM's moderate approach smoothed its relations with the regime, it was less popular with the masses. As *The Observer* averred, 'groups like New Forum began to find themselves on the wrong side of the tracks, urging restraint where the crowd wanted resolve, and caution where the crowd wanted action' (Hawkes, p.79). The cleft between CM and 'crowd' was not simply over degrees of militancy but reflected divergent attitudes to the SED and to East Germany's independence (as opposed to unification with the FRG). CM leaders were committed to reforming the existing state, and many envisaged a pivotal role for themselves in the process. Moreover, most CM activists were highly critical of West German capitalism. The CM therefore comprised the more patriotic and socialist section of the mass movement; those committed to curing rather than euthanasing the GDR. Or, as Schwanitz said to Modrow, 'New Forum etc. are, like us, for democratic socialism, so we should be able to achieve consensus.'

To return to the narrative: in late November, Modrow's attempt to persuade CM leaders to cooperate in the restitution of social order centred on the offer of a place at 'Round Table' negotiations between CM, church, and parties of the old regime. The offer pitched CM leaders into a quandary. On the one hand they rightly suspected that the Round Table would have negligible influence on policy, given that the government would still control the main levers of power. On the other, it seemed to offer them the prospect of a degree of influence whilst avoiding the uncertainties inherent in the more radical course of mobilizing for the overthrow of the regime.

In the first week of December the choice before the CM was illuminated in stark relief. Modrow's offer lay still unsigned on the table when a group of workers persuaded Karl-Marx-Stadt New Forum to call for a political general strike. The New Forum national leadership was aware that this brought the opportunity to sweep aside the SED-regime. The slogan 'Power to New Forum!' had been gaining broad popularity on demonstrations. Despite its prevaricating stance New Forum still possessed massive support, while the government's legitimacy was evaporating. A widespread readiness for industrial action was reported by activists — in Saxony it was 'overwhelming', according to New Forum leader Jens Reich (in Joppke, p.163). Delegations from several major factories had approached New Forum, saying 'We're prepared to strike; just give us the signal.'[5] New Forum leaders had to decide which way to jump: general strike or Round Table; the fate of the revolution hung in the balance. After a somewhat confused debate they opted for the latter, and took their seats at the Round Table. 'Our goal was not to usurp power,' insisted Jens Reich (in Joppke, p.163), so 'we tried to calm them [the workers] down.'

Unification

By binding CM leaders into the bureaucratic machinery which it controlled, the SED government had neutralized the immediate threat to its rule. Not content with this success, SED leaders began to reconsolidate their power. They refounded the SED under a new name, organized pro-communist demonstrations, and postponed the promised dissolution of the Stasi. This was a high-risk strategy — and it did not pay off. Despite CM leaders' repeated appeals for calm and for the defence of the state, the mass movement resurged. Many parts of the country experienced their largest and angriest demonstrations yet. Particularly galling to protestors were the delays in the dissolution of the Stasi, and news of perks promised to retiring functionaries. Political strikes over these issues occurred in several cities, while in Berlin hundreds of building workers marched on parliament to press for the abolition of the Stasi. The following days saw yet more marches on Stasi buildings, and the storming of its national headquarters.

By now the demonstrations were thick with West German flags, unification had become the prime demand. Unification bore the prospect of economic prosperity, of hard currency to reward hard work. It held the promise of institutionalized political freedoms. Above all, it implied the deracination of the 'SED-Stasi State' — as Ulrich Beck has argued, East Germans demanding unification were *acting, within the horizons of the GDR,* in a revolutionary way; for they helped to power the rival system' (Beck, p.24).

The regime had failed to placate the movement. Faced with the choice between intransigently defending GDR sovereignty, which would provoke further radicalization, or bowing to the call for unification, Modrow chose the lesser evil and announced his conversion to pan-German nationalism.

Outcomes

How does one assess the outcome of a revolution? Usually by describing institutional changes. For East Germany these may be summarized as the transition to parliamentary democracy (winter 1989-90), the exit from Warsaw Pact and Comecon, and unification (autumn 1990). Viewed solely through the institutional lens, however, one may conclude that collective action had no, or only marginal, impact. After all, other Communist states such as Hungary departed the Soviet Bloc, instituted market reforms and parliamentary democracy, and all with scarcely a whisper on the streets. Perhaps for this reason many analyses belittle the role of protest in 1989. Exemplifying this tendency, Claus Offe has argued:

> The GDR-revolution was an 'Exit-revolution', not a 'Voice-revolution'. The East German state was not brought down by a victorious *collective* struggle for a new *political* order; instead, massive and suddenly unstoppable *individual* emigration destroyed its *economic* foundations (p.293).

Although it is easy to refute Offe's interpretation, identifying the precise effects of collective struggle is necessarily somewhat speculative. Would democratic reform have occurred in the absence of protest? And unification? One suspects so, albeit with unknowable tempo and trajectory. But there are two other consequences of the movement that have, in my view, been gravely neglected. Firstly, it affected conflict elsewhere, most obviously by inspiring protestors throughout Eastern Europe, and in the 'West'. In 1990, African democracy campaigners assailed their home-grown Honeckers with cries of 'Stasi out!'; British anti-poll tax campaigners made similar connections before toppling their local despot. Struggles in one country remind regimes worldwide of the potential threat from below. The 1989 revolution was itself partially determined by the struggles of Polish workers and Afghan guerrillas which helped impel the Kremlin towards *perestroika*. The GDR uprising in turn influenced the strategies of other East European regimes. But 'western' regimes were affected too, most obviously the FRG. Chancellor Kohl was seriously worried that the unification movement might radicalize further. In October 1989 he said to 'Mr. General Secretary Krenz',

> In your important and very, very difficult task I wish you the best of luck and success ... In our interest, in my government's interest, and above all in my own interest, the situation in the GDR must not develop in such a way as to make a calm, sensible development impossible (Stephan, p.180).

Clarifying his meaning, Kohl added that the last thing he wanted was 'to awake expectations which would raise the pressure; that wouldn't help either of us'. Later, in November, he assured Krenz that:

> I have always emphasized that I see every form of radicalization as dangerous ... We needn't discuss what sort of danger that might be, anyone can easily work it out (Stephan, p.245).

The second unquantifiable and neglected — but important — consequence of the uprising is its impact on consciousness.[6] East Germans, especially participants in collective action, were powerfully affected by the experience. In 1989, habitual rules of social activity — which had come to be experienced as inevitable — were cast aside, exposing the 'natural' order as frangible artifice. Those who for decades had stooped to authority discovered the strength to rise up, to 'make the continuum of history explode'

(Benjamin, p.253). Countless statements in memoirs and interviews testify to the potency of the experience:

> That was really some feeling, being in that mass of people, that was so liberating ... Even now tears come to my eyes when I see film of it on television. I'm actually a very hard bloke, but that was quite an experience, it was fantastic! (Lindner/Grüneberger, p.34).

For some, perhaps, these memories will linger merely as recollections of heady days, filed alongside school reunions and the like. For many, however, they will influence practice, particularly participation in collective action. The most extensive survey of former protestors suggests that in 1989 people experienced a leap in their confidence to engage in protest (Opp and Voß). In interviews, former protestors commonly describe how 'politicized' they became, how the rapidly changing events constantly forced them to rethink their ideas, discuss what was happening, educate themselves. Many experienced a marked rise in self-assertiveness. For example, one hotel worker who was, before 1989, so afraid of speaking in public that she took tranquilizers before attending even small workplace meetings was amazed to find herself two years later mounting a podium to address thousands at an anti-fascist rally — and with no chemical assistance. In barely visible ways the experience of collective action has fertilized those vital resources — such as confidence — that enable active resistance to injustice and oppression. Combined with the democratic transformation of the polity, it has resulted in a dramatic increase in the level of collective action compared with the pre-1989 levels.

This may be the most important legacy of 1989. Eastern Germany today reveals extensive dissatisfaction with the economic and social consequences of unification. One recent survey suggests that a majority of the Eastern population are disappointed by unification, while an astonishing number compares the old regime favourably with the new (*Spiegel*, 3.7.95). One worker even complained that 'Nothing remains of the ideals which we took to the streets for.' (Klein, p.209). With poverty has come insecurity and fear, competition has atomized society once more. According to one former protestor, 'Many people are once again scared to open their mouths for fear of being fired; they've withdrawn back into their shells.' But, he adds, 1989 bore not only the threat of renewed fear, but hope for future struggles: 'The street has always been powerfully effective. It's important that that doesn't get forgotten' (in Lindner/Grüneberger, p.105).

Acknowledgement

Thanks to all interviewees, especially Ramona, Antje, Andrea, Steff, Gabi, Bert, Klaus Wolfram, Tina Krone and Uwe Rottluff.

References

Anstiftung zur Gewaltlosigkeit, (1991), Impuls, Magdeburg.

Bahr, Eckhard, (1990), *Sieben Tage im Oktober*, Forum, Leipzig.

Barker, Colin, (1995), 'The Muck of Ages', *Studies in Marxism*.

Baule, B. in Loew, Konrad, (ed.), (1991), *Ursachen und Verlauf der deutschen Revolution 1989*, Duncker & Humboldt, Berlin.

Beck, Ulrich, 'Opposition in Deutschland', in Giesen, B, and Leggewie, C, (eds.), (1991), *Experiment Vereinigung*, Rotbuch, Berlin.

Benjamin, Walter, (1992), *Illuminations*, Fontana, London.

Doehnert, A. and Rummel, P. in Grabner, J. et al (eds.) (1990), *Leipzig im Oktober*, Wichern, Berlin.

Eyerman, R. and Jamison, A. (1991), *Social Movements*, Polity, Cambridge.

Fantasia, Rick, (1988), *Cultures of Solidarity*, University of California, Berkeley.

Hartung, Klaus, (1990), *Neunzehnhundertneunundachtzig*, Luchterhand, Frankfurt.

Hawkes, Nigel, (ed.), (1990), *Tearing Down the Curtain*, Hodder & Stoughton, London.

Hirschman, Albert, (1993), 'Exit, Voice, and the Fate of the German Democratic Republic', *World Politics*, Vol.45, No.2.

Joppke, Christian, (1995), *East German Dissidents and the Revolution of 1989*, Macmillan, Basingstoke.

Klein, Olaf Georg, (1994), *Ploetzlich war alles ganz anders*, Kiepenheuer & Witsch, Cologne.

Kuhn, Ekkehard (1992), *Der Tag der Entscheidung*, Ullstein, Berlin.

Lang, Ewald (ed.) (1990), *Wendehals und Stasi-Laus*, Heyne, Munich.

Liebsch, Heike, (1991), *Dresdener Stundenbuch*, Peter Hammer, Wuppertal.

Lindner, B. and Grüneberger, R. (eds.), (1992), *Demonteure*, Aisthesis, Bielefeld.

McFalls, Laurence, (1995), *Communism's Collapse, Democracy's Demise?*, Macmillan, Basingstoke.

Marcuse, Peter, (1991), *A German Way of Revolution*, Dietz, Berlin.

Meinel, R. and Wernicke, T. (eds.), (1990), *Mit tschekistischem Gruß*, Babelturm, Potsdam.

Mitter, A. and Wolle, S. (eds.) (1990), *Ich liebe euch doch alle*, Basisdruck, Berlin.

Offe, Claus, (1993), 'Wohlstand, Nation, Republik', in Joas, H. and Kohli, M. *Der Zusammenbruch der DDR*, Suhrkamp, Frankfurt.

Opp, K-D. and Voß, P.*Die Dynamik gewaltloser Revolution*, Survey data.

Opp, K-D. et al (1993), *Die volkseigene Revolution*, Klett-Cotta, Stuttgart.

Pond, Elizabeth (1993), *Beyond the Wall*, Brookings, Washington.

Przeworski, Adam, (1991), *Democracy and the Market*, Cambridge University Press.

Rein, Gerhard, (ed.) (1989), *Die Opposition in der DDR*, Wichern, Berlin.

Reuth, R. and Boente, A. (1993), *Das Komplott*, Piper, Munich.

Riecker, A. et al, (1990), *Stasi intim*, Forum, Leipzig.

Rule, James, (1988), *Theories of Civil Violence*, University of California.

Scott, James, (1990), *Domination and the Arts of Resistance*, Yale, New Haven.

Simon, Günter, (1990), *Tisch-Zeiten*, Tribüne, Berlin.

Stephan, Gerd-Rüdiger, (ed.), (1994), 'Vorwaerts immer, rückwaerts nimmer!', Dietz, Berlin.

Zimmermann, B. and Schütt, H-D. (1992), *ohnMacht*, Neues Leben, Berlin.

Zwahr, Hartmut, (1993), *Ende einer Selbstzerstoerung*, Vandenhoek and Ruprecht, Goettingen.

7 Shirkers in revolt – mass desertion, defeat and revolution in the German army: 1917–1920

Nick Howard

Introduction: 'Fleeing the Colours'

During World War One, the collective response of German deserters to danger, hunger, fear of punishment, or war weariness was shaped more by their war time experiences than by ideology or party. In 1918, despite the intensely personal motives for their actions, they were driven collectively into headlong conflict with a defeated ruling class over the future of the German state. This study examines those experiences, assesses the scale of desertion, its impact on the war effort and records the part played by deserters in the revolution that followed. The concept 'desertion' is based upon the Kaiser's amnesty decree for peace-time deserters in August 1914. Under military law, the *'Fahnenflüchtiger'* (deserter from the colours) was either a foreign legionnaire, a draft-dodger or was considered AWOL, absent without leave. If guilty of 'degradation', presumably as a homosexual, or in prison or if he fought against Germany in the war, he received no pardon.

The decree's definition of desertion is widened in this study to cover those who were enlisted for war but avoided active service under cover of the bureaucratic regulations of the 1916 Auxiliary Service Law. It includes mutineers at the front who organized their own retreats or surrendered *en masse* in defiance of orders, during the last battles. During the war the generals blamed shirkers among the troops for their own military failures but they admitted no responsibility for the sharp decline in recruitment in the second half of the war and they never recorded the actual numbers of deserters. The real amount was hidden under the general heading of a shortage of reserves.

According to Guards Lieutenant Herbert Hartwell, in 1914 there was no excuse for failing to heed the call to arms. 'Conscientious objection was an unknown category in the German army'.[1] Conscripts in 1914 amounted to 1.3 million men, mostly aged from 20 to 22 years. A mixture of anxiety and enthusiasm greeted their enlistment.

> People cried and sang at the same time. Entire strangers, men and women, embraced and kissed each other; men embraced and kissed each other. Nobody, not even the strongest and most determined spirit, could resist that ebullition of feeling.[114]

Germany mobilized 13.25 million men throughout the war. Two million were killed, over four million were wounded and one million were taken prisoner or went missing. Three million enlisted men were exempted from field service as essential workers in munitions, mining and transportation, half of whom in any crisis were required to be ready as a reserve for the field armies. Officially, the field armies in the front lines and forward bases at war's end numbered just under three million.[3]

Draft dodging among the youngest age groups began to show in the recruitment figures in 1917. Nevertheless, in the spring of 1918, nearly 8 million Germans were under the colours. Almost four million were on active service in the field of war. More than a quarter of these had become a casualty by the end of hostilities. Another three million stayed behind in essential employment. Half of these were on the active reserve list and repeated calls for them to serve at the front were increasingly resisted. By war's end the number of deserters approximated to over half the army's surviving strength.

From 'hidden military strike' to revolution: the historical impact of German desertion

Mass desertion in the west European sectors of World War One was a key factor in the break-up of the German army in 1918, though it is overlooked by most historians who recognize its exceptional impact upon the collapse of the Austro-Hungarian and Russian armies.

Most histories of the war point to hard fought battles with very high casualty rates on all sides, right up to the Armistice of 11 November 1918, as indicative of no movement by German soldiers to desert the battle in the last year of the war. German nationalist historians glorified the 'front soldier' and falsified the army's record in the field by creating the myth of 'the stab in the back' which alleged that liberals, pacifists and socialists in the homeland alone were responsible for Germany's defeat. British historians who dismiss this myth, nevertheless give it weight by praising the German army as the one that never cracked.[4] Mutiny in the German army is also downplayed. Historians locate the naval mutiny at Kiel as the main factor in the collapse of the Imperial regime and allocate a conservative role to the rank and file of the army. Nevertheless, 10,000 revolutionary soldiers' councils[5] were built by deserters and mutineers in the last weeks of the war.

Ludendorff, leading general on the High Command complained of *Drückebergerei* (shirking) after each military setback. His own figures showed that enlistments to the infantry fell from 4.27 million men in the first two years of the war to 2.17 million in the final two years.[6] In 1917-1918 more than two million servicemen deserted. According to parliamentary researches in the 1920s by Major Erich Otto Volkmann, up to a million of these took part in a 'hidden military strike'.[7] Though peasant soldiers were predominant among those who deserted from the Austrian and Russian armies, German deserters from the towns and cities overstayed their leave (*Überlaufen*) or prolonged their deferment as essential workers. Draft dodging, desertion in the field and mutiny in the base camps brought the war in the west to a halt six months before the final battle in the summer of 1919, that was anticipated by the high commands on both sides.

After the exultation of 1914, disillusionment set in quite rapidly. 'The great desire for the ardently expected peace' recorded by British intelligence in a letter found on a dead German soldier in August 1916, showed evidence of war weariness.[8] Large public meetings in the *Heimat* (homeland) calling for peace followed the imprisonment for anti-war activities of Karl Liebknecht, socialist member of parliament. Most soldiers longed for peace throughout the war, but believed initially that only victory would bring it. Such feelings changed throughout 1916, after the horrific slaughters at the Somme and Verdun. The British agent in Holland whose task was to buy information from deserters reported that one pseudonymous contact

> ... had a genuine grievance against the German authorities. He told me about his wife and three children in Berlin: how for months they had lived on nothing but turnips and watery potatoes. He had a greater responsibility towards his family than to the Kaiser and the military clique who were driving Germany to its ruin.[9]

The German generals responded to the change in mood shown by the dramatic decline in recruiting (see Table 1). In March 1917 they withdrew the western armies to specially prepared defences 25 miles to the east of their furthest advance into France. A programme of morale raising patriotic education was imposed on the troops. Discussion groups and the circulation of pamphlets were banned, to shield the armies from 'everything which is likely to prejudice the morale of the troops'.

Desertion was not triggered, as in eastern Europe by extreme shortages of almost everything a mass army required. By contrast on Germany's western front, medical supplies, clothing and weapons were in adequate supply, though food shortages and unequal rations between the officers and other ranks provided a continual cause for indiscipline, disaffection and ultimately a class based hatred of the officer corps. Social democrats were more likely to desert than staunch nationalists and conservatives, but the will to survive was uppermost among those who refused to confront the juggernaut of war. The demand for minority national rights that inspired the sudden mass desertion of Czech soldiers from the Austrian armies was not so dramatically asserted by Poles and Alsace-Lorrainers, thousands of whom nevertheless deserted the German army in France. Despite the prevalence of war weariness from 1916 onwards, politicians of all the main parties continued to support the war and endorsed the German Emperor's demand for a commitment from each soldier to die for his country. The German SPD (*Sozialdemokratische Partei Deutschlands*) voted for war credits throughout, in the belief that its political survival and the economic advancement of its working class voters depended entirely upon victory for the German Empire.

In the final weeks of the war, the deserters' movement collectively spread mutiny throughout the rank and file. The revolutionary disbandment of the German army by its own soldiers influenced the course of the strategic struggle in the west. British political leaders called suddenly for a halt to their efforts to destroy Germany's military strength entirely. In the War Cabinet on 10 November 1918, Churchill surmised, 'We might have to build up the German army, and not destroy the only police force available for maintaining order in Germany, as it was important to get Germany on her legs again for fear of the spread of Bolshevism. General Smuts shared this view'.[10] Their views, had they been broadcast, would have seemed a mockery to the families of the millions of French, American, British and colonial servicemen who over four years had sacrificed their lives against that army. But the possibility of rank and file German soldiers taking on a policeman's role in the wake of their mass desertion was extremely remote. In the last phase of the war:

> deserters in Belgium were so numerous that the German military police gave up all attempts to round them up. Almost half the army returning from Belgium in the first week of November 1918, 'consisted of deserters who for over two months had been keeping themselves hidden in the vilest districts of Antwerp and Liége'. On the trains into Germany deserters actively incited non-deserters to mutiny against their officers.[11]

Their presence in Belgium was sufficient to thwart any remaining plans of the German High Command to keep Belgium under occupation as a bargaining counter in peace negotiations. The deserters' uprising raised the prospects in the west of the bolshevism that Churchill most feared. As the British War Cabinet considered the occupation of a defeated Germany, Prime Minister Lloyd George observed that:

> Marching men into Germany was like marching them into a cholera area. The Germans did that in Russia and caught the virus. It would be most undesirable to march British miners to Westphalia if Westphalia was controlled by a Bolshevist organization.[12]

From 1917 onwards desertion by stay-at-homes and shirkers had drastically reduced the offensive capacity of the German armies in the west, forcing them on some sectors of the front into a disorganized rout in the last weeks of the war. Others withdrew in a fighting manner but once it became clear that the armistice was pending, the German deserters at the front and on the army's lines of communication became sufficiently organized to persuade the non-deserters into showing tacit support for their actions. They were equally as instrumental in fomenting major political changes as were their Russian counterparts. The soldiers' councils formed by mutineers and deserters challenged the monarchy, and the political structures of the republican state formed by social democrats after they were given powers of government by the defeated generals and the demoralized middle classes on 9 November 1918.

Though many deserters retained their arms, two million of which were later recovered by the authorities, most refrained from using violence. Only in cases where officers resorted to arms were weapons used against them. The fear of violence against the officers during the wave of mutinies in the last weeks of the war prompted the High Command to order their officers not to provoke unrest by the use of weapons against mutineers, 'or against their own kind'. An exception, rarely applied, was made in the case of looters.

Orders to that effect on 9 November were signed by General Hindenburg.[13] Everyone, he instructed, should obey their superior officers. Calling instead for equality and for elected commanders, the soldiers removed all symbols of authority from their officers. However, they subsequently failed to assert their own authority sufficiently to prevent the revival of the officer corps and to resist the order issued by the social democratic parties, to restore badges of rank. The temporarily servile 'don't shoot' tactic of the generals, struggling to maintain their authority, seemed incredible at the time to many right wing officers who nevertheless complied with their instructions.

The outcome of the deserters' subsequent failure to overturn the military state reveals the weaknesses of their movement. Largely spontaneous acts which removed the authority of the officer corps and ejected state bureaucrats from their offices, gave way to a period of inactivity to await parliamentary methods of change. In practice this switch marked a strong tendency to political abstentionism among deserters as they disbanded the army. The majority social democrats, the SPD, took control away from the soldiers' councils in order to limit their actions. Like Germany's enemies, they feared the inrush of bolshevism, believing it could be prevented by maintaining continuity and despite the revolution, by preventing too much political change. They sought the election of a constituent assembly to consolidate the parliamentary republic. To this end, the SPD called for support from right wing army officers who seized the opportunity to massacre food rioters and demonstrators supporting the soldiers' and workers' councils.

The deserters' movement subsequently turned into an immense unplanned rush for the self-demobilization of the armed services, operating under the much reduced powers of the councils. Its impetus placed in great jeopardy the economic policies of the SPD. After the expulsion of the Kaiser on 9 November 1918, a joint governing council was formed from the right and left social democrats, the SPD and the independent minority USPD. On 11 November the council, nominated as peoples' delegates, ordered the restoration of the officers' powers of command, but called on them not to use weapons against their own kind. The rebellious servicemen wrongly believed that this urgent call 'under no circumstances to fire on the revolutionaries'[14] came from parties in sympathy with their demands to dismantle the powers of the officer corps. But the order of the new social democrat government was effectively the same order as Hindenburg's of 9 November, but now signed by the revolutionary people's council. Both the people's council and the High Command failed to stop the rush to desert the military in the remaining weeks of 1918. By January 1919, the army in the west had disappeared, six months before the victorious allies ordered the reduction of its ranks to one hundred thousand, under the imposed Peace Treaty of Versailles.

To pacify the rising threat from mutineers and deserters, in December 1918 the USPD gained a legal pardon for all deserters, though in the heat of the revolution this step meant little to millions of men who were flouting military law with impunity. In practice, the move for a general amnesty for deserters helped to restore the authority of the officer corps. Relieved by the social democrats of the task of having to take proceedings against the deserters, senior army officers like General Maercker, were licensed by Noske, the new SPD minister of war, to mobilize the *Freikorps* (paid voluntary paramilitaries) in preparation for the violent suppression of the joint councils of revolutionary soldiers and organized workers.

Shirkers and stay-at-homes — the quantitative effect on the war effort

Estimates of the extent of desertion are obscured by the huge and controversial discrepancies in war-time casualties, comprising those killed, injured, captured or missing. No official figure was ever provided. The most accurate figures come from the initial head count at the barracks on recruiting days, compared with the diminished numbers on field service in the last year of fighting. Of the 119 divisions on the most active sectors of the western front in October 1918, 31 were seriously reduced in strength. Nine had less than a quarter of their normal complement of troops, six of which reported only a few elements remaining. Twenty had less than a third and the remaining two less than two thirds of their field strengths. Another 32 had been disbanded entirely.[15]

Though these diminished strengths suggest heavy battlefield losses, which by September were declining steeply, they also point to the failure to replenish these by combing-out the non-combatant servicemen and the 17 to 50 age groups of the male population for replacements. Those eligible for war service were divided into four categories. The young, trained and fit for active service were labelled 'k.v.', the initials for the German word that described their status. Others were allocated 'g.v.' status for garrison and lines of communication duties. The remainder were allocated to 'a.v.' or manual and administrative employment for base and supply duties while the residue was classed as permanently unfit, 'd.u.'.[16] Many frontline deserters longed for a change of classification from 'k.v.' to any other status.

Each year 700,000 18 year olds were eligible for military service. However, the huge casualty losses in 1915 and 1916 forced the generals constantly to comb through the non-'k.v.' categories to find more fighting soldiers, while not depriving industry of its skilled labour force. Two factors dogged their plans for military conquest. By the end of the war they were increasingly dependent upon re-cycling the recovered injured or combing out exempted skilled men as well as the older age groups of civilians who had been directed to administrative, communication and transport duties. Secondly, the shortage of skilled industrial workers forced the generals to release up to 3.0 million conscripts after call-up, as exempted workers in mining, rail transport and the munitions industry. Half of these were classed as k.v. by the end of 1917.121 In April 1917 and January 1918, hundreds of thousands of them joined the nationwide strikes of industrial workers against the food ration, rising prices and for peace.

The generals punished the strikers by sending them to the trenches, where many of them spread the idea of refusing to fight, thus striking a blow against the prolongation of the war. Those not punished in this way went on 'go-slows' to prolong their stay at home, away from the war zones. Despite the strikes, the generals' plans for munitions production were too successful, in fact. The monthly output of gunpowder trebled during the war but by autumn 1917, the output of light artillery and mine-throwers had to be constantly cut back 'because there were not enough men at the front to use them'.[18]

Ludendorff's figures showed a decline of 2.1 million in enlistments to the infantry from the mid-point of the war onwards, despite the enlargement of the eligible age groups from 20 to 45 year olds to 17 to 50 year olds.[19] Table I quantifies the effects on the western front of this drastic reduction, after Russia's revolutionary withdrawal from the war. The previous year's army intake declined by well over a half. Enrolments fell from 1.4 million in 1916 to 0.6 million in 1917.

Table 1 — German military manpower losses and intakes 1915-18

Year	Losses in the West (Military Casualties)	Total Intake. (All recruits, comb-outs and returned injured)	Balance for All Fronts (Reserves for Active Duty)
1915	337,000	1,070,000	733,000 (+)
1916	549,000	1,443,000	894,000 (+)
1917	510,000	622,000	112,000 (+)
1918	1,498,000	405,000	1,093,000 (-)

(a) Casualties comprize killed, injured, POWs and the missing.
(b) Source; Table up-graded entirely from data in Winston S. Churchill (n/d), *The World Crisis — 1911-1918*, Odhams, London, Vol.2, pp.963, 968-9.

In late 1916, the Auxiliary Service Law was brought in to counter-act the losses from battlefield casualties, by drafting civilians of both sexes to munitions work, thus increasing the male reserves available for the front without upsetting the balance of labour required for war production. The act had the opposite effect on the provision of reserve contingents and in its application provided increased avenues for desertion. When put into effect, the act doubled the number of skilled and unskilled workers exempted from field service in 1917.[20]

There were close to three million deferred men of all classifications at the start of the spring offensives of 1918. Joint committees of employers and trade union leaders could withdraw skilled engineers and miners from service at the front for a period. They could train women or unskilled workers to replace them thus enabling the release of soldiers for the battlefield. Though the new law ostensibly put the direction of labour under military control, nevertheless as a result of civilians working to rule, additional numbers of exempted k.v. men managed to stay-at-home as essential workers. Table 2 shows that over half of them were of combat readiness. It estimates the numbers who were able to shirk the call to the front, from the proportion of those deferred men sent to the war from munitions work.

For example, in December 1916 the generals had called for 200,000 front-line volunteers from among almost 2.0 million exempted men. Only 60,000 came forward, together with a similar number of civilians to fill the resultant vacancies in munitions. By the end of May 1917 there were 260,000 trained troops staying at home under exemption procedures, who were required at the front.[21] 80,000 workers of both sexes and of non-military age groups were found as work place substitutes but only 36,000 k.v. men went to the front. Thus the estimated proportion of fifty percent who managed to maintain deferment and avoid front line service is probably an understatement of the actual position. However, what is made clear from these figures is that conscripted men could not use the complex Auxiliary Service Law as a means to avoid front line service without the assistance of civilian shirkers.

Table 2 — Deferred military servicemen — the position on 24 March 1918 and estimated stay-at-homes — 50% of all k.v. exempted men

Designation	Total (Prussia, Bavaria, Saxony and Wurtemberg)	Of which k.v. men
Skilled	1,714,539	771,097
Unskilled	1,243,438	771,696
Totals	2,957,977	1,542,793

Summary Estimate:-
Desertion rate, stay-at-homes (50% approximation) **750,000**

(a) Sources; *Statistisches Jahrbuch für das Deutsche Reich*, (1924/25) Verlag für Politik und Wirtschaft, Berlin. Vol.44, pp.24-26; tables 1-3, 6. In the same *Jahrbuch*, 2.7 million servicemen were reported to be remaining in the homeland on 11 November 1918.
(b) Gerald D. Feldman, Princeton University. See footnote 20 for bibliographical details.

General Groener, Ludendorff's assistant at the War Office in charge of war food supplies argued that 'certainly under the headings of exempted k.v. men there were deserters of all classes, but the numbers scarcely covered the necessary demand in industry for all the needed skilled workers'. Against this view, General Ludendorff in September 1917 complained to the Imperial Chancellor, that:

> the output of the workman, particularly exempted men had dropped by thirty or forty percent. This is not a question of food. It is due to passive resistance and, in the case of the exempted men, the desire to make work last longer so that calling-up can be avoided.[22]

Although most losses of enlisted k.v. men to field service came about by restrictive trade union practices, deserters could also plead the vital nature of their war work and thus move about the labour market. Exempted men could also prolong deferment in cases of illness or hardship at home. Among the wealthier classes, social influence and bribery fuelled sympathetic responses to requests for continuing deferment. From 1916 to 1918 the numbers exempted under the Auxiliary Service Law rose from approximately one million to three millions, half of whom were k.v. men.

The High Command attempted to counteract blatant civilian shirking by drafting forced labour from Belgium and after declaring Poland to be an independent but federal monarchy, men were sent from Posen and Silesia. The physical weakness of the Belgians and the resentments of the Poles turned these measures into fiascos[23] and added particularly to the numbers of Polish speaking soldiers who deserted. Those previously exempted were 'combed out' for the front-line and desperate to maintain battlefield strengths, the High Command turned to the untrained and to those recovered from injuries sustained in previous battles.

Deserting the Kaiser's war: stay-at-homes and strong refusers at the front

As the stay at homes came to predominate, the decline in recruits of k.v. capability left the generals with a deficit in men for field service, of over one million in the last year of the war. 100,000 men already in the army were combed out from the lines of communication in 1917, by what one German veteran called '*General Heldenklau*', the 'hero's claw'. In early 1918 it reached into the army ranks at the bases, hospital and orderly rooms to send several hundred thousand to the front.[24] 3.6 million men were mustered for the 'Spring Offensive' of 21 March 1918, of whom 1.0 million attacked the Allies on a fifty mile section of the western front. Most of the subsequent heavy losses were not replaced and Ludendorff later complained that he had needed another 200,000 for the attack. Summaries of sixteen divisions on 7 May showed infantry losses of from 40 percent to 60 percent. According to General von Kuhl, army divisions fell to half the infantry levels of 1914. After June 1918, no replacements could be found from the army of *Drückeberger*. By the early autumn of 1918, Rupprecht, the commander of the 6th and 17th Armies reported to the interim government leader Max von Baden, that the bases harboured thousands of pillagers and shirkers and that the strength of the army divisions under his command was one-twelfth of the number each division had put into the field in 1914.[25]

There were many ways of organizing the process of desertion. Such as getting hold of the medical 'ticket' which exempted the wounded on sick leave from further service at the front. Fighter Pilot Rudolph Stark visited an injured friend in the artillery while on leave in August 1918. Discussing his return, he was told 'I've no intention of going back; I'm not quite mad. My wound is one that just enables me to dodge active service. I shall put in a bit of time at the depot and then go my own way'.[26] Others took the more drastic course of acquiring a self-inflicted illness. At a court martial in 1916, against a gunner who contracted gonorrhoea after visiting a forbidden brothel, the defence of the accused was that he and five others had bought pus from an infected infantryman to smear on themselves. In that same year, the number of suicides in the army reached 1,831.[27] In the ranks, soldiers constantly applied for re-training courses or for compassionate leave and some low-ranking officers even colluded in the process of desertion:

> On the Russian Front in early spring 1918, my captain called me to his office and said to me 'I see that you haven't had any leave yet. I'll give you your pass now and if I can give you secret advice, go home and don't come back.'.[28]

Half a million soldiers were transferred from Russia after the October Revolution, but 50,000 of these deserted. A message from Moscow on 25 May 1918 reported:

> ... serious unrest among the German soldiers stationed at Dvinsk. Two divisions have refused to leave Russia for the French front. Prince Leopold of Bavaria has come to open an enquiry. Several soldiers have been hanged and some dozens sentenced to penal servitude for life.

An estimated 5,000 men refused to join the transports.[29] Of those who did arrive, Lieutenant Brüning, in command of a machine gun detachment on the western front, commented:

> It was soon clear to us that the hope that the peace treaty with Lenin and Trotsky would bring us a great number of divisions from the east, though certainly fulfilled in terms of numbers, in reality only paved the way for the subversion of the west front.[30]

Almost all journeys between, to and from the fronts were by train and reports and orders from the General Staff in the autumn of 1917 complained of unrest and mutiny on the trains and that ten percent of replacement soldiers went astray during rail journeys. Many such deserters found refuge in neutral countries such as Holland and Switzerland, or went into hiding in the larger cities of Belgium and Germany. In April 1917, over 100,000 deserters were reported living openly in Holland and Switzerland, and by October 1918 50,000 deserters were living in the working class districts of Berlin. In May 1918 the Swiss Government tightened its controls over the 25,000 German deserters to whom it gave sanctuary, as the Bolsheviks were instigating many of them to become 'world revolutionaries'.[31]

Desertion on these scales weakened the war effort by attrition. Ludendorff, anxious to shift responsibility from himself for the loss of the war, complained that before the offensive of spring 1918:

> ... the recruiting situation need not have been so bad. The loss by desertion was uncommonly high. The number that got into neutral countries — e.g. Holland — ran into tens of thousands, and a far greater number lived happily at home, tacitly tolerated by their fellow-citizens and completely unmolested by the authorities. They and the shirkers at the front, of whom there were thousands more, reduced the battle strength of the fighting troops, especially of the infantry, to a vital degree.[32]

Ludendorff observed that 'many offences were committed in order to escape regimental duty and fighting, by undergoing punishment'.[33] An anonymous soldier recorded in his diary for 1918:

> April 12th Arrested at the station at Sains for having stolen some bread.
> April 23rd Brought up for stealing bread.
> May 1st I had some really good news today, viz. that on account of that damned bread business I got 48 hours 'middle arrest', must start my sentence immediately. But I'll get my own back on the blighters as soon as we get into the front line.[34]

In some cases, deserters went across no-man's land to inform their enemies of forthcoming attacks. Two men from Alsace-Lorraine deserted to the British to let them know the timing of the German March offensive. In early June 1918:

the number of German deserters suddenly increased, a sure symptom in 1918 that an offensive was imminent. Other information received on the 8th made it certain that an attack was imminent, while a deserter who came in on the night of 8th/9th finally revealed the exact date and hour.[35]

The massed array of German guns well provided with ammunition was prepared for one final offensive on 15 July. Over the previous fortnight, German deserters crossed over to the French lines to give every detail of the forthcoming attack. The French evacuated the first line trenches, nullifying the impact of the German offensive.[36] The favour was returned on 11 July by French deserters who had crossed the lines to tell German soldiers that they were to be attacked on 18 July.[37]

Disobedience at the front became commonplace. In the German 7th Army on 27 May 1918, the French towns of Soissons, Fismes and the village of Pévy were captured but had to be evacuated 'for fear of excesses and the breakdown of discipline' as men looted wine-cellars. 'One saw melancholy sights and cases of serious drunkenness', wrote one German officer. Three days later, five divisions failed to attack. Three 'strongly refused to do their attacking duty' while the failure of the other two was 'ascribed to their having come from the Russian front.'[38] In mid-1918, three air force officers and a civilian war resister, deserted from Berlin to Denmark, in service aeroplanes, to raise the call for a peace without indemnities and to warn of the coming revolution in Germany.

After the failure of five divisions during the German attack in May, Germany's last offensive came to a halt in mid-July, according to Ludendorff for want of 200,000 men who had deserted the call to the colours. On 8 August 1918, six or seven divisions quit the battlefield under cover of fog during an Allied attack. Even a Prussian division failed badly on that 'black day for Germany'. Ludendorff later complained to the cabinet,

> Shouts of 'Blackleg, You're prolonging the war', were heard as refusers met up with reserve divisions moving to the front. Whole bodies of our men had surrendered to single enemy troopers. In some units, the officers lost all influence and fled with their men. One commander thought he had bolsheviks under him, not German soldiers.

Six days after the collapse of these divisions, Ludendorff reported to the Kaiser that the army had experienced a set back, due to low morale and falling reserves. The Kaiser recommended:

> There must be a more effective combing-out to re-man the front. In Berlin there are still a lot of fellows loafing about. Enheartening speeches must be made by persons whose voice carries weight with the public.[39]

Ballin, the great shipping magnate was suggested, but in discussions with the steel baron Stinnes, Ballin was told that 32,000 men had deserted during the Allied offensive and that Stinnes own preference would have been to open peace talks at once.[40]

On 13 August Scottish gunner, William Carr reported that 'the road through the wire was black with retreating men, I could scarcely believe my eyes. It was like a crowd leaving a football match'.[41] Gunner Carr's battery fired on the 'football' crowd. When he saw the results he broke down in tears and was so sickened that he refused to fire another shot. He was sent home from the British army in the field. Such events show that high desertion rates and high battlefield casualties were inter-linked phenomena in World War One. The war in 1918 had become an open war of movement and manpower losses reverted to the appallingly high levels previously reached in 1914. To avoid them, on September 3rd, entire regiments of German guardsmen surrendered, applauding each company with hand-claps and laughter as they were herded into Allied POW compounds.[42] By mid-September 1918, deserters at the front were leaping aboard the ambulance trains in hundreds, returning to Germany and disappearing in the big cities.[43]

Reaching the critical level; counting the cost of desertion

In the last two months of the war German officers gave up making casualty returns and at the end of the war a discrepancy of half a million unrecorded casualties was discovered in the official statistics.[44] Statistics handed to the Allied powers after the cessation of hostilities revealed a figure of three quarters of a million troops unaccounted for, an amount that equals Volkmann's estimate of the scale of desertion from March to November 1918,[45] shown in Table 3.

The heavier losses in the field suffered by the Germans in the last eight months of the war were not in themselves sufficient to explain the almost total disappearance of the company and battalion strengths of many divisions serving at the front. Allied advances were never so rapid or so extensive that divisions in reserve behind the lines were over-run and captured. They had simply disappeared, or were hanging around the *étappe*, the base areas, waiting to leap on trains for the homeland.

Table 3 — All desertions — 1918

Military Desertions 1918. (a) Volkmann's estimate, averaged to include voluntary surrenders at the front.	0.875m
Draft Dodging — Class of 1918. (b) Churchill's estimate: call-up year group: 700,000 less actual intake.[46]	0.295m
Shortfall in 1918 comb-out of k.v. and g.v. reserve men (c) Ludendorff, The General Staff and Its Problems.[47]	0.200m

Summary estimate - total desertions, military and draft dodging 1918
1,370,000

The comb out of g.v. men was only effective before the end of March 1918.

The losses from all forms of desertion in 1918 approximates the figure for all losses from military casualties in the same year. However, the figures quoted above do not cover the shortfalls in the class of 1917, nor do they cover the failures in 1916-17 of Groener's call for volunteers after the introduction of the Auxiliary Service Act in August 1916.

Table 4 shows the change in field army and ration strengths from March to November 1918, during which period there were 1.4 million battlefield casualties of all kinds. After a call for enlistment of conscripts in early September 1918 from the mines, railways and from labourers for the harvest, Ludendorff had to admit to the war cabinet on 9 October that he had failed by 640,000 men whom he required at once. Another 300,000 would be needed for training in readiness for battles six months hence, but he admitted that 'the g.v. men will not fight now'. Thus approximately 1 million men behind the lines refused to heed his call for a last ditch battle on 25 October 1918. After this failed to evoke any response, Ludendorff was dismissed to a lower office but deserted his post and fled to Sweden until the revolution was brought under control in February 1919.

Table 4 — German desertions: Totals from 1917 to 1918 — by official statistics

(a) Front line strengths of German armies on all fronts - 21 March 1918	4,353,598
(b) Military Casualties March - November 1918	1,372,074
(c) = (a)-(b) Final ration strength German field armies, W and E fronts	2,981,524
(d) Enlisted army strength Nov. 1918, field armies and occupied territories	5,300,000
(e) = (d)-(c) Front line Shortfall against numbers enlisted	**2,318,476**

Source: *Statistisches Jahrbuch* (1925), Vol.44, p.24. *Jahrbuch* footnote: From 2 February 1918 onwards, in place of fighting and ration strengths, a single statistic under one heading of field strength, corresponding with the ration strength was reported.

Of the total number of men in the field when the shooting ended, almost an equivalent number had deserted in one way or another. But few of those still at their posts during the armistice period wanted any longer to wait in line for army rations. Aware of the threat of famine at home, made more desperate after the armistice by the British and French prolongation of the war-time food blockade, mutineers and deserters took the army's food stocks to distribute to the civilian populations they were rejoining. They set up soldiers' councils to co-ordinate these tasks.

'The spark of insurrection leapt across the contaminated bases'

'Equal Rations! Equal Pay! then the War can stay away', chanted
Oskar Hippe's mutinous unit as they marched up to the Belgian front,
there to commandeer a train to take them back to Brussels in
September 1918. At night they had another chant for the barracks,
that threatened the officers with the knife to within an inch of their
lives.[48] Lieutenant Brüning ordered his machine gun unit to project its
gun barrels through closed train doors in a vain attempt to prevent
the mutineers from taking over the railway stations. The officers,
demoted by the rank and file, became aware that their main enemy
was no longer the English. German military representatives at the
armistice talks, on being told that they must surrender the bulk of
their armaments to the victors, begged the Allies to allow them to
keep 5,000 machine guns, because in the words of the French
Marshall Foch, 'they would have insufficient to fire on their own
men'.[49]

When, in August 1918, tens of thousands of servicemen from all
parts of Germany had been hiding from the trenches in the big cities
and in the forests of Silesia, where working women provided them
daily with food, Volkmann commented, 'It is worth noting that the
General Staff saw itself as incapable of calling a halt to this mass
desertion, by suitable methods'.[50] General Groener told the High
Command in early November 1918, that August should have been the
month for setting up the notorious *Freikorps*, to enforce discipline
against deserters and mutineers.

The spark of insurrection, in General Maercker's apt description,
that turned mass desertion from mutiny into revolution, was lit by
the news of the Kiel uprising and fell upon the tinder spread by the
rebellious soldiers across eastern France and Belgium. The flint was
armed in opposition to the call from the army and naval High
Commands to mobilize the diminished ranks for an all-out last battle
to stave off Germany's total defeat. The mutinous soldiers
spontaneously organized a revolutionary withdrawal from Belgium.
70,000 men fought with their officers at the Beverloo base camp and
at the Maas bridges after a further exchange of fire with their
officers,[51] then crossed peaceably into Holland after negotiations

with the Dutch authorities, carting back to the homeland hundreds of thousands of tons of army food stores. Others, leapt into red-ribboned officers' cars and spread their uprising to Brussels, Namur, Liége and Antwerp, completely overthrowing the German military government in Belgium.[52] The mutineers, carrying huge stocks of army stores, rations and food supplies, commandeered trains to re-enter Germany where they briefly seized power in most of the towns and cities.

Upon their return, the rebellious deserters organized the confiscation of hidden civilian food stores. Wilhelm Necker of the 9th Grenadiers chaired the Stargard Soldiers' Council.

> The next thing was to control the great estates of *'Hinter Pommern'*, east Pomerania. It was known to us that the great estates had many more cattle and pigs than were in the compulsory register. The surplus was impounded by us and we had enough food for the garrison and the new troops arriving in the town. There was a threat of famine for a long time after the war. We had to take control of food supplies.[53]

The movement posed an insurrectionary threat, not only to the generals, but to the SPD, to whom political authority was handed by the generals' nominee, Prince Max of Baden. In their movement to the homeland and upon their arrival in the towns and cities, the mutineers freed POWs and political prisoners, seized and occupied town halls, law courts and government offices, unlocked black market food stores, took control of rail stations and networks, ran wireless-telegraphy services and newspapers. The great symbol of their triumph was their forced removal of the officers' insignia of rank. In Berlin entire regiments of deserters were formed into a 'Deserters' League' demanding amnesty, back pay, food, clothing and discharge papers, all of which they won for the entire movement.[54]

In Berlin, despite the efforts of the High Command, no regiment could be found to defend the old order. The problem for the mutineers was the centralization of their new authority, which many of them had not considered. The right wing social democrats however, were well prepared. At a mass delegate conference in Berlin on 10 November 1918, 3,000 soldiers' delegates, some with their officers from the barracks of the royal regiments in Berlin and well briefed beforehand by the SPD, voted to hand over power to a coalition government, pending the general election of a constituent assembly. In contrast to the actions of the mutineers, the Berlin conference of soldiers' council delegates allowed the officials of the monarchical state to remain in office. Nor did the USPD supported workers' councils, that linked up to the soldiers' councils, insist on the immediate dismissal of the Kaisers' war time bureaucrats. The Independents believed that their transitional demands for more socialization of the economy had to be fought for politically, in a parliament elected for the first time in German history under a universal franchise.

The Independents accepted the demand for the maintenance of the state bureaucracy, on condition that the soldiers' councils should sit in with the old authorities in an advisory capacity. The spontaneity of the soldiers' movement proved unequal to this task, which in the minds of the mutineers called for nothing less than the removal of the officers, whether in military or in bureaucratic service to the state. The soldiers' actions increasingly became street actions, along side crowds of civilian demonstrators. On 7 November army mutineers joined a 200,000 strong demonstration in Munich. They launched an attack on the barracks and the prisons and then entirely overthrew the royal government of Bavaria.

The same potential existed everywhere. But it was held back by the workers' councils. In Berlin an earlier call for a similar demonstration and a general strike was postponed for a week by the shop stewards district committee. Before it could take place, revolutionary crowds occupied the streets, but the social democrats were in office and the immediate threat to the generals was removed.

Postscript — the price of disorganization

Leaderless, the rebellious soldiers' movement turned into the largest demobilization mutiny on record. By the spring of 1919, the deserters had disbanded the greatest German army in history. After their rapid return home to an inflation-wracked economy of scarcity, the mutineers in civilian clothing, despite the efforts of the High Command to buy off their discontent by persuading employers to give them any work at any cost, were dragged into civil war. The officers were ordered by the High Command firstly to infiltrate and then to disband with force, the soldiers' and workers' councils, whose growing militancy was seen by the SPD, the defeated German ruling class and the victorious Allies as a carrier of the contagion of bolshevism. The USPD resigned from the revolutionary council after the massacre of mutinous soldiers and sailors at Christmas 1918. The SPD then endorsed the creation of the *Freikorps*, which mobilized middle class university and high school students from the classes of 1919 and 1920. Draft dodging was ended by the SPD government which extended the call-up.

In Berlin, in March 1919, the soldiers' and workers' councils were ferociously suppressed by right wing officers, using aircraft and machine guns remitted to them by the British and tanks captured from them. The struggle re-ignited the spark of working class revolt that alternatively spluttered and flared for the next five years.[55] In the general strikes of 1919 and against the Kapp Putsch, the generals' coup of March 1920, the remnants of the rebellious movement of deserters and mutineers confronted the continuing efforts of the SPD to maintain the diminished prestige of the generals and of the officer corps. They defeated the coup but despite suffering great bloodshed from a revived but right wing republican German army, they prevented the immediate return of the generals and admirals to absolute power. However, once again the SPD secured defeat from their victory and a generation later, placing themselves at the service of the Nazis, Germany's army and naval High Commands re-built their armed forces for another era of mass destruction.

134

Notes

1. Recollection recorded in the Peter Liddle Collection, Brotherton Library, Leeds University. Box on German Forces in the Field.
2. Koettgen, J. (translator) (1917), *A German deserters wartime experience*, Grant Richards, London, p.13.
3. *Statistisches Jahrbuch für das Deutsche Reich*, (1925) Verlag für Politik und Wirtschaft, Berlin, Vol.44, 1924/25, pp.24-26.
4. For counter argument see - Eckstein, Modris (1989) *Rights of Spring*, Bantam Press, London; Middlebrook, Martin (1978), *The Kaiser's Battle*, Allen Lane, London; Winter, J. M. (1989) The Experience of World War I, Guild Macmillan, London.
5. See Howard, Nick (forthcoming) 'The German Revolution Defeated - Fascism Deferred: the Servicemen's Revolt and Social Democracy at the end of the First World War: 1918-20', in Kirk,Tim and McElligott,Tony (eds.) *Community, Authority and Opposition to Fascism in Europe*, Cambridge University Press. Numbers of soldiers' councils in Goerlitz, Walter (1953) *The German General Staff*, Praeger,New York, p.206.
6. Ludendorff, Erich (1922) *Kriegführung und Politik*, Mittler und Sohn, Berlin, pp.108-9.
7. See Volkmann, Erich Otto (1925), *Der Marxismus und das Deutsche Heer im Weltkriege*, Reimar Hobbing, Berlin. The phrase appears in an article by Deist, Wilhelm (1992) Verdeckter Militaerstreik im Kriegsjahr 1918?, in Wette, Wolfram, (ed.), *Der Krieg des kleinen Mannes: Eine militaergeschichte von unten*, Munich, pp.149-50.
8. War Office, 22.8.16. SS.473, 1a/19703, in A. A. Laporte Payne papers. Peter Liddle Collection.
9. Landau, Henry (1934), *All's Fair - The British Secret Service behind the German Lines*, Putnam, New York. p.97.
10. War Cabinet minutes, PRO CAB 23/14 WC500a, pp 300-1, 10 November 1918.
11. Brüning, Heinrich (1970), *Memoiren 1918-1934*, Deutsche Verlags-Anstalt, Stuttgart, p.30.
12. Public Record Office, War Cabinet Minutes CAB 23/14, WC 550a, pp.310-11, 10 November 1918.
13. Volz, H. (1942), *Novemberumsturz und Versailles 1918-1919*, Berlin, Part 1, pp.393-4.
14. Brüning, op.cit., p.28.

15. See Index and German map of 30 October 1918 published by the British General Staff (1919) in *The German Forces in the Field 11 November 1918,* War Office, A. 2266, London.
16. A complete description of the enrolment system is to be found in British General Staff (1919), *The Handbook of the German Army in War April, 1918,* War Office, S.S.356, London.
17. Groener, Wilhelm (1957), *Lebenserinnerungen,* Vandenhoeck & Ruprecht, Goettingen, p 356.
18. Feldman, op.cit., p.494.
19. Ludendorff, Erich (1922), *Kriegführung und Politik,* Mittler, Berlin. pp 108-9.
20. Feldman, Gerald D. (1966), *Army, Industry and Labour in Germany - 1914-1918,* Princeton UP, New Jersey, p 301.
21. Feldman, op.cit., pp.303-4.
22. Ludendorff, Erich (1920), *The General Staff and its Problems,* Hutchinson, London. Vol.1, p.111.
23. Feldman, op.cit., p.308.
24. Middlebrook, op.cit., pp 58-9.
25. Letter from Kronprinz Rupprecht to Chancellor Prince Max. In von Baden, Max (1968), *Erinnerungen und Dokumente,* Ernst Klett Verlag,Stuttgart, p.439.
26. Stark, Rudolph (1931), *Wings of War,* (English reprint 1988) Greenhill, London, p.104.
27. Edlef Koeppen (1931), *Higher Command,* Faber & Faber, London, pp.235-6.
28. Hans Feibusch, Recollections, Peter Liddle Collection. Interviewed by Michael Hammerson.
29. Daily Review of the Foreign Press, (1918) War Office, London. Series 7, p.227. A similar incident also recorded in Richard Bessel, (1988), 'The Great War in German Memory', *German History,* Vol.6, No.1, p.24.
30. Brüning, op.cit., p.20. Brüning became Reich Chancellor from 1930 to 1932, ruling by emergency powers.
31. PRO, FO 371:3255, fn 232754. 7 December 1917. FO 383:464, fn. 115259 1 May 1918.
32. Ludendorff, Erich (1921) *My War Memoirs,* Hutchinson, London, vol II, pp.585-7.
33. ibid. 611-2.
34. German Forces in the Field, Recollections, Peter Liddle Collection.

35. Edmonds, Brigadier General Sir James E. (1939), *Official History of the Great War, Military Operations, France and Belgium 1918*, Vol 3, Macmillan, London, p 172. Edmonds quoted extensively from German monographs of the *Reichsarchiv* parliamentary research unit.

36. Volkmann, Erich Otto, (1922), *The Great War*, Berlin, cited in Koppen, op.cit., p.380.

37. Edmonds, op.cit., p 241.

38. Edmonds, ibid., pp.118-9, 142.

39. Quoted in Ludwig, Emil (1935), *Hindenburg and the Saga of the German Revolution*, Heinemann, London, p.166.

40. Petzold, Joachim, (ed.) (1970), *Deutschland im ersten Weltkrieg*, Akademie-Verlag, Berlin, Vol 3. p.418.

41. Gunner William Carr, (1985), *A Time to leave the Ploughshares*, Robert Hale, London, pp.165-7.

42. Gibbs, Philip (1938), *Realities of War*, Hutchinson, London, Vol. II p.459.

43. Volkmann, op.cit., p.193. Maercker, (1921), *Vom Kaiserheer zum Reichswehr*, Koehler, Leipzig, p.19.

44. See report on this discrepancy in Winston S. Churchill, op.cit., p.962, f.n. 2.

45. For details see Howard, N. P. 'The Social and Political Consequences of the Allied Food Blockade of Germany, 1918-19', *German History*, Vol 11. No.2 1993. p 172.

46. Churchill, op cit , p.968. Churchill over estimated the numbers in the class of 1918 by 100,000.

47. Ludendorff, *The General Staff and Its Problems*, Vol.I p.138.

48. Hippe, Oskar (1991), *And Red is the Colour of Our Flag*, Index Books, London. pp.29-30.

49. Quoted in Lloyd George, David (1936), *War Memoirs*, Odhams Press, London, Vol II, p 1983.

50. Volkmann, E. O. (1929), 'Die sozialen Mißstaende im Heer waehrend des Weltkrieges', quoted in Deist, Wilhelm, (1970) *Militaer und Innenpolitik im Weltkrieg 1914-1918*, Droste Verlag, Düsseldorf, Vol.2, p.458.

51. Maercker, op.cit., p.20.

52. See press reports of the uprising in Brussels, Liége, Namur and Beverloo, datelined 11, 13 and 18 November in *Koelnische Zeitung* and in Pester Lloyd, 14-15 November. Quoted in Buchner, E. (1921), *Revolutionsdokumente*, Deutsche Verlag für

Politik und Geschichte, Berlin, pp.202-4.

53. Howard, Nick (1993), 'Essay in Oral History, Der Wilde Necker, A Weimar Republican recalls the years from 1918 to 1934', *Labour History Review*, Vol 58, No. 3, p.41. For details of the work of the soldiers' councils against the famine see, N. P. Howard, *German History*, op cit, pp.161-188.
54. Gordon Harold J. (1957) *The Reichswehr and the German Republic 1919-1926* Princeton University Press, New Jersey, p.21.
55. For an account of these five years, see Harman, Chris (1982) *The Lost Revolution*, Pluto Press, London.

8 Militant and the failure of 'acherontic' Marxism in Liverpool

Alan Johnson

CONSIDERING, That the emancipation of the working classes must be conquered by the working classes themselves ... ('The Provisional Rules of the First International', 1866, in Marx, 1974).

Flectere si nequeo supros, Acheronta movebo — If I cannot change the Powers above, I shall set the Lower Regions (Acheron) into motion (Virgil's *Aeneid*, VII, quoted in Draper, 1992 p.245).

A Labour Party activist last year accompanied a prominent Labour councillor receiving a delegation from tenement tenants in Liverpool 8 — 'Toxteth' to the rest of the country. The tenants — two of whom were party members — were arguing the case to be allowed to stay in their community as a community. The councillor responded by saying he had the keys to the city's best ten council houses in his pocket and that if he were to throw them on the floor the members of this 'community' would tear at one another to get their hands on them (Allen 1986b, p.19).

Introduction

From 1983 to 1985 the city of Liverpool was the site of one of the most remarkable political struggles of the Thatcher years as the local Labour council, led by the Trotskyist Militant Tendency, clashed with the Conservative government over the question of local government finance. This chapter critically examines the role of Militant in Liverpool and challenges both the 'enormous condescension' of those commentators who have seen only the 'capture' of a moribund party and a crude 'blackmail and bankruptcy' strategy (Belchem, 1992, p.20) designed by diabolic Trotskyists 'to inflict a painful lesson on the people of Liverpool', (Callaghan, 1987, p.203) and the self-promotion of those supporters of Militant who, invoking Wordsworth, have compared the campaign favourably with the French Revolution of 1789 (Taaffe and Mulhearn, 1988).[2]

Militant was no 'bed-sit Trotskyist' imposition on the body politic of Liverpool. There was an organic relationship between Militant supporters and sections of the Liverpool working-class which had developed a reputation for militancy since the 1960s. In broad outline no city in the country so confirmed the political perspectives of the Militant Tendency. Yet those perspectives, developed by Ted Grant, (1989, pp.413-456) had changed little in over thirty years and were philosophically a species of vulgar determinism, (Matgamna, 1966; O'Mahony, 1985) a prediction that 'History' would, 'within ten to fifteen years', produce socialism or barbarism. This would involve an unfolding process of (1) capitalist economic crisis, producing (2) the radicalization of the working class, and (3) the expression of that radicalism within the traditional organizations, the Labour Party and Trade Unions, into which the workers would move en masse, creating a ripening political differentiation and a 'mass left wing' and finally, (4) the growth of Marxism to a position of leadership within those organizations.

After a periodization of the collective action of the Liverpool working class since the nineteenth century, (influenced by the work of Davies, 1988) I explore the relationship between the political economy of Liverpool in the 1970s and 1980s. and the political perspectives of Militant. While I refuse any easy dismissal of those perspectives or of the practice which flowed from them — 'entrism', or revolutionary socialists working within the Labour Party — I also argue that Militant's crude determinism and divisive sectarianism were responsible for the collapse of the council campaign in 1985. The tragedy of Liverpool was two fold: first, and outside the scope of this chapter, is the isolation of the council by the Labour and Trade Union leaders, and by the other 'left-wing' Labour councils, and second, the 'acherontic Marxism' of the Militant Tendency itself, which ensured that the remarkable popular support for the council was treated at best as a stage army, and at worst as the 'enemy within'. The chapter concludes by exploring the significance of the principle, central to classical Marxism, of 'self-emancipation' for the political leadership of popular protest.

Accumulation and collective action in Liverpool: a periodization

Collective action is rooted in the character of a local regime of accumulation but is constructed by politics: a form of 'structured agency'. The concept of 'regime of accumulation', developed by Aglietta (1979) but modified by Therborn (1983, p.42) refers to 'the specific form of capital accumulation established in a particular locality viewed from the angle of the class relations of power', and focuses attention upon the fact that 'capital may be successfully accumulated in a large number of ways, but with widely varying effects upon working class collectivity'. The concept of 'capacities' (Therborn, 1983) refers to resources and powers possessed by collective actors and understood as the outcome of both the position of the collective actor in the regime of accumulation ('intrinsic strength') and the degree of self-consciousness and organization ('hegemonic capacity') the collective actor possesses. These capacities are historically and spatially variable and both materially determined and politically constructed. The regime of accumulation does not 'decide' the kind of collectivities which will emerge but it does set the terms, limiting and enabling, for the kind of collectivities that political practice is able to construct. The notion of class as objective and subjective, as intrinsic strength and self-identification, and the concept of 'capacities', understood as the outcome of these two registers of class taken together is, I believe, the key to a non-reductionist notion of determination. Together they provide an analytical 'hinge' to connect the two registers of class and guide empirical enquiry into the conditions and dynamics of collective identity and action.

From the 19th century 'founding moment' to the 1930s

Liverpool's regime of accumulation was based upon the economic activity surrounding the Port: a vast *entrepot*, and the 'gateway to empire' (Lane, 1987). Working class formation took the form of successive waves of immigration, and pre-existing identities and prejudices, far from being dissolved, actually functioned as the basis for labour market, residential, and political segmentation until the post-second world war period. This local regime of accumulation was the material basis for the chronically delayed unification of the working class, ensuring that its intrinsic strength, seriously weakened already because of casualism and segmented labour markets, was never realised, displaced as it was by nationalism and religion, cowed by deferential submission, and fragmented by ethnic closure. The dominant collectivities were rooted in a lived experience of religious, occupational and spatial division and conflict within the working class. This was inimical to the emergence of a class collectivity or 'labour vision' (Davies, 1979-80; Shallice, 1980; Smith, 1980) and was the basis of the political hegemony of Tory Democracy and Irish Nationalism, political formations which, in turn, worked to reproduce those divisions, not least by the use of gerrymandering (Davies, 1995). The comment of Georg Lukacs that 'the structuring of pre-capitalist societies into castes and estates means that economic elements are inextricably linked to political and religious factors' (in Callinicos, 1987, p.173) is apposite for capitalist Liverpool. Labourism struggled to emerge, resting on a thin layer of workers whose experience was conducive to the vision and formal representational politics of the Labour Party. Unlike in Glasgow, this native labourism was unable to transcend the particularistic collectivities produced by divided economic, cultural and socio-spatial structures. The marriage with Catholicism in the late 1920s (Shallice, 1982) saw Labour absorbed by one of those particularisms. Bossism, with its mix of the clientalism, patronage and the whiff of corruption, emerged as a characteristic of Labour politics in the city at this time (Baxter, 1969).

From the 1930s to the 1970s

After 1914 the structural decline of the service and manufacturing specialisms of the city, and the downturn in international trade, produced local economic crisis (Davies, 1992). From the 1930s there began a serious attempt by the state, first locally and then nationally, to induce a new regime of accumulation based upon branch plant manufacturing industry and the creation of new estates on the city's rim. The resulting economic and socio-spatial restructuring ruptured the collectivities, common-senses and politics of sectarianism, and so the intrinsic strength and hegemonic capacity of the working class were enormously enhanced. However this was also the period of a ripening 'crisis of representation' between those class collectivities and a shrinking Labour Party unable to articulate an alternative political project to the Tories. The early 1970s marks the high point of Labour's estrangement as its technocratic and managerial modernism, allied to support for rent increases, resulted in the rapprochement of the Liberal Party with 'middle Liverpool' via 'community politics' and low rates.

From the mid 1970s to the mid 1980s

In the 1970s and 1980s both the Port and the Branch Plant regimes collapsed leaving a de-industrialized city to cope with mass unemployment and its attendant social problems (Parkinson, 1988). The public sector became the dominant employer and politics was subsumed by the question of the city's 'managed decline'. The context of the rise of Militant was the revival and radicalization of the Labour Party itself as the militants who had fuelled the 'revolt from below', faced with the limits of workplace militancy and community politics in the face of global slump, turned to politics, the Labour Party and the Militant, and a genuine, if partial, rapprochement between the party and sections of the class was effected, albeit via an intensification rather than a transcending of labourism.

The Drama: the political economy of Liverpool and the political perspectives of Militant

Militants rise in Liverpool then, far from being a 'coup' or a 'capture' of a moribund party, or a simple reprise of 'boss politics', was rooted in underlying shifts in the local regime of accumulation. Indeed, far from being a sectarian fantasy, Grant's five-part schema roughly predicted the dynamics of a series of working class struggles, throughout the 1970s and 1980s, which transformed the capacities, institutions and the political affiliations of the Liverpool working class.

Stage (1) 'the twilight of capitalism': organic capitalist crisis

The new organic crisis which is maturing marks a new stage in the development of post-war capitalism. It opens up a new period of struggle between the classes over the next five, ten or twenty years which poses the problem of the entire fate of mankind (Grant 1977, in 1989, p.420).

Militant's perspectives for the 1980s (see Grant, 1989, p.482-528) were predicated on the idea that the contradictions of the post-war long boom could no longer be suppressed, and the productive forces on a world scale were now stagnating. In this 'twilight of capitalism', economic crisis would 'engulf the workers in poverty, want and penury'. Mocked as 'catastrophism' (Callaghan, 1987) Grant's perspective spoke directly to the lived experience of the working class in Liverpool facing the collapse of both the older regime of accumulation based on the Port, (Merseyside Socialist Research Group, 1980; Cornfoot,1982; Stoney, 1983) and the newer state induced branch-plant economy which had carried all the inflated hopes of the 1960s (White, 1975; Lloyd and Dicken, 1977 and 1978; Parkinson, 1988). Between 1979 and 1984 the city lost 40,000 jobs, and a full one-third of manufacturing employment. From 1976 to 1984 the Transport and General Workers Union alone lost 41 per cent of its Merseyside membership. In addition, the sharply declining population, Liberal neglect, and Conservative Government policy conspired to shrink the city's rate base until, as Parkinson (1985, p.10) put it, 'by the mid-1980s cuts in Government financial support had turned economic failure into fiscal crisis and brought Liverpool to the edge of bankruptcy'.

The very speed of this economic collapse, and the depth of the fiscal crisis, made confrontation the **common-sense** response (Ridley, 1986) among a population which, having experienced a process of depopulation (Lawton, 1982) selective by class, was now the most proletarian city in Britain. Moreover the city was reliant upon employment financed from public funds, (Daniels, 1982) and by the mid 1980s over 50 per cent of Merseyside's trade unionists were public employees. This development produced a shift in the focus of the class struggle from production and the workplace to collective consumption and the city. This, in turn, fostered a spatial expression of the class struggle — 'Fortress Liverpool against Westminster' — which allowed the council to draw upon deep resources of local chauvinism in a city which had always claimed no less than a world significance (Lane, 1987; Wainwright, 1987, p.130).

Stage (2) 'the whip of necessity': the radicalization of the working class

In 1977 Grant predicted economic crisis would act as a 'whip of necessity', producing 'inevitable disillusionment with capitalism' and a 'class awakening' (1989, p.420).

> Experience will teach the workers en masse as they move into activity, which will be forced on them by the struggle against unemployment, for shorter hours, better conditions etc., in defence of living standards and for their improvement. They will come up against the granite barrier of the world crisis of capitalism. More and more broad sections will begin to understand that capitalism is responsible for their daily problems and anxieties (Grant, 1977, in 1989, p.506).

In fact it was in conditions of boom that post-war Liverpool experienced an explosive 'revolt from below' in the workplace and the union; from the ebullient unofficial movements on the docks (Hikins [ed.], 1973; Hunter, 1994) and in the seafarers union (Wailey, 1985) to the 'new unionism' of the new manufacturing industries on the outer estates (Beynon, 1973; Spencer, 1989) and the rise of 'white collar militancy'. Community solidarity, released from its sectarian cocoons, had flourished in groups campaigning around fair rents and tenants' rights in the face of inner urban blight and new estate anomie. This revolt was facilitated by the arrival of new manufacturing industry and the creation of new estates which ruptured hitherto dominant economic and socio-spatial structures such as casualized labour, segmented labour markets and residential stability in neighbourhoods defined by religious sectarianism. The revolt drew on the organic 'democratic temper' of waterfront Liverpool, now given a wider legitimacy by national cultural trends, the opportunity presented by a tighter labour market, and geographical reach due to spatial scattering as a result of slum clearance (Lane, 1987). The 'natural democrats' of dockland Liverpool, freed from geographical confinement, religious particularism, and from the chains of the most severe poverty stuck out their chests and strutted across the city transforming the institutions of the working class, first the unions and then the Labour Party, in their own image. Certainly, this image was white and male, and the 'revolt from below' was experienced differently by gender and 'race', but to reduce this process to either the capture of a 'moribund party machine' by Militant (Belchem, 1992, p.20) or to the 'whip of economic necessity' is equally simplistic.

Drawing upon the organizational capacities developed during the revolt from below there was a tremendously high level of **resistance** to the onset of mass unemployment, forcing on it the status of a public and political scandal rather than a natural disaster or individual failing. In the late 1970s and early 1980s Liverpool was a living laboratory of forms of working class resistance to slump. Methods ranged from strike action (Bean and Stoney, 1986) community action (Liverpool CDP, 1975) factory occupations, workers plans (McTiernan, 1986), International combine committees, Co-Ops (Eccles, 1981; McMonnies, 1985), a network of Unemployed Centres funded by a levy on employed unionists, and Welfare Rights Advice Centres (O'Neill, nd.). A new politics linking labour and community also began to emerge in which women were central, for instance in the Health Service (Leighton, 1979). Ian Williams (1985b) has written of Liverpool's artistic and cultural vibrancy born of slump: plebeian, anti-authoritarian and decidedly 'unofficial'.

Liverpool's working class possessed abundance what Miliband calls 'desubordination' (1978), a cultural capacity of collective 'solidarity in mutual adversity'. This democratic temper, constitutive of both the revolt from below and the later resistance to slump, was harnessed in campaigns for electoral success and occupancy of the Town Hall in 1983. However, it was distrusted by Militant thereafter, unless expressed in traditional ways through the 'traditional organizations' and according to a timetable laid down by them. The attempt by Militant to force what was by nature an ebullient anti-authoritarian impulse into the narrow confines of the 'perspectives' and the centralized control of the Tendency, was to result in the fragmentation of the council's base of support and the use of the capacity of desubordination against the council itself.

Stage (3) 'the inexhaustible reservoir of support': the radicalized workers turn to their traditional organizations

If one idea distinguished the Militant from other groups on the far left it was the expectation that a radicalized working class would turn to its 'traditional organizations', the Labour Party and the Trade

Unions:

> ... the working class will find that industrial action is not enough to solve their problems, and that political action is necessary...**Once they take the road of political action, there is only one way in which they can go**, and that is to try and change the organization which was built by the unions, to move into the Labour Party with the purpose of transforming it to meet their needs (Grant, quoted in McGregor, 1986, p.69, emphasis added).

In fact the 1960s had seen a gulf open up between economics and politics in the Liverpool working class. As the 'DIY reformism' of the union militants and community activists developed momentum, it grew estranged from a local Labour Party so decayed that it gave birth to the theory of a universal 'decline of working class politics' (Hindess, 1971). Beynon (1973) for instance, found the shop stewards at Ford Halewood in 1967 'avowedly anti-political'. Politics was seen to 'get in the way of the job'. As one steward told him:

> Most of the lads think you can forget about the Labour Party y'know. Forget about it because it's never going to do anything for the working class. The general feeling on the [shop] floor is that we're on our own y'know. We've got to fight our own battles, do everything ourselves from now on (1973, p.228).

All this was to change in the 1970s as the cold wind of economic crisis blew the activists toward an attempt to reclaim the Party for some kind of socialism. This was a common enough phenomenon across Britain. Liverpool was different in two regards: the class composition of the new recruits and the presence of Militant. Within a very short space of time the Labour Party became the very fulcrum of working class politics in the city. The revolt from below reached the limits of its own practice, unable to translate ebullient factory consciousness and neighbourhood organization into a strategic response to a slump which had global causes. Indeed validation of Grant's view that, in Britain, socialists should seek to be members of the Labour Party as the mass party of the working class stands out as the most obvious, but little remarked upon, 'lesson' of the Liverpool experience. Layers of Transport and General Workers Union shop stewards began to actively back the Labour left locally (McGregor,

1986). The economic militancy of the council workforce in the face of attempts by the Liberal-Tory coalition to cut jobs in the late 1970s, took a similar political turn in the 1980s. Ian Lowes, a leading General and Municipal union activist and a Militant supporter, recalls the dynamic at work:

> Initially we fought on the basis of trade union militancy, 1979-1983. (...) Then we started relating to the political struggle and fought privatization as a political issue not an economic issue. We got involved with the Labour Party to get a Labour council elected. We needed a change in council politics. So we ran a joint campaign with the Labour Party. We called workplace meetings to discuss the issues. We got [a couple of hundred GMBATU] people to join the Labour Party. We argued it was in the interests of the workforce to kick out the rightwingers in the Labour Party and influence the direction of the Labour Party (in McGregor 1986, p.72).

Stage (4) 'As events demonstrate their correctness': the growth of Militant in Liverpool

> In this atmosphere, it is entirely possible for the ideas of Marxism to secure a powerful hold within the traditional organisations of the class at a time when the crisis of capitalism is deepening (Grant, 1979, p.425).

By the late 1930s 'Liverpool had been a base for the Trotskyists for some tim", centred on one of the first families of Liverpool socialism, the Deane's (Bornstein and Richardson, 1986, p.5; Taaffe and Mulhearn, 1988, p.33-34). When Grant was driven out of the unified Trotskyist group, the Revolutionary Communist Party, in 1950 by Gerry Healy, he took the Liverpool Trotskyists with him, and though elsewhere his group was feeble throughout the 1950s, in Liverpool a base was built in Walton where a magazine *Rally* was edited by Pat Wall, and Ted Grant was almost adopted as the parliamentary candidate. In 1955 the Grantites formed The Revolutionary Socialist League (RSL) as the British Section of the European based Fourth International and Grant hoped that Liverpool 'could be a base to spread out in Lancashire, then London and nationally' (quoted in Crick,1986 p.42). In fact Militant did not grow nationally until they were handed control of the Labour Party youth section by the other Trotskyist groups who left or were expelled in the late 1960s. (Atkinson, 1992) and reached a *modus vivendi* with the Labour Party bureaucracy, presiding over the least troublesome youth movement in Labour's history (Matgamna, 1992). Militant used these structures as their own private recruiting ground throughout the 1970s, growing slowly and organically. Matgamna sums up this process:

> The network of Labour Party Young Socialists branches connected to the constituency Labour Parties gave Militant a large base for its propaganda and a trelliswork — subsidised by the Labour Party! — on which to thread its own growing organisation, together with a stable routine of meetings and national affairs. Its manner of growth must be unique in the history of self-proclaimed revolutionary organisations (1992, p.11).

However, the pattern of growth was very different in Liverpool where Militant had deep roots in the local Movement and had been central to the energetic rebuilding of a hollowed out Party from the mid-1970s (Taaffe and Mulhearn, 1988). Militant won a position of leadership locally by the mid-1980s as a result of its interaction with the Liverpool working class over a period of four decades. The most relevant 'exceptional circumstance' in Liverpool, apart from the scale of the economic crisis, was **the presence of a layer of experienced and respected Marxists who had not isolated themselves from, but were at the heart of, the existing Labour Movement.** As Ian Williams, a fierce opponent of the Tendency in Liverpool, admitted:

> The typical Liverpool Militant is not necessarily the callow youth of legend, reciting the slogans to the Zen rhythm of one hand clapping. They are members of many years standing ... commanding respect in their own fields. In many wards they were significant in rebuilding Labour's organisation (Williams, 1985a, p.13).

In 1960 the Apprentices Strikes saw Militant activist Terry Harrison play a leadership role in Merseyside and recruit some of the key activists. Led by Harrison and Mulhearn, Militant were involved in a series of struggles led by the Trades Council and Labour Party, not least against anti-trade union legislation in the late 1960s and early

1970s and alongside tenants groups for fair rents against the right-wing Labour Group. These struggles discredited the Labour right and prepared the Liberal victory of 1973. Militant continued to draw into the Labour Party layers of trade unionists engaged in struggle, for instance from the fire fighters strike of 1977, the campaign to save Western Ship Repairers in 1978, the Typists strike of 1982, and the fight against the privatization of council services. By the late 1970s Militant were 'a serious political force in Liverpool' (Crick 1986, p.222) with seven councillors, and, by 1982, hegemony in the all powerful District Labour Party. In that year four Militant supporters, Harrison, Mulhearn, Fields and Hatton, were selected as Prospective Parliamentary Candidates, and the local Party adopted Militant policy for local government of no cuts in jobs and services, no massive rate rises and a campaign to force the Government to make up the shortfall: the strategy of mobilization and confrontation. Ignored in most academic accounts (e.g. Ridley,1986; Belchem, 1992) are the mass campaigns of canvassing and recruitment which transformed the local Party further in the late 1970s and early 1980s:

> The mass door-to-door canvassing in Wavertree in 1982 was typical of the local campaigns carried out at this time. Two hundred, predominantly Young Socialists, converged on the area. Three quarters of the constituency was canvassed in a weekend! The same approach was adopted in other Liverpool constituencies. Thousands of new members were won to the party. Connections were cemented with the shop stewards and active workers in union branches by the tireless work of the parliamentary candidates and councillors in support of workers fighting to prevent redundancies etc. (Taaffe and Mulhearn, 1988, p.65).

It was this mass political canvassing and discussion, in which canvassers were 'asked into houses or kept for 20 or 30 minutes on the doorstep discussing political issues', (Taaffe and Mulhearn, 1988, p.88) set against a backdrop of economic crisis, which saw Militant supporter Terry Fields defy national trends and win Liverpool Broadgreen in the general election of 1983 on a 2 per cent swing from the Conservatives to Labour (Taaffe and Mulhearn, 1988 pp.84-100; also see Johnson, 1987, for a case study of this style of election campaigning). Unlike many other cities the resulting influx of new members to the Labour Party was composed not of the tired ex-revolutionaries of 1968 but young workers and unemployed people eager to fight back against local economic and social crisis (Ridley, 1986). When, in 1983, the Labour Party won a clear majority for the first time in ten years in a landslide victory increasing its share of the vote by 40 per cent (Taaffe and Mulhearn, 1986, p.82), the political core of the group, and the strategy were provided by Militant. The essence of Grant's schema seemed to have been confirmed: capitalist crisis was being resisted by a radicalized working class which had joined the Labour Party in large numbers, pushed it leftwards, and thrust Marxists into positions of leadership. In Liverpool, the scene was set for a practical test of the politics of the Militant.

The campaign: 1983-1985

Labour's manifesto commitments, of job creation, house building, rent reductions and better conditions for council employees did not match its resources. The gap of about 25 million was to be made good not by rent or rate rises or redundancies but by a political campaign to force the government to give the city the funds to carry the programme through. After an extensive series of meetings, rallies and publicity aimed at explaining the situation,in November 1983 20,000 people joined a march to support the council's stand. On 29 March 1984, Budget Day, despite a one-day strike by council workers and a mass demonstration of 50,000 at the City Hall, Labour's 'unbalanced' no-cuts budget was defeated by three right wing Labour councillors voting with the Liberals and Tories. All other budgets were also defeated. council elections in May 1984, saw Labour win a further seven seats, with seven new Militant supporters becoming councillors, and a solid majority within the new group for the deficit budget. However that budget was not put again to council and the mass campaign was wound down. As Taaffe and Mulhearn admit, 'negotiations behind the scenes recommenced' with the Government (1988, p.149). In July a compromize deal was struck which involved a 17 per cent rate rise, a budget reduction or cut of 13 million from £231 million to £218 million, and a capitalization of housing repairs, while the Government conceded £10 million and removed the threat of clawing back a further £17 million in penalties. Militant called this a '95 per cent victory' though others have described it more accurately as 'an old-fashioned compromize'

(Gyford, 1985, p.99). Militant's critics on the left (*Socialist Organiser* 1986; Watson, 1986) have argued that 1984 was the great missed opportunity of the campaign, a squandering of the chance to link up the tremendous popular support for the council's stand — according to a Poll published in June 55 per cent of Labour voters would have backed a general strike if the Government sent in the commissioners — with the Miners' Strike raging nationally.

In March 1985 the Miners were forced back to work. Although the council had registered significant achievements in the fields of house-building, urban regeneration and education (see Taaffe and Mulhearn, 1988, p.157-179) the financial crisis created by central Government remained. Liverpool first delayed setting a budget then, in June, after all the Labour councils, with the exception of Lambeth, climbed down and set legal rates, proposed a 20 per cent rate rise and some financial juggling to see the council through the year. After the council Trade Unions overturned this plan the council set an unbalanced budget, but no clear campaign of action. In September the council announced it was about to run out of cash and would issue 90 day redundancy notices to all employees as a 'legal device'. After the council Unions protested the notices were withdrawn, and the council shop stewards called a ballot for an all out strike. When the vote was lost 47 per cent to 53 per cent the council leaders sent out the redundancy notices again, some, to circumvent an NUT picket line, by the infamous fleet of hired taxis lampooned by Neil Kinnock at the Labour Party Conference in October. NALGO members took strike action against the council and, after the NUT won a legal action, the redundancy notices were withdrawn again, only for the council to propose laying off the entire workforce from 1-28 January. In November, as the national Labour Party set up an inquiry into Liverpool District Labour Party, the council announced a deal: a secret loan from a Swiss Bank had been agreed as long ago as August and would be released on the condition that cuts were made and the council agreed to 'stay legal' in the future. Most of the required cuts had been made anyway during the run down of services in the preceding months. In March 1986 a court declared the Liverpool Labour councillors must be surcharged and disqualified because of their delay in setting a rate. In October 1986 the Labour Party conference approved the expulsion of Derek Hatton and other leading Militant supporters in Liverpool from the Party, the only opposition coming from the hard left. Martin Thomas has argued

152

there is a direct connection between the twists and turns and the bizarre 'tactics' of the council and the mechanical political perspectives of the Militant Tendency:

> Victory is inevitable in the long term; so why take risks now ? If the situation is favourable now, it will certainly be more favourable in the future. And it makes no sense to risk positions, prestige, and propaganda platforms for the sake of 'ephemeral' struggle. So Militant tried to maintain a delicate balance: on the one hand giving Liverpool a profile as a fighting, socialist council: on the other trying to make sure they kept the council in office and themselves in the leadership of the council...contrary to all intelligent tactics they have tried again and again to postpone the crunch and extend the time in which the council stands in opposition to the government but not quite in collision with it (*Socialist Organiser*, 1986, p.5).

The Tragedy: the 'acherontic' Marxism of the Militant Tendency

Peter Taaffe, the editor of Militant, wrote in an internal bulletin of the criteria by which the Militant would judge the success or failure of the campaign in Liverpool:

> There is no guarantee, according to the Marxists that 'success' will result from their stand, if success or otherwise is to be judged by whether the Tory Government backs down or not. The Marxists have always argued that the criteria for any struggle, particularly a struggle which can be isolated because of the role of the national labour and trade union leaders, is whether it meets the twin objectives of raising the level of understanding, the consciousness of the proletariat as a whole and also strengthens the position of Marxism in the eyes of the broad mass of the working class (Taaffe, 1984).

It would be wrong to understate the enormous difficulties faced by Militant in Liverpool. The brute fact of defeat in 1985 was made certain by the preparedness of the Government to mobilize the powers of the central state and the political isolation of Liverpool after the national Labour Party and Trade Union leaders, and the other Labour councils, retreated and refused to support the agreed policy of confrontation (see O'Neill, nd. *Socialist Organiser*, 1986; Taaffe and Mulhearn, 1988). But the **manner** of the defeat — the Joint Shop Stewards Committee wrecked, widespread contempt for 'municipal Stalinism' and the 'Tammany tendency', and the alienation of one of the most oppressed black communities in the country from the labour movement - must be explained primarily by the character of the Militant Tendency itself.

Militant's politics are best understood as a combination of the mechanical determinism of the maximalist-rationalist segment of the Second International and a crudely sectarian and vanguardist interpretation of Trotskyism (International Communist League, 1977). The roots of these politics lie in the theoretical understanding of the emerging Stalinist satellite states of Eastern Europe developed by Jock Haston and Ted Grant, then members of the Trotskyist Revolutionary Communist Party, immediately after the Second World War. The new theory committed them to the view that the essence of a workers state was nationalization, irrespective of who carried out the nationalizations, how they had been enacted, for what purpose and in whose interests. This confusion of formal juridical property forms for the substance of new social relations necessitated a redefinition of socialism, no longer the self emancipation of the working class, but a particular level of stratification. This has been the real 'unbroken thread' in Grant's Marxism ever since, and has shaped Militant's conceptions of the content, agency and organization of socialism (Matgamna, 1966; O'Mahony, 1985 pp.18-58; McGregor, 1986, p.60-64).

The **content** of 'socialism' necessarily became confused with the stratification of society. According to Grant, 'the whole essence of the problem is that where we have complete stratification, quantity changes into quality, capitalism changes into its opposite', so 'a state can be a proletarian state on the basis of...the economy' (quoted in McGregor, 1986, p.60-61). In Britain 'socialism' was identified with 'the nationalization of the top two hundred Monopolies' by a Labour Government passing an Enabling Act through Parliament (Taaffe, 1981). In Liverpool itself, one critic summed up Militant's vision as 'socialism *is* the Labour Party running the local authority' (Thompson, 1984, p.1). This centralist and bureaucratic conception possessed an elective affinity to some older, native traditions of the post-war Liverpool Labour Party, embodied in the figure of Tony

Byrne, the powerful Chair of Finance and architect of the Urban Regeneration Strategy. Figures like Hatton and Mulhearn were not simply agents of Grant's Marxism but rather brokers between it and these native traditions of Liverpool labourism. The resulting mutation stabilized around an understanding of stratification as the essence of socialism, the Labour Party as the adequate and only acceptable form of political organization, and a conception of the working class as sociologically narrow as it was politically bureaucratic: a stage army to be wheeled on to 'change the powers above'.

Grant's world-view also displaced the working class as the **agency** of socialism albeit in favour of 'History' itself. Marxism was reduced to a positivistic 'science of prediction', a vulgar evolutionism, in which the 'needs of economic development' replaced the hurdy-gurdy of the class struggle. In 1989 Grant wrote:

> Lenin hammered home the point that in the transition from feudalism to capitalism the dictatorship of the rising bourgeoisie was reflected in the dictatorship of one man ... under certain conditions the dictatorship of the proletariat could also be realised through the dictatorship of one man (Grant, 1989, p.245).

This analogy between the bourgeoisie revolution and the proletarian, central to orthodox Trotskyism, forgets that when the working class lacks political power then stratification in itself does not mystically 'express' the rule of the working class and indeed has no socialist content at all (Shachtman, 1962; Draper, 1992, p.2-34). Moreover, while 'one man' can indeed reflect the rule of the bourgeoisie, this is because the social power of that class lies ultimately in the unconscious operation of the market and the law of value. The 'rule' of the working class, in contrast, is conscious and collective, and therefore democratic, or it is a legal fiction. Grant's theory of the Colonial Revolution (1989 pp.275-371) saw him join Deutscher atop the 'watchtower', looking down sagely on an epoch of progressive 'proletarian Bonapartism' (i.e. Stalinism) which would develop the productive forces while using the masses as cannon fodder. Stalinism occupied a similar place in Grant's world-view to the place of the bourgeois revolution in pre-1917 social democracy: a progressive force for a whole historical period, (O'Mahony, 1985) although this assumption was commonplace not just to the Communist Parties but most left-wingers from the Fabians in the 1930s through to latter-day Deutscherites such as Perry Anderson (see Anderson, 1983).

In Britain Militant developed organizationally as a sect making abstract propaganda counterposed to involvement in struggles alongside other socialists (Bradley,1989) its internal life marked by an absence of mechanisms for internal democracy, cultist relationships between members and leaders (see the testimony of ex-members in Crick, 1986 pp.173-185) and a membership schooled to deride all activity outside 'the traditional organizations'. Militant had been alone on the far left in ignoring the radical upsurge outside the Labour Party in the late 1960s, failing even to mention the massive anti-Vietnam war protests in their newspaper. This pattern was repeated with movements for sexual liberation, abortion rights, anti-fascism, and with the peace movement (McGregor 1986, p.65; Bradley, 1989). Nationally, Militant did not so much challenge labourism as use its structures as both a protective shield from the world outside and a womb in which to grow organically. One ex-member recalls: 'we kept our heads down and pushed the general programme of Militant' (McGregor 1986, p.67).

Liverpool and the five strains of 'acherontic' Marxism

The term 'acherontic' was used by Hal Draper (1914-1990) in his seminal essay, 'The Principle of Self-Emancipation in Marx and Engels' (1992, pp.243-271). Draper's central contribution to Marxist thought was his extended redefinition of Marxism as the theory and practice of 'socialism from below', contrasted to various strains of 'socialism from above'. Draper claimed that even most Marxists had missed Marx's most fundamental innovation: his fusion of the socialist idea and the democratic idea by the redefinition of socialism as the self-emancipation of the working class. In discussing this innovation Draper drew upon the passage from Vigil's *Aeneid* to highlight a form of socialism which rejecting Marx's innovation, sees the working class only as an object, an 'acheron', or stage army, wheeled on to threaten 'the Powers above' but never to be a subject, a self-controlling agent of social change in its own right. Draper's insight seems to me useful in considering Militant's role in Liverpool, where five strains of 'acherontic' Marxism can be identified: bureaucratism, paternalism, workerism, sectarianism, and bossism, which , in combination shaped the manner of the defeat in Liverpool.

Bureaucratism and paternalism

In Liverpool Militant were an entrist organization who, paradoxically, were also Labour Party loyalists. The existing structures of the Labour Movement, controlled tightly by the Militant-dominated District Labour Party, were defined as the only legitimate channels of participation in the campaign. A Liverpool Party member and non-Militant Marxist, Kevin Feintuck (1984, p.10) pointed out that a local rebellion against Westminster could hardly be organized through the ward parties:

> The campaign in Liverpool had succeeded in mobilising tens of thousands for days of action. But these have been essentially isolated incidents, with the vast majority of activists being used as a stage army to be wheeled on and off at the whim of the local bureaucrats. What has been lacking has been a broad based campaigning body with roots throughout the whole of the working class. Such a body, organised from the base upwards, would have guaranteed the active ongoing participation of many people who are neither members of the Labour Party nor of affiliated unions.

This perspective was more appropriate to the multiplex character of the popular support for the council but was never supported. John Bohanna, a shop steward at Fords, spoke accurately when he drew attention to the local pride which underpinned the council's popularity: 'every Scouser loves Scouseland, they regard it as their city. That's what was at stake: our city, not the Labour Party, not Militant' (in Wainwright, 1987, p.130). In fact Militant ignored voices outside the Labour Party while using its control of the District Labour Party to 'laugh in the face' (Hatton, 1988) of opposition within the Party, to control policy, and to select and reject those who stood for council, much in the style of the old Labour right (Tribune, 1986).

Efforts to decentralize and democratize local government, pursued enthusiastically elsewhere, (Hoggett and Hambleton, 1986) by-passed Liverpool. Thompson and Allen, (1986, p.8) describe Liverpool as an example of 'mobilization without participation' and 'a combination of client and mobilization practices, with a minimal emphasis on participation', though they do not criticize those councils which simply cut their budgets as an alternative to mobilization per se with or without participation. Allen (1986b, p.22) complained of the emergence in Liverpool of:

> ... an unholy alliance between vanguardism and municipal paternalism both of which share a suspicion-bordering-on hostility of independent initiatives, whether they be black organizations, tenant groups, the voluntary sector, or working class housing co-operatives.

Again, while such critics tend to remain silent about that other unholy alliance — between a rhetoric of 'empowerment' and 'participation' and a practice of cutting services — the damage done by bureaucratic paternalism to the campaign is undeniable. In Speke for instance, Labour sought to close the local Community Centre and Adventure Playground as part of the Urban Regeneration Strategy. In the face of local opposition a leading councillor addressed a meeting of local people and said, '... this is not a proposal, this is what you're going to have'. The result was the formation of a local Action Group, the occupation of the Community Centre, the forging of links with the Black Caucus and other groups who were moving into reluctant opposition to the council, and direct action to disrupt council meetings, (Meegan, 1990) a striking example of bureaucratic paternalism turning the cultural resource of desubordination inwards against the council itself. The aspirations of the activists were clear:

> This place is important for the people. It's the only community centre within five or six miles. There's nowhere else for the people — where else can they go? All the groups using this place have been here since 1963, when it was opened. In some cases, five — yes, five — generations have used this place. It's home for them.

> It's sad that they [the council] thought we were dispensable. But we weren't — we just fought the buggers back. I was proud of this community the way it fought over the 'commy' (Meegan, 1990).

Gyford (1985) describes the Militant as practising 'pseudo-participation' aimed at 'mobilizing people into support for the policies of those already in power'. Initiatives originating outside the DLP were beyond the pale. Housing Co-ops were defined as 'anti-socialist', decentralization was rejected out of hand, and the voluntary sector laboured under the threat of 'municipalization'. The stated aim of the Urban Regeneration Strategy was to leave tenant organization 'rendered superfluous by a highly effective method of consultation with individual tenants' (DLP Housing Policy Statement, 1985, p.11-12) and it was matter of policy that the council would not meet with organized tenant groups but only individuals. Other local party members, though in practice hostile to the council's strategy per se, did advance valid criticisms of the absence of public involvement in planning decisions, the denial of the value of anything other than low rise housing, the scrapping of a black elders housing project despite Government commitment to pay 75% of the cost, and the way the Urban Regeneration Strategy (URS) swallowed up all the government provided urban programme funds (Saren, 1986, p.23).

Workerism: Militant and the black community

Militant had an organic relationship to certain sections of the Liverpool working class: white and blue collar (Ridley, 1986) and to a certain political culture in which, as Hatton put it 'there is no place for the faint-hearted' and 'you have to be absolutely ruthless'. But Militant failed to develop a politics, at the level of either ideas or organizational forms, which was capable of addressing **difference** — of experience, identity, aspiration and organization — within the working class, and this was seen most tragically in the council's relationship to the Liverpool black community.

District Labour Party 'aggregates', which all members could attend, took place in the headquarters of the Transport and General Workers Union, only a couple of miles from the heart of Liverpool's black community. Yet on many occasions an audience of hundreds would contain no black Liverpudlians at all. The great exception to the ebullient revolt from below which rolled across so much of the city in the 1960s and 1970s was the black community, as racism ensured its continued confinement to sharply segmented labour and housing markets and to racist policing (Gifford, 1989). This discrimination produced a rise of independent 'black consciousness' organizations in the 1970s (Wilson and Womersley, 1976, p.92) and the disturbances of 1981, but no significant involvement in a labour movement which was itself implicated in the reproduction of discrimination via the practice of trade union nomination rights. Militant's strategy to combat racism was summed up by Keva Coombes, a councillor and former leader of the Merseyside County Council in evidence to the Gifford Enquiry into racism in Liverpool:

> I think the dominant analysis in my own party membership among councillors between 1983 and 1987 was that the only way successfully to achieve and maintain improvement in employment practices and the council's policies generally, so far as they affect Black people, was to make sure that class interests were properly protected. In blunt terms, it was said,it was a class issue not a race issue. If you built houses and if you preserved jobs, there would be a direct benefit to the Black community. That was all you needed to do, and anything else was a diversion from that (in Gifford, 1989, p.55).

In fact in 1989 the Commission for Racial Equality (CRE) issued a non-discrimination notice against the council after research (CRE, 1989; Seager, 1989) proved it had, during the Militant years of 1984 to 1986, 'discriminated both directly and indirectly in the way it nominated members of ethnic minorities to poorer properties'. The 'Sam Bond Affair' cemented the alienation of the black community from the Labour Movement. In 1984 Bond, a 26 year old building surveyor from London, and a Militant supporter with little experience of anti-racist struggle, was appointed as Liverpool's Principal Race Relations Advisor. The opposition to Bond's appointment was immediate and spread across virtually the entire Labour Movement and every other oppositional social movement in the city. The local non-Militant left spoke of 'a massive rift between the District Labour Party and both the black community and the rest of the local Labour Movement' (*Merseyside Labour Briefing* 1985, p.2). Militant however, while comparing Bond to Malcolm X, denounced the Black Caucus as an 'unrepresentative clique' using 'alien methods' who were 'enemies of the labour movement' and 'increasingly lumpen' (*Militant*, 1985). Militant's racial politics in Liverpool (see the exhaustive treatment in Liverpool Back Caucus, 1986) proved unable to cope either with divisions within the working class nor with the need to construct a political bloc between the Labour Movement and the resistance of oppressed groups.

Sectarianism

Hilary Wainwright has argued that Militant put 'the aggrandizement of its own organization' before the needs of a 'courageous and popular resistance', the classic definition of sectarianism (1987, p.126). The claim can be judged by examining the collapse of support for the council in the white-collar union NALGO and the disintegration of the Joint Shop Stewards Committee (JSSC) in 1985. Established in 1979, the JSSC had co-ordinated the resistance of council workers to redundancies, privatization and school reorganization. JSSC activists leafleted en masse for Labour in 1983 and joined the Labour Party. Spencer claims the episode as a practical demonstration that 'active participatory trade unionism alongside the pursuit of working class politics can have a politicizing effect on the general population' (1989, p.93). Peter Creswell, a local socialist and NALGO leader, has written of the role of NALGO in 1984:

> Throughout the first half of 1984, Liverpool NALGO ran a campaign — 'Our City—Our Fight' — which was unparalleled in NALGO's history. It was designed to gain support for the City Council's stand against Government cuts, and was the biggest campaign run by any union in the City. On almost every demonstration, NALGO's was the biggest single union contingent, and the strike on 29 March was almost 100% solid among NALGO members (Creswell, 1985, p.1).

Yet by September 1985 only 1,500 NALGO members out of a membership of around 6,000 voted to take strike action in support of the council. This collapse of support was due to the deterioration in relations between NALGO and the council in the intervening year. First, the settlement of 1984 was sold as a 'massive victory' by Militant with a surge in publicity and recruitment to the Tendency. But, as Creswell commented later 'we at least expected to be told the truth' (in Wainwright, 1987, p.131) and the truth was that the deal was a compromize achieved because the Government did not want to open up a second front while the Miners were on strike. The sectarian need of Militant to present Liverpool as their 'jewel in the crown' which had 'humbled Thatcher by the might of the local working class' seriously miseducated local trade unionists and made it doubly difficult in 1985 to generate enthusiasm, or even a sense of realism, in the campaign. Second, the opposition of NALGO to the appointment of Sam Bond from October 1984 led to 'an unprecedented campaign of lies and slander against NALGO' by Militant in defence of 'their man', leaving NALGO positioned 'fighting on two fronts', with the council against the Government, and with the black community against the council (Creswell, 1985). Third, Militant's crude 'Marxism' dovetailed with the tendency of some GMBATU stewards to see in NALGO, infamously, 'wimps' and 'penpushers' (*Merseyside Labour Briefing*, 1985 p.5). Fourth, throughout 1985 the unions were treated as a stage army to be moved around in a game of bluff with the Government, as first 90 day redundancy notices and then a one month lay-off were threatened, causing confusion and alarm amongst union members. As Spencer argues, 'the decision to call for an all-out stoppage also became entangled with the redundancy notices issue' (1989, p.90). Militant blamed the defeat of the strike vote on the treachery of NALGOs local leaders, ignoring the fact that, despite everything, those leaders had supported the strike call (Taaffe and Mulhearn, 1988, p.291).

Bossism: the 'Tammany Tendency' and the 'ethics of revolution'

A Socialism that is not completely, and to the very roots of its being, honest has not got a hope (Geras, 1986, p.xv).

I was a virtual prisoner. They knew my every move, my phone calls were vetted and vital information was kept from me (John Hamilton, 'Leader' of Liverpool Council, *Today*, 30/3/87 p.18).

By the end of 1985 Liverpool was being compared to Chicago more often than Petrograd as the abuse of municipal funds and powers became a source of mistrust and division in the local party. 1985 began with the 'Asda Affair' in which a District Labour Party with policy commitments against retail development in Enterprise Zones was persuaded by Militant to support Asda's application to build a hypermarket in the Speke Enterprise Zone. There was surprise and confusion when it was discovered that Hatton had, one month before, been on holiday in Tangiers with Tony Beyga, the Public Relations Officer with Merseypride, the company which owns the proposed Asda site (Williams 1985, p.12). The drip of stories in the local press about 'jobs for the boys and girls', of which Bond was only the most prominent, demoralized the council's supporters while some local community workers felt the council was using the Urban Regeneration Strategy, 'as a shield to undermine valuable voluntary initiatives' (Allen, 1986a p.19). Some delegates complained of an intimidatory atmosphere at District Labour Party meetings, pointing to the way members of the Static Security Force or 'Hatton's Army' as they were called locally, attended in uniform and behaved officiously (*Tribune*, 1986, though see Taaffe and Mulhearn, 1988 p.170-172, for an alternative view). Certainly Mike Allen has alleged that:

At the DLP executive of 22 November [1985] local trade unionists (including Labour Party members) were named as targets for removal. It was stated that certain people would be 'got rid of' and that if redundancies were to take place then 'we know who they are (1986a, p.8).

Minimally, the Marxist is committed to what Geras, following Trotsky, calls the 'efficacy principle'; 'That is permissible ... which really leads to the liberation of mankind'. In other words not every means will do, because many means will lead away from the ends desired. In Liverpool Militant simply did not pass the efficacy test. The means of patronage, manipulation, bluff and bluster, were not really means to the ends of the campaign, but to the ends of the short-term self-aggrandizement of Militant. The appointment of Sam Bond, like the appointment of Militant supporters to jobs as Student Union officials in Further Education colleges, or the use of council powers to set up Merseyside Action Group to undermine the local black community, or the censoring of John Hamilton's critical remarks in his speech to the 1985 Municipal policy conference (see Black Caucus, 1986, pp.95-97 for the two versions of his speech) served only to fatally undermine the broad coalition of support which had sustained the council in 1983 and 1984.

Conclusion: Marxism and the principle of 'self-emancipation'

Does the failure of Militant in Liverpool indicate a deeper failing in the entire Marxist tradition as many of the 'new urban left' claim? (Gyford, 1985; Lansley et al, 1989). The theoretical underpinning for such a conclusion can be seen in the work of Alberto Melucci who, in an influential discussion of collective action in contemporary societies, (1989) has claimed that Marxism *per se* is incapable of addressing the question of how objective class-in-itself becomes subjective class-for-itself, as it reifies rather than investigates collective action, collapsing the empirical reality of a variety of collective identities under the single identity of class. Moreover, it assumes this will be delivered automatically as 'a unified datum' by the economic contradictions of capitalism. Marxism is tied to the 'naive premise ... that 'interests' are the motivating force of collective action', and is incapable of addressing the three questions at the heart of identity formation and collective action today:

> Through what processes do actors construct collective action? How is the unity of the various elements of collective action produced? Through which processes and relationships do individuals become involved in — or defect from — collective action ? (1989, p.192).

Melucci suggests that to answer these questions the old opposition between structural determination and individual agency is inadequate and suggests a shift in focus to an intermediate level comprising 'the processes through which individuals recognize that they share certain orientations in common and on that basis decide to act together' (1989 p.30) in recognition that:

> ... a social movement is not a unified 'subject' but always a composite action system, in which widely differing means, ends and forms of solidarity and organisation converge in a more or less stable manner (1989. p.28).

There is much of relevance here to the Liverpool experience. The base of the victories of 1983 and 1984 was a composite of different collectivities, identities and aspirations. The attempt, increasingly crude and coercive, to force that multiplex base into the centralist and 'acherontic' strategy and timetable set by Militant, and the untransformed structures and culture of the Labour Movement and the city council, was guaranteed to fragment and divide the campaign. But is any of this a challenge to Marxism *per se*? The assumption is that classical Marxism dealt with a simple world marked by the elemental and transparent struggle of 'class versus class', and is of little use in today's more complex world. In fact, the classical Marxist tradition dealt with diverse collectivities embedded in complex social formations in which power relations were far from transparent but were actually saturated by ideological codes and symbols, and in which the non-correspondence (if not the autonomization) of economics and politics was taken for granted. The need for a **politics** able to foster alliances within the working class and between it and other social forces were the abiding concerns of the classical Marxists (see the discussion in Wood, 1986 and Callinicos, 1989).

Is it not possible that Melucci and the Militant, superficially opposites, actually **concur** in a reduction of the classical Marxist tradition to a caricature? Take Melucci's treatment of Rosa Luxemburg whose rich contribution to the theory and practice of collective action is reduced to this:

> ... the Luxemburgian model attributes to individuals a spontaneous capacity to mobilise on the basis of discontent, injustice and deprivation..disregarding the fact that individuals define themselves as collective actors by means of a variety of negotiated interactions (1989, p.32).

In fact *The Mass Strike* (Luxemburg, 1970, pp.152-218) to speak only of that work, contains not 'spontaneism' but a complex and empirically grounded account of precisely those 'negotiated interactions' which can construct unity (see Geras, 1976, pp.111-1131; 1990 pp.89-92). What distinguishes the classical Marxism of Luxemburg from Melucci is not a belief in the unproblematic character of collective identity formation and collective action but a hard headed strategic insight into the kinds of material conditions and forms of political mediation which stand a chance of creatively developing such identity and action. Luxemburg's insight was that socialist collective action is the creation of struggle, and the 'method of motion' by which **socialist** collective identity and action could be developed was the 'living political school' she called the Mass Strike (1970, pp.153-218). She viewed the very errors of a real movement on the move as 'more fruitful than the infallibility of the cleverest central committee' (1970, p.130). Geras has called this the principle of 'interiority'; the idea that struggle can itself be productive of changes which could be called instrumental — the breaking of the power of an oppressor — and developmental — the breaking of the subordinate consciousness of the working class (1994). The role of political leadership, though important, is necessarily circumscribed in this perspective for, as Geras has argued:

> ... just because what is envisaged is an emancipation, those carrying it through have to be free in their constructive enterprise (...) There can be for [Luxemburg] no authoritative blueprint; no 'pre-established schema' vouchsafed by doctrine. Authoritative is only the democracy of the agents themselves, struggling, differing, failing, learning; endeavouring to make another world, in light only of some egalitarian, communist and — yes — liberal critical principles (1994, p.100).

Militant also engage in this violent reduction of classical Marxism to a caricature. For example, the racial politics of Militant can be usefully contrasted to the lengthy and complex discussions among the American Trotskyists in the 1920s about the racism of the white working class and the struggle for socialism (Trotsky, 1978). James P. Cannon, for instance, mocked the idea that the oppression of black people was simply 'an economic problem, part of the struggle between the workers and the capitalists; [and that] nothing could be done about the special problems of discrimination and inequality this side of socialism' as nothing more than, 'a formula for inaction ... and a convenient shield for the dormant racial prejudices of white radicals themselves'. Trotsky himself, while seizing every opportunity to promote unity in struggle, said '99.9% of the American workers are chauvinists, in relation to the Negroes they are hangmen', and accordingly saw a role for the self-organization of black people to the extent of raising the question of a black political party and even a black republic (see *Socialist Organiser*, 1986b).

The deeper unity between Melucci and Militant, and between the New 'True' Socialism of academic 'discourse theory' (Wood, 1986) with some contemporary 'Trotskyism' more generally, is this impoverishment of the richness of the classical Marxist tradition. The two sides differ only on whether to put a positive or negative sign next to the caricature they both recognize as 'Marxism'. They respond to the non-correspondence of economics and politics, and to 'difference', in remarkably similar ways: the former embracing an absolute indeterminacy in which 'anything goes', the latter clamping on ideological blinkers to shut out the complexity of the world: an absolute idealism clashing with a mechanical materialism like the 'ignorant armies' in Arnold's poem *Dover Beach*. The historian Bryan D.Palmer, has argued as a result, 'what has been killed along the way is any appreciation of the complex interaction of economic structure and historical agency, of imposed necessity and cultivated desire' (Palmer, 1990, p.126). What has also been killed off is an understanding of the potential (no more, but equally, no less) for the self-emancipatory **struggle** of self-controlling agents in the face of exploitative and oppressive social relations, to act as a sorting house in which differences can be negotiated and points of contact and solidarity developed into more durable **unities**.

There were glimpses of this potential in 1983 and 1984 in a struggle which in truth was neither a 'grotesque chaos' nor the recreation of Petrograd on the Mersey. The early experience of the campaign hinted briefly at the kind of radical and popular politics of self-emancipation championed by Luxemburg and should be rescued from commentators who have trivialized the campaign and the role Militant played in generating it. The campaign's decline and the ignominies of 1985 were the inevitable outcome not of 'impossibilist politics' but of the combined opposition of the Government and the Labour leaders which left Liverpool isolated, and the 'acherontic' Marxism of Militant which, treating the working class as a stage army or worse, and unable to address divisions within the working class, ended up with what Ridley (1986, p.134) has rightly called 'a remarkable failure of coalition-building'.

Notes

1. I am grateful to Debbie Williams, Martin Thomas, John McIlroy, Paul Kennedy, and Paul Reynolds for constructive criticisms and fruitful suggestions.
2. My standpoint is not that of the so-called 'new urban left' associated with the GLC and other similar Labour councils of the 1980s, whose many criticisms of Militant were advanced as part of a drive against the entire strategy of refusing to implement Government cuts by mobilization and confrontation adopted by Liverpool, in favour of the 'dented shield' approach proposed by Neil Kinnock. My use of specific criticisms advanced by the 'new urban left' whether about gender, 'race' or local democracy, should not be read as support for this larger project. The goal here is to contribute to the elaboration of a more adequate class politics. (see *Socialist Organiser*, 1986a).

References

Aglietta, A. (1979), *A Theory of Capitalist Regulation*, New Left Books, London.

Allen, Mike (1986a), 'On the Mersey Beat', in *Chartist*, 1986.

Allen, Mike (1986b), 'Two-tone politics hit voluntary groups', in *Chartist*, 1986.

Anderson, Perry (1983), 'Trotsky's Interpretation of Stalinism', in *New Left Review*, No.139.

Atkinson, Julian (1982), 'Labour's Youth Movements' in *International*, May/June 1982.

Ayres, Pat (1990), 'The hidden economy of dockland families: Liverpool in the 1930s', in Hudson, Pat and Lee, W. R. (eds.), *Women's Work and the Family Economy in Historical Perspective*. Manchester University Press, Manchester.

Baxter,R. (1969), *The Liverpool Labour Party 1918-1963*. (D.Phil. Oxford).

Bean, Ron and Stoney, Peter (1982), 'Strikes on Merseyside: A Regional Analysis', in *Industrial Relations Journal*.

Belchem J. (ed.) (1992), *Popular Politics, Riot and Labour. Essays in Liverpool History 1790-1940*, Liverpool University Press, Liverpool.

Bornstein, S. and Richardson, A. (1986), *War and the International:*

A history of the Trotskyist Movement in Britain 1937-1949, Socialist Platform, London.

Bradley, Clive (1989), 'Is Militant Marxist ?' in *Socialist Organiser* No.397 and 398.

Callaghan, J. (1987), *The Far Left in British Politics*. Basil Blackwell, Oxford.

Callinicos, A. (1987), *Making History: Agency, Structure and Change in Social Theory*. Polity, Oxford.

Commission For Racial Equality, (1989), *Racial Discrimination in Liverpool City Council: Report of a formal investigation into the Housing Department*. CRE, London.

Cornfoot, Trevor (1982), 'The Economy of Merseyside, 1945-1982: quickening decline or post-industrial change ?' in Gould, W. T. S. and Hodgkiss, A. G. (eds.) *The Resources of Merseyside*, Liverpool University Press.

Creswell, Peter (1985), 'Nalgo will fight on both fronts!', in *Merseyside Labour Briefing*, No 18 February/March.

Crick, M. (1986), *The March of Militant*. Faber and Faber, London.

Daniels, P. W. (1982), 'Services: the growth sector of the 1980s ?' in Gould W. T. S. and Hodgkiss, A. G. (eds.) *The Resources of Merseyside*, Liverpool University Press.

Davies, J. (1988), 'Class Practices and Political Culture in Liverpool', Lancaster Regionalism Group, Working Paper 37.

Davies, Sam (1979), 'The Liverpool Labour Party and the Liverpool Working Class, 1900-1939' in *Bulletin of the North West Labour History Society*, No.6.

Davies, S. (1992), *Genuinely Seeking Work*, Countywise, Merseyside.

Davies, S. (1995), *Liverpool Labour: Social and political influences on the development of the Labour Party in Liverpool, 1900-1939*, Keele University Press, Keele.

Draper, H. (1992), *Socialism From Below. Essays selected, edited and with an Introduction by E. Haberkern*, Humanities Press, New Jersey.

Eccles, T. (1981), *Under New Management*. Pan, London.

Federation of Black Housing Organisations (1986), 'Furnace in the Pool' in *Newsletter*, Vol.2 No.2.

Feintuck, Kevin (1984), 'Liverpool: half a victory' in *Socialist Organiser*, No.187, 12 July.

Friedman H. and Meredeen S. (1980), *The Dynamics of Industrial Conflict: Lessons From Ford*. Croom Helm, London.

Geras, N. (1976), *The Legacy of Rosa Luxemburg,* Verso, London.

Geras, N. (1986), *Literature of Revolution: Essays on Marxism,* Verso, London.

Geras, N. (1990), *Discourses of Extremity:Radical Ethics and Post-Marxist Extravagances.* Verso, London.

Geras, Norman (1994), 'Democracy and the Ends of Marxism' in *New Left Review,* 203.

Gifford, Lord, et al (1989), *Loosen the Shackles. First Report of the Liverpool 8 Inquiry into Race Relations in Liverpool,* Karia Press, London.

Gyford, J. (1985), *The Politics of Local Socialism,* George Allen and Unwin, London.

Grant, T. (1989), *The Unbroken Thread:The Development of Trotskyism over 40 Years,* Fortress Books, London.

Hallas, Duncan, (1982), 'Revolutionaries and the Labour Party', in *International Socialism,* Vol.2. No.16, London.

Hatton, D. (1988), *Inside Left:the story so far,* Bloomsbury, London.

Hikins, H. (ed.) (1973), *Building the Union: Merseyside 1956-1967,* Toulouse, Liverpool.

Hindess, B. (1971) *The Decline of Working Class Politics,* MacGibbon and Kee, London.

HMSO (1965), *The Problems of Merseyside,* London.

Hoggett, P. and Hambleton, R. (eds.) (1986), *Decentralisation and Democracy. Localising Public Services,* School for Advanced Urban Studies, Bristol.

Hunter, B. (1994), *They Knew Why They Fought: Unofficial Struggles and Leadership on the Docks 1945-1989,* Index Books, London.

International Communist League, (1977), 'Democracy in the Labour Party' in *International Communist* No.2/3.

Johnson, A. (1987), *Back To Basics: The Lessons of Wallasey's Election Campaign,* Socialist Organiser, London.

Lane, T. (1987), *Liverpool:Gateway of Empire,* Lawrence and Wishart, London.

Lansley, S., Goss, S. and Wolmar, C. (1989), *Councils in Conflict. The Rise and Fall of the Municipal Left,* Macmillan, London.

Leighton, Jane (1979), 'Fighting for better health services:the role of the Community Health Council', in Craig G. and Mayo, M. Sharman, N. (eds.) *Jobs and Community Action,* Routledge and Kegan Paul. London.

Liverpool Black Caucus, (1986), *The Racial Politics of Militant in Liverpool*, Merseyside Area Profile Group, Liverpool.

Liverpool CDP, (1975), *The Fight for jobs at Tate and Lyle*, Liverpool.

Lloyd, P. and Dicken, P. (1977), 'Inner Merseyside Components of Industrial Change in the Corporate Context', *N.W.I.R.U. Working Paper* No 4, Manchester.

Lloyd P. and Dicken, P. (1978), 'Inner Metropolitan Industrial Change, Enterprise Structures and Policy Issues: Case Study of Manchester and Merseyside', *Regional Studies*, No.12.

Marx, K. (1974), *The First International and After*, Pelican, London.

Matgamna, S. (1966), *What we are and what we must become* (unpublished Militant internal bulletin)

Matgamna, S. (1992), *Labour's Misspent Youth. The seedbed of the Left: the origins of today's far Left Groups*. Socialist Organiser, London.

McGregor, Sheila (1986), 'The history and politics of Militant' in *International Socialism*, Series 2, No.33, London.

McMonnies, D. (1986), *Trade union attitudes towards Co-ops: A Merseyside case study*. Working Paper No. 14, Department of Politics, Liverpool University.

McTiernan, M. P. (1986), *Workers Alternative Plans: A Case Study At United Biscuits Liverpool Plant*. Warwick Papers in Industrial Relations, No.7, University of Warwick.

Meegan, Richard (1990) 'Merseyside in Crisis and in Conflict', in M. Harloe, C. Pickvance and J. Urry (eds.) *Place, Policy and Politics:Do Localities Matter?* Unwin Hyman, London.

Melucci, A. (1989), *Nomads of the Present:Social Movements and Individual Needs in Contemporary Society*, Hutchinson Radius, London.

Merseyside Community Relations Council, (1984), *Black Linx*, (Special issue, Racism and the City Council) Liverpool.

Merseyside Community Relations Council, (1986), *Annual Report 1985/6*. Liverpool.

Merseyside Socialist Research Group, (1980), *Merseyside In Crisis*. Birkenhead.

Miliband, Ralph (1978), 'A State of Desubordination' in *British Journal of Sociology*, Vol.29, 4.

Militant, (1985), 'Sam Bond: The Real Truth' (leaflet) Liverpool.

O'Mahony, J. (1985), *Afghanistan: Militant's Policy and the 'Colonial Revolution': an analysis* (Socialist Forum, No.3) Socialist

Organiser, London.

O'Neill, M. (n/d), *Counter Apparatus*. Merseyside Trade Union, Community and Unemployed Resource Centre, Liverpool.

Palmer, Bryan D. (1990), 'The Eclipse of Materialism: Marxism and the Writing of Social History in the 1980s' in R. Miliband and L. Panitch (eds.) *Socialist Register 1990: The Retreat of the Intellectuals*. Merlin Press, London.

Parkinson, M. (1985), *Liverpool on the Brink*, Policy Journals, Hermitage.

Parkinson, Michael (1988), 'Liverpool's fiscal crisis: an anatomy of failure' in M. Parkinson, B. Foley and D. Judd (eds.) *Regenerating the cities: the UK crisis and the US experience*, Manchester.

Ridley, F. F. (1986), 'Liverpool is different: Political Style In Context', in *The Political Quarterly*, Vol.57, 1986.

Saren, Jane (1986), 'Putting on a style', in *Chartist*.

Shachtman, M. (1962), *The Bureaucratic Revolution*, New York.

Seager, Richard (1989), 'Race:Liverpool's lesson to others' in *Race and Housing* July/August 1989.

Segal, Lynne (1988), 'Hose 'em down', a review of 'Inside Left:The Story So Far' by Derek Hatton in *New Statesman*.

Shallice, Andy (1980), 'Orange and Green and Militancy: Sectarianism and Working Class Politics in Liverpool 1900-1914', in *North West Labour History Bulletin*, No.6.

Shallice, Andy (1982), 'Liverpool Labourism and Irish nationalism in the 1920s and 1930s'; in Bulletin of the *North West Labour History Society*, No.8.

Smith, J. (1980), *Commonsense Thought and Working Class Consciousness: Some aspects of the Glasgow and Liverpool Labour Movements in the early years of the Twentieth Century*. PhD. University of Edinburgh

Socialist Organiser, (1986a), *Liverpool:What went wrong ?*, London.

Socialist Organiser (1986b), 'Labour council's 12m cuts', in *Socialist Organiser*, No.279, 14 August.

Socialist Organiser, (1986c),'Pandering to Prejudice' in *Socialist Organiser*, No.296,11 December.

Spencer, Bruce (1989), *Remaking the Working Class? An examination of Shop Stewards Experiences*, Spokesman, Nottingham.

Stoney, P. J. M. (1983), 'The Port of Liverpool and the regional economy in the twentieth century', in Anderson and B. L. and

Stoney, P.J.M. (eds.) *Commerce, Industry and Transport:Studies in economic change on Merseyside*, Liverpool University Press, Liverpool.

Taaffe, P. ('Tom Pierce'), (1984), 'Liverpool: the role of Marxist Leadership', in the *Bulletin of Marxist Studies*, London.

Taaffe, P. (1986), *Militant: What we stand for*, Militant Publications, London.

Taaffe, P. and Mulhearn, T. (1988) *Liverpool:A City That Dared To Fight*, Fortress Books, London.

Therborn, Goran (1983), 'Why Some Classes Are More Successful than Others' in *New Left Review*, No.138.

Thompson, Paul (1985), 'Liverpool Council rules O.K.?' in *Chartist*, July.

Thompson, Paul and Allen, Mike (1986), 'Labour and the local state in Liverpool' in *Capital and Class*, No. 27, Winter.

Tribune (1986), 'Liverpool: why Labour had to hold an enquiry' (evidence submitted to the National Executive Enquiry by Merseyside Labour Co-ordinating Committee) 24 January.

Trotsky, L. (1978), *Leon Trotsky on Black Nationalism*, Pathfinder, New York.

Wailey, T. (1985), *A Storm From Liverpool*, Liverpool University, Ph.D.

Wainwright, H. (1987) *Labour: A Tale of Two Parties*, The Hogarth Press, London.

Warlock, D. and Sheppard, D. (1989), *Better Together. Christian Partnership in a Hurt City*, London.

Waters, Mary-Alice (1970), *Rosa Luxemburg Speaks*, Pathfinder Press, New York.

Watson, M. (1986), *Liverpool: Lessons for the Left*, London.

Williams, Ian (1985a), 'Town Hall Troubles', in *New Statesman*, 22 February.

Williams, Ian (1985b), 'The Quality of Mersey', in *Marxism Today*, September.

Wilson H. H. and Womersley, L. (1976), *Change or Decay: Final Report of the Liverpool Inner Area Study*.

Wood, E. (1986), *The Retreat From Class: A New 'True' Socialism*, Verso, London.

White, S. J. (1975), *Unemployment on Merseyside*, Liverpool Council for Voluntary Service.

9 Business enterprises as agents of cultural and political change: the case of green/ethical marketing

Paul Kennedy

> Our products reflect our philosophy. They are formulated with care and respect. Respect for other cultures, the past, the natural world, our customers. It's a partnership of profits with principles (Roddick, 1990).

> It may well be the case that late twentieth-century Western consumerism contains within it far more revolutionary seeds than we have hitherto anticipated (Nava, 1991, p.171).

Introduction

Some business enterprises have always been prepared to adopt the mantle of corporate social responsibility by assuming certain non-economic activities, supporting charities, founding educational trusts and so on. No doubt their primary purpose has been to legitimize their quest for profit and enhance their public profile. However, I suggest that certain kinds of businesses have recently begun to be propelled much further in this direction, whether by choice, necessity or both. Indeed, the evidence from the empirical study on which this paper is based suggests that some businesses are in the process of becoming key agents of cultural and political change in their own right and so are contributing, often unwittingly, to the formulation and dissemination of certain utopian ideas that may prove ever more relevant in the coming years. This evolution in the role of certain businesses needs to be contextualized in terms of major, long term social and cultural changes that have been gathering pace in Western societies during the last two decades or more. Here, it is necessary to draw on recent sociological thinking. In doing so we can ascertain several reasons why the sphere of green-ethical business is especially likely to generate a convergence of interest and concerns between citizen-consumers and some capitalist interests; an increasingly interactive, negotiated market relationship that locks both parties into a mutually validated cultural embrace.

Firstly, according to Beck (1992, Chapter 8), the bourgeois sphere of markets and technology, once regarded as the world of non-politics, only accessible to citizens as purchasers or investors, is now being opened up to full democratic scrutiny to an extent that was not previously possible when labour and capital fought over issues of wealth and income distribution but neither class questioned the relentless pursuit of material development as a valued goal per se. This questioning has recently become both possible and necessary partly because of the sheer magnitude of accumulated human-made, environmental hazards and risks. But the greater social as well as environmental insecurities generated by late industrialization, and now endemic to the 'risk society' (Beck,1992), have increasingly 'liberated' many citizens from older class, family and community structures, propelling them towards greater self-determination. Meanwhile, greater access to education in knowledge-based economies and the spread of information technology has enabled many to acquire a certain competence or 'lay expertise' with regard to scientific and other matters. Beck (1992) argues, therefore, that a growing number of individuals are both equipped and motivated to create and demand new forms of participation while insisting on their right to question the aims of science, corporate capital and material progress whether as consumers or as citizens who participate in various social movements.

Secondly, the ascendancy of green concerns, either in their milder, reformist, 'environmentalist' version or the more radical, Deep Green 'ecologist' one (Dobson, 1990), has been accompanied and sometimes underpinned by a number of earlier movements. Each of these tended to embody, by implication or design, a certain antipathy to capitalism: the resurgence of interest in cooperative enterprises from the early 1970s (Mellor et al, 1988 and Thornley, 1981); the rise of vegetarianism and veganism alongside the growing interest in 'wholefoods' and in 'healthy' organic and additive-free diets (Atkinson, 1980 and Beardsworth and Keil, 1992); the growth of the animal rights and welfare movements and the desire for cruelty-free products; and the concern with fair trading practices with respect to Third World goods. There is also a sense in which these movements are in the process of converging with, and being invigorated by, the wider green movement.

Thirdly, and at the same time, consumption and leisure practices remain central to the lives of most postmodern citizens manifested, for example, in the weekend trip to the ubiquitous shopping mall or arcade (Shields 1992), the compulsive but creative construction of private lifestyles and the search for personal identities among the 'floating signifiers' of contemporary popular culture (Featherstone 1987, p 57, but see also; Baudrillard 1988 and Tomlinson 1990). The predominance of cultural pursuits and identities (Crook et al 1992) in postmodern society is, in turn, inextricably intertwined with and underpinned by the political economy of an increasingly deregulated, disorganized and globalized capitalism; one that is sustained by a rising volume of credit and debt transactions, highly dependent on information technology and international communication systems and characterized by the continuing shift to various service and leisure industries. This unity of culture and economy in a global setting is neatly captured by the title Lash and Urry (1994) have given to their recent book; The Economy of Signs and Spaces. Given that the core of postmodern society revolves around a fundamentally materialist culture it has been inevitable that the economy and business enterprise have become major targets for the expression of environmental concern.

Lastly, several sociologists see these changes as highly dependent not only on the growing fear and awareness of environmental hazards but also on the increasing exercise of reflexive social action - that is, creative, self-monitoring, agent-led behaviour - by post or late modern citizens. Reflexivity is said to involve different dimensions: an underlying basis in cognitive/learning processes, knowledge and lay expertise (Giddens,1990 and 1991); it may also involve a critical element of moral awareness (Beck, 1992); alternatively, or in addition, reflexivity may contain an important element of expressive or aesthetic competence derived from participation in various forms of popular culture, especially film and television (Lash and Urry 1994). Here, presumably, the lifestyle preoccupations and narcissism embodied in postmodern signifying culture may nourish as well as educate citizen awareness of wider political issues especially through the informing role of the mass media. Whether, to what extent and precisely in what sense reflexive citizen actions are different from earlier forms of agent-led behaviour, and/or more numerous and powerful in their impact, remains unclear so it is necessary to be wary of these claims. Nevertheless, they raise interesting and suggestive questions that deserve further analysis. They also have a certain resonance with respect to the present discussion.

One key location where all these changes appear to have operated to some effect is in the market interface between business enterprise and the consuming public. This market interface has generated new market opportunities but is also marked by certain constraints. Chief among the latter is the currently rather narrow mass market base for genuinely green and ethical products in Britain compared to countries, such as Germany, Holland and Sweden. However, whereas the majority of British consumers may remain reluctant to engage in 'deep' and sustained green purchasing (Irvine 1989), partly because of the higher prices such goods command, a growing minority of highly informed and ethically aware consumers have created new market opportunities in this sector.

Of course, there are a number of powerful additional forces at work compelling companies to adopt more ethically and environmentally responsible practices, although these, too, are partly explicable in terms of wider socio-cultural changes: the recent escalation of national and supranational regulation; the influence increasingly exercised by various stake-holders such as investors, directors, employees and client firms; the need to avoid future legal or financial liability regarding possible, later claims for damages and the resulting pressure from banks and insurance companies; and the economic benefits of improved waste management, energy conservation schemes and so on. Nevertheless cultural change has been critical and many firms, especially 'Blue Chip' companies, have been well aware of its implications. For example, in 1989 the CBI commissioned a study on the rise of green concern among school children and the likely market consequences for British business while many firms now recognize that consumers increasingly base their marketing decisions on 'entire company philosophies and policies' (Charter, 1992, p.27) and no longer simply select particular brand goods.

This study suggests that the changes outlined above have generated certain significant consequences for firms operating in this market sector, a compulsive and partly externally-imposed logic, which most need to confront. To different degrees, the outcome has been to propel many of these enterprises towards adopting certain campaigning characteristics that are not normally associated with capitalist businesses. What are these mutually reinforcing pressures for change?

1. Commercial pressures

Virtually all such enterprises, are driven by considerations of survival, growth and profit. They need to retain their present market share by accommodating the demands of consumers and interested citizen groups while seeking to expand through participating directly in the process of 'converting' those consumers who remain relatively unresponsive to green-ethical concerns.

2. Exposure to external cultural pressures

These firms are engaged in exploiting market niches that require the commodification of ethicality. Accordingly, their business strategies may become both dependent upon and exposed to many external pressures from the consuming public and from a variety of non governmental organizations (NGOs), citizen networks and community groups, radical research and publishing organizations, specialist industry and professional groups, the media and others. But the rationale of such groups is largely moral, political and cultural rather than technical or economic; their agendas are not commercial ones. The discussion will identify exactly how and why such pressures operate so as to penetrate some aspects of business activity and decision-making.

3. Internalized moral and political intentionality

Our research identified another route through which some enterprises, primarily those designated as 'radical' (see below), may become active participants in processes of wider cultural change: namely, the existence of leading figures in a company who possess a considerable degree of personal green or ethical commitment on their own account and which they consciously seek to express through

179

various aspects of business endeavour. Clearly, such an internal momentum for change is likely to reinforce and interact with both points 1 and 2 above. The specific entrepreneurial responses generated by this internal ethicality are likely to vary considerably in degree and form. At one extreme business operations will continue to be partly and perhaps mainly driven by profit considerations. Other enterprises may be motivated by moral and political considerations to the greatest extent that may be compatible with the very survival of the 'business' itself as an organizational vehicle for conducting what has become almost entirely a campaign rather than a profit-oriented enterprise. Many intermediate positions are also possible.

The study and its methodology

The paper draws on the findings derived from a study conducted between May 1993 and June 1994. This involved conducting in-depth interviews with the leading figures in 74 enterprises located mostly in Northern and especially North-West Britain; 38 were based in and around the Manchester conurbation with most of the remainder (apart from 7 firms) situated in West Yorkshire (19), Merseyside (4), or north Derbyshire (6). The enterprises selected for interview were ones that directly or indirectly served the market niches created by final consumers for a wide range of such green-ethical goods and services as the following: re-cycled textiles, clothes, plastics, wood and paper products (20 firms); cruelty-free, non animal-based body products, cosmetics, soaps etc. (4); environmentally-friendly, biodegradable chemicals and cleaning agents (5); organic, vegetarian 'wholefoods' and beverages (24); printing, publishing or retailing of radical or alternative materials (5); services such as ethical finance, investments or loans, green consultancy, architecture and accountancy (10); and general purpose retailing of a range of green-ethical goods, educational materials, fair-trade Third World craft products etc. (6).

Of these firms, 15 were worker's cooperatives, 5 were community or social enterprises (charities or friendly societies), there were 27 limited liability companies and 27 partnerships or sole proprietorships. Most (61) were founded after 1976 and more than half (38) were established in the period of rising public concern with environmental issues that was notable from 1988 onwards. Manufacturing was the primary activity in the case of 32 firms, 19 enterprises were engaged in the service sector, there were 5 wholesale distributors and the remainder (19) were retailers. The sample is in no sense a random or representative one; a lack of resources severely circumscribed the geographical area available for investigation and, as far as the author is aware, there is no available data base, at present, capable of identifying a reliable pool of green-ethical enterprises. Thus, the sample was partly obtained by consulting national magazines, newspapers and directories (for example, the *Ethical Consumer, The Globe, Cahoots* and the *Green Directory* for 1989) and partly by employing a 'snowball' approach, following up leads obtained from our initial sample of self-styled green-ethical enterprises concerning their suppliers, market outlets and so on. Approximately two thirds of the enterprises encountered in these ways were included. Apart from a few intrinsically interesting cases we avoided contacting very large international companies and national chains, including supermarkets, because their head offices were situated outside our geographical area, many were foreign-owned and they were only marginally involved in genuine green-ethical marketing. We have no way of estimating how many other firms there may be of whose existence we remain ignorant but which were theoretically eligible for inclusion.

For purposes of analysis the sample is divided into two main groups according to their modes of business orientation. First, there was a group of approximately 30 enterprises designated as 'mainstream'. Most were medium or large in their scale of operations and might be one of a group of affiliated companies. Their management structures were hierarchical, specialized and professional. Assets were privately owned and remuneration was highly unequal as between employees. Involvement in green-ethical business activity normally generated only a part of their sales turnover and was motivated first and foremost by profit considerations though other pressures had begun to intrude at the same time, as we will see. A second group of about 33 enterprises are designated as 'radical'. Their proprietors and/or members displayed most of the following orientations: a strong leaning towards democratic and equalitarian organization and work practices; a wide-ranging and deep commitment to green-ethical business activities; the tendency to give political and moral considerations a nearly equal or sometimes greater priority than narrow commercial ones; and a preference for alternative, relatively non-materialistic lifestyles in their private non-work relationships and leisure preferences.(1)

Clearly, enterprises meeting such criteria are still rather exceptional and it may not be possible to extend their experiences and the study's findings to the generality of businesses. Nevertheless, it could be argued that the changes such 'front line' firms may be accommodating today may presage the kinds of pressures that will gradually engulf more and more enterprises and economic sectors in the coming years.

The commodification of ethicality and its likely consequences

Most of these businesses were driven either partly (the radical firms) or primarily (the mainstream enterprises) by an economic rationale. This includes their motivation for responding to cultural pressures; it is a necessary route to ensuring business survival and profitability, a market ploy. In this respect they are no different from any other capitalist enterprise.

1.   Nevertheless, the successful exploitation of green and ethical market niches may both generate and require certain additional practices and relationships. Thus, whatever else such businesses are engaged in selling - the provision of quality goods at reasonable prices capable of fulfilling certain utility functions, the means for satisfying consumers' social, individual aesthetic or lifestyle aspirations - it is clear that they are also providing products perceived by consumers as embodying some elements of political or moral credibility. Thus, they are engaged, among other things, in the commodification of ethicality: in marketing the proofs of their own virtue as well as those of their customers. This generates several further important consequences to which we now turn.

2.   The commodification of ethicality, in turn, depends on the moralization of some consumer practices. Here, what is important is that minority groups of highly informed, discerning and ethically conscious consumers have increasingly emerged whose spending and lifestyle practices express their moral or political as well as other preoccupations. Many reject the 'normal' consumer role of relative passivity, where they exercise a certain postmodern 'free' choice in their personal selection of predetermined signifiers from an array of

market-researched products but have little say in the way goods are actually produced, packaged and presented. Instead, this growing minority of consumer are engaged in developing a demanding and participatory role as agents in the various stages of the economic decision-making process, especially those of production and the disposal of waste, spheres from which they were previously excluded.

3.   Selling virtue as a market strategy also requires the adoption of certain minimum criteria of green-ethical purity in terms of what is permissible to use by way of ingredients in the production process, the ways in which production and organization are conducted and the range of goods and services that are legitimate to market. Such purity criteria may be adopted with varying degrees of strictness and may cover a narrow, wide or even complete range of products. Compromises may need to be justified not only to discerning customers but in terms of the prevailing enterprise ethos.

4.   A further consequence of involvement in green or ethical business is not just the likelihood of much greater exposure to a widening range of external non-economic pressure groups and interests than is normal in conventional business sectors but also the prospect of increased dependence on these external forces. This may involve several dimensions.

Coping with reflexive consumers

Businesses need to accept a greater degree of accountability since the people who buy their goods are likely to be more scrupulous in their demands and rather better informed than the majority. This is particularly the case when, as often happens with such goods, they are more expensive than their non-ethical-green equivalents and command premium prices. Thus, selling goods that embody certain green or ethical claims invites scrutiny and calls for proof. Customers may also need to convince themselves of their own lack of culpability, requiring evidence of their personal, ethical credentials.

Scrutiny from interested groups

At the same time, there is every likelihood that enterprises will become exposed to increasing amounts of detailed examination and political pressure from a wide range of NGOs, local voluntary groups, colleges and schools, the media and consumer research organizations such as the Ethical Investment Research Service (EIRIS) and many others concerned with these issues. Other companies offering contracts for supplies are also likely to demand reassurance concerning the 'clean', environmentally valid nature of enterprise operations. This is especially true in the case of large companies such as Tesco and British Telecom which are engaged in trying to enhance their own reputations for green-ethical correctness. Indeed, making some kind of public commitment with regard to wider green-ethical issues probably attracts more rather than less scrutiny. Virtue may be its own reward, as the old adage reminds, but it also betokens the assumption of new responsibilities. The recent controversy surrounding the Body Shop would appear to substantiate this claim.

Verification requirements

These businesses must be able to cope with the knowledge and verification implications of green-ethical marketing. This is especially the case since such information is constantly being revised in the light of new research findings or further twists in the complex debates surrounding the supposed environmental consequences of alternative production systems (for example, the relative environmental merits of using re-cycled paper or virgin pulp obtained from 'managed' and 'sustainable' forests) and as these find their way into the media and so the public domain. Businesses need to be thoroughly informed in order to keep abreast of such developments or risk losing the credibility and trust of customers and green-ethical pressure groups. To assist them in their constant search for such new and reliable information (including data on their own suppliers and client firms), the enterprises included in the study, even very large and wealthy companies, could not always rely solely on their own resources but required outside technical advice. Only organizations with similar interests - including other businesses operating in the same area of marketing - and/or that specialize in assimilating and presenting relevant research findings may be capable of providing sufficiently trustworthy information. Among the organizations and publications on which these enterprises relied for information were the following: various NGOs, government-sponsored agencies, the *Ethical Consumer* and *The Globe* magazines and the London-based EIRIS and Women's' Environmental Network.

The need for special resources

These enterprises may also require the special training facilities or financial assistance that only sympathetic support agencies working in similar or related fields are willing or able to provide. More conventional organizations were often less understanding or even distant with regard to the aims and concerns of green-ethical businesses. Alternatively, they were simply unable to offer assistance given the rather narrow parameters within which they operated. Examples of networking with sympathetic support agencies included obtaining loans from organizations such as the Industrial Common Ownership Movement (ICOM), Christian Aid, the Quaker Loan Fund or Mercury Provident. These are private or voluntary agencies with a strong preference for assisting enterprises with a leaning towards social and ethical goals. Some enterprises had also secured technical advice or grants from Labour Councils whose commitment to furthering local economic initiatives might include the desire to help enterprises with ethical or social goals. Some of the mainstream firms had also drawn upon 'official' industry-based or government sponsored organizations with specialist interests and knowledge such as the National Recycling Forum, the Producer Responsibility Group (set up as a result of an initiative by John Gummer), the Institute of Environmental Assessment and various chambers of commerce operating in conjunction with local training and enterprise councils.

The need for inter-personal trust

Businesses need to be in a position to trust the claims of their own suppliers that the inputs provided meet the required ethical standards and guaranteed quality demanded by their own clients further down the production chain or by final consumers. Here, it is important to note Giddens' (1990) argument to the effect that a good deal of social interaction in late modernity is increasingly made possible not by ascriptive and close face-to-face relationships but by largely impersonal arrangements and contracts based on technical or professional trust. This enables social relations to be stretched across time and space, (a phenomenon he defines as dis-embeddedness).

185

However, the evidence from the study suggests that the 'trust' between business contacts required in this particular field of enterprise may also rely critically on personal loyalties generated and maintained by shared ethical commitments and facilitated by frequent contacts and the evolution of 'friendships' based on genuine mutual liking. Such close and pleasurable relationships not only created openings for genuine displays of trust but also offered fertile ground for persuasion and conversion, for the dissemination and reinforcement of values. In the case of the radical firms (and those who had occasion to deal with them) such good relations might also help to ease financial stress since they tended to pay their invoices promptly, so foregoing the 'normal' business practice of loading unpaid debts from purchasers on to suppliers.

Direct dependence on citizen initiatives

Among the mainstream manufacturing enterprises included in the study, half (15) were directly dependent in one or more ways on the political or moral activities of particular groups or institutions for either their supplies of raw material, their market outlets or both. Supplies of re-cycled inputs were often drawn from some combination of the following sources: the voluntary campaigning actions of members of the public operating either as house holders, employees participating in workplace (university, hospital or city office) re-cycling schemes or as members of community, church or school groups; the financial, organizational and advertising support provided by local authorities involving various 'kerb side' schemes; the leadership skills, campaigning drives and permanent collection sites provided by NGOs such as Friends of the Earth and various private charities like Oxfam; and the non-profit-driven initiatives supported by some large corporations or responsible business associations. Secondly, these businesses had relied partly or entirely on an increasing degree of public awareness concerning green-ethical issues for a large part of their market. As they acknowledged, this had been generated, in turn, largely through the activities of assorted NGOs, schools, leading companies that had earlier assumed a high environmental profile or the voluntary attention and free advertising they had received from sympathetic media coverage. Thirdly, some mainstream enterprises sold some or most of their products directly to the trading sections of various pressure groups such as Friends of the Earth or Greenpeace or were dependent on other much more radical and committed green-ethical enterprises as their key buyers.

Enterprise responses; towards the campaigning business?

As enterprises become more exposed to the pressures for change described in the previous section, so it is possible that their organizational strategies and goals, and the way they prioritize these, may undergo important modifications. In particular, they may be increasingly propelled towards demonstrating the following characteristics and practices. Firstly, they may engage in spreading. This involves the tendency for purity criteria, and their operationalization, to become generalized or diffused away from the immediate cutting edge of consumer demand. Thus, other aspects of business organization may also become ethicalized, such as employee-management relations (for example policies concerning gender and ethnic equality of recruitment and fair wage practices) or the wider application of environmentally-responsible policies perhaps with regard to packaging, waste disposal or energy use. This spreading effect may enable enterprises to make further legitimate claims for greenness or ethicality.

Secondly, firms caught in the logic of green or ethical marketing may find it both necessary and advantageous to nestle within, and to seek dealings with, a network of sympathetic, like-minded business contacts and support agencies sharing the same preoccupations and problems. This embeddedness is likely to further consolidate or deepen their green or ethical commitments. However, this does not by any means preclude a continuing and parallel dependence on more formal or conventional organizations (high street banks, solicitors, etc.) that do not engender or display such commitments.

Thirdly, as the boundaries of business organization become more permeable, more open to outside influences, less separate from the wider society and the cultural stream of change so, in the process, enterprises may become less narrowly focussed solely on economic concerns. Instead they may assume additional activities of an overtly or quasi moral, educational or political nature, especially in dealings with clients. In so far as this qualitative change takes place we could, perhaps, claim that enterprise activity is becoming progressively less specialized and more multi-functional and simultaneously somewhat radicalized in its concerns.

Some theoretical underpinning for this phenomenon can be found in the recent writings of sociologists such as Crook (1992), among others. In late capitalist society, it is said, the process of structural differentiation whereby highly specialized institutional processes and life experiences have become clearly demarcated by function and ethos, characteristic of the earlier period of modernization, culminates in a state of hyper-differentiation or extreme social fragmentation. Indeed, many activities, institutions and interests have now become so fractionalized that citizens have found it both meaningful and possible to generate counter-tendencies towards de-differentiation. They are discovering ways to fuse together previously separate practices across and within social, political, economic and cultural institutions thereby forging new processes and meanings. That it has become both possible and desirable for postmodern citizens to engage in these processes has been helped by the following: the increasing opportunities for many citizens to plan their own biographies due to rising incomes, greater education, the expansion of leisure time and the progressive de-linking from community, class and family; the rise to dominance of cultural concerns associated with the immense proliferation of media images, the growth of the cultural industries and the corresponding influence of the so-called new cultural intermediaries in popular culture, journalism, advertising and so on; and the tendency for citizens to increasingly express their ideological and personal concerns not through formal political processes but in the new social movements.

There is a very real sense in which this argument has a certain resonance with respect to the present discussion. Thus, to a greater or lesser extent, the majority of the enterprises included in this study revealed clear demonstrations of moves towards de-differentiation at the very heart of the capitalist project; they were combining cultural, quasi political and educational functions - the features of a campaign — with narrow economic ones. And yet their motives for doing so were largely and unavoidably instrumental; to retain and expand market share and to accommodate the demands of pressure groups and reflexive consumers, operating with quite different non-commercial agendas, to whose gaze they had become exposed and to whom they were increasingly accountable. In this sense, the increasing permeability of their organizational boundaries, tendencies towards de-differentiation and radicalization were inextricably linked aspects of the same process. What is the evidence from our study for such campaigning activities?

The mainstream enterprises

One third of the mainstream enterprises (10 firms) manifested only minimal evidence of campaigning activity. They provided clear information concerning the authenticity of their green or ethical products reinforced by a presentation emphasizing images of simplicity and 'naturalness'. They were also well aware of their market dependence on the cultural stream of moral or political awareness. But they revealed little or no direct involvement in the public debate on green issues or any attempt to demonstrate a wider commitment to these questions by overtly wooing public concern. In short, they remained indirectly dependent for part of their business success on powerful independent forces but evinced no campaigning features. This minimalist response was normally explicable in terms of one or more of the following situations: their rather marginal involvement in green or ethical marketing; the tendency to rely on supplying 'own brand' goods to supermarket or other chains where they were protected from 'front line' exposure to final consumers; or their dependence on an established and mainly working class market niche where customers were more concerned with obtaining 'value for money', 'whiter than white' clothes and sparkling homes than with environmental or ethical priorities.

In contrast, two thirds of the mainstream firms (20) were either directly dependent on the cultural stream of ethicality and greenness for some raw materials, information, technical assistance, networking facilities or market outlets and/or they were also engaged in developing some kind of pro-active stance with respect to rising public awareness. To some degree, this latter group (15 mainstream enterprises or half of this group) were endeavouring to demonstrate their willingness to assume the role of agents, committed to assisting in the generation of wider change in their own right. This took various, and sometimes overlapping, forms. Eight firms had adopted an informative, educational profile with respect to schools, colleges and the general public. This involved producing highly professional films, videos and brochures demonstrating the role that their firms, and industry, could and were playing in adopting improved environmental management; holding and attending exhibitions, craft fairs or industry events that were designed to inform consumers and the general public about green-ethical issues; hosting regular school and college visits; and making company facilities and its environmental expertise available to local educational curriculum programmes and student placement schemes. Six enterprises were engaged in targeting and gaining the support of different interest groups: for example, by participating in voluntary schemes designed to promote environmental awareness in conjunction with green pressure groups and local or central government initiatives and/or providing financial sponsorship, active organizational support or free advertising and communication facilities for one or more NGOs. Nine companies had taken steps to attract and employ a core of professional managers or technicians who combined environmental training and a degree of personal commitment to such issues. These employees had then been given considerable scope, in terms of investment and company facilities, to develop and enhance the firm's environmental activities and public profile. Finally, at least three enterprises were involved in sponsoring local, community activities of a voluntary and ethical nature such as helping to finance a nature reserve.

Of course, businesses have always utilized cultural themes as a market resource, carefully insinuating such wider meanings into their products through their use of advertising techniques. There is also a long history of companies exercising various forms of corporate responsibility. However, there are important differences between these older expressions of business responsibility and those we describe here. For example, there is now a much stronger compulsion to communicate, convince and interact directly with the immediate consumer as a key part of this process of demonstrating corporate responsiveness. Nor have citizens been so predisposed, until now, to look so critically and knowledgeably into the ethical and environmental implications of so many aspects of business activity or to regard companies as clearly culpable where such questions are concerned. Also, the pressure groups with which businesses may now need to interact are sometimes rather alternative, even anti-capitalist in their orientations yet they enjoy very wide public support and considerable media coverage.

Clearly, the evidence from these mainstream enterprises of moves in the direction of campaigning activity is slight and it was almost certainly motivated originally by commercial considerations. Yet, given the nature of green or ethical production and marketing and increased exposure to community groups, NGOs, and their like, such enterprises may gradually find themselves subtly bound into a web of obligations and unfamiliar loyalties that generate their own logic. Here, one kind of commitment presupposes and engenders others while exposing a firm's own activities to ever more compelling demands for detailed investigation. Should the cultural stream of greenness and ethicality continues to flow and to deepen its impact, then, an increasing number of these and other firms may eventually cross some kind of threshold between business action that is purely profit-driven and that which begins to be propelled by a genuinely felt quasi political or moral commitment for its own sake. If so, then we might expect the campaigning characteristics manifested by these enterprises to intensify. Indeed, they might begin to resemble the radical firms which operated much more overtly and extensively as campaigning businesses because they were driven by a third momentum for cultural change; namely, an internalized political or moral ethos.

The radical enterprises: campaign or business?

The proprietors and members of the radical enterprises not only displayed a very high degree of personal commitment to their firms' green and ethical goals but this had been present from the very outset; the histories of these enterprises were 'saturated' with their chosen ethos. The desire to make a living without the necessity to compromise personal morality was what had drawn most of these entrepreneurs and members towards the goal of founding or working in a radical business in the first place. Although most were endeavouring to run a reasonably profitable business, and so were bound by commercial considerations, they were simultaneously dedicated to the attainment of wider non-economic goals. These were 'profit-plus' businesses or as one informant expressed it: "this is so much more than just a business". Another remarked that he and his cooperative members had never been sure whether the business existed in order to run a campaign or the campaign operated so as to promote the enterprise.

Several consequences followed from the above. Firstly, the radical enterprises adhered very strictly to whatever criteria of purity were relevant to their particular sphere of green or ethical business. Compromises with principle were rare and might engender bitter internal disputes. In addition, the attempt to operationalize purity criteria was extended to all or most areas of business activity, unlike the situation prevailing in most of the mainstream firms. For example, and especially in the cooperatives, the working environment was invariably rather equalitarian, democratic and participatory; jobs were rotated as far as possible, special skills were not given any particular recognition and there were opportunities for regular consultation. They were also likely to display a wider commitment to environmental responsibility, including participation in voluntary re-cycling schemes, engaging in energy-saving activities such as operating a door-to-door bicycle delivery service to customers' homes and using re-cycled stationary and other paper products in routine business operations. A strong commitment to community service was also evident in some instances.

Secondly, the evidence of embeddedness was also rather more pronounced in the radical enterprises since their overt moral or political ethos made them especially dependent on a network of like-minded suppliers and support agencies who were reliable and trustworthy. Thirdly, and most importantly, the evidence for moves towards de-differentiation - assuming a high campaigning profile - was particularly marked, especially, though not only, in the case of retailers who are located in the 'front line' where committed final consumers have to be directly confronted. Here, it is important to stress that the radical enterprises' willingness to offer a combination of economic, cultural and community services was not motivated solely by moral or political considerations, powerful though these normally were. Rather, business survival depended on the ability to attract customers in competition both with other radical firms and with mainstream businesses. The latter present an especially powerful threat since it has become increasingly possible - as most respondents explained in considerable detail - for consumers to purchase much cheaper green or ethical substitutes from supermarkets, large book sellers and health food, pharmaceutical and other chains. It is the willingness of consumers to buy from the radical enterprises at premium prices that largely keeps them in business although a convenient location may be an additional business advantage. According to the respondents their regular clientele of 'repeat' customers were mostly middle class, youngish, educated, often professional people who shared their concerns. Some were said to be affluent people involved in 'two-career' relationships for whom the higher prices charged by radical enterprises presented few problems. But others, it was claimed, tended to be on low incomes; students, members of the caring professions, nurses, teachers, social workers, or citizens dedicated to a more 'alternative, new-age' lifestyle who were poor because they were marginalized, whether by choice or necessity, from the mainstream economy. Price considerations probably remained critical to this second group despite their otherwise radical commitments. Moreover, even for customers such as these, and certainly in the case of the majority of more conventional consumers, it seems likely that the postmodern appeal of shopping malls and arcades as sites for what Shields (1992) calls "the enactment of lifestyle" (p.16) and "zones of permitted, legitimate pleasure" (p.8) retain certain attractions.

Consequently, what helped to provide the radical enterprises, especially the retailers, with a much-needed market edge was precisely their ability to offer something that their much larger and cheaper rivals along with the glitzy shopping malls were unable to provide to anything like the same extent: an all-encompassing experience of alternativeness including evidence of personal and business commitment to the importance of the campaign. In fact, they may have little or no choice but to foster and promote such a total cultural package. Many of their clientele expect nothing less; a busy, interesting atmosphere of social warmth and personal attention, the enjoyment of community feeling, the opportunity for personal networking with various quasi political groups and, of course, the opportunity to affirm their own private, green or ethical credentials. These 'proofs' of both personal and business responsibility may take various forms: the back-up information supplied with the commodities and the simplicity of the packaging, resonant, perhaps, with images of naturalness and simplicity; the milieu in which goods are purchased with its emphasis on wholesomeness and informality; an abundant supply of information concerning radical petitions, actions and movements and invitations to support housing cooperatives, local charities and so on; and the cultivation of an atmosphere of friendliness where customer's own ethical commitment is acknowledged, validated and valued.

In all these ways those running the radical enterprises were actively engaged in constructing and presenting instances of multi-functional social practice. Their efforts in this regard were pursued much more self-consciously than was the case in most of the mainstream firms. At the same time they were acting in the capacity of cultural intermediaries, as inventors and purveyors of meaning. And their capacity to do so required the active complicity of their customers.

Notes

1. The remaining eleven proprietors' motivations for establishing a business were based on individual or family health concerns (for example, allergies to dairy products, food additives or the incidence of asthma), a strong fascination with artistic or craft expression or religious preferences. That such activities had generated certain environmental or wider ethical advantages was therefore largely coincidental and unintentional. This group is therefore excluded from the discussion.

References

Atkinson, P. (1988), 'The symbolic significance of health foods', in Turner, M. (ed.) *Nutrition and Lifestyles*, Applied Science Publishers, London.

Beardsworth, A.and Keil, T. (1992), 'The vegetarian option; varieties, conversions, motives and careers', *Sociological Review*, 40 (2).

Beck, U. (1992), *Risk Society; Towards a New Modernity*, Sage, London.

Charter, M. (1992) *Greener Marketing*, Greenleaf Publishing, Sheffield.

Crook, S, et al (1992), *Postmodernization; Change in Advanced Societies*, Sage, London.

Baudrillard, J. (1989), *Selected Writings*, edited by Poster, M., Polity Press, Cambridge.

Dobson, A. (1990), *Green Political Thought*, Unwin Hyman, London.

Featherstone, M. (1987), 'Lifestyle and Consumer Culture', *Theory, Culture and Society*, 4 (1).

Giddens, A. (1990), *The Consequences of Modernity*, Polity, Cambridge.

Giddens, A. (1991), *Modernity and Self-Identity*, Polity, Cambridge.

Irvine, S. (1989), 'Consuming fashions? The limits of green consumerism', *Ecologist*, 19 (3).

Lash, S. and Urry, J. (1994), *Economies of Signs and Spaces*, Sage , London.

Mellor, M. ;Hannah, J. and Stirling,J. (1988), *Worker Cooperatives in Theory and Practice*, Open University Press, Milton Keynes.

Nava, M. (1991), 'Consumerism reconsidered; buying and power',

Cultural Studies, 5 (2).

Roddick, A. (1990), Body Shop Promotional Literature.

Shields, R. (1992), *Lifestyle Shopping*, Routledge, London.

Thornley, J. (1981), *Workers' Co-Operatives; Jobs and Dreams*, Heinemann, London.

Tomlinson, A. (1990), *Consumption, Identity and Style*, Routledge, London.

10   Daring to dream: idealism in the philosophy, organization and campaigning strategies of Earth First!

Jonathan Purkis

Introduction

It is a Sunday afternoon in a well known 'Do It Yourself' store somewhere in a city in the northwest of England. There is the usual flow of families wheeling trollies around the spacious aisles. Anybody who was paying attention to the kind of people passing through the turnstile would notice a sudden influx of half a dozen obviously overdressed customers, followed by a steady stream of slightly unorthodox looking young men and women who, upon entering the premises, disperse themselves to different parts of the large store. Several minutes pass and then a young voice calls out loudly from the back of the store, demanding everybody's attention. From the vantage point of an in-store trolley he informs people of the fact that the store stocks illegally logged mahogany products which have been extracted and produced at enormous social and environmental cost to indigenous peoples in Brazil. The demonstration of which he is a part is demanding that the store agrees to cease importing mahogany altogether. As he has been speaking, other activists have locked themselves to mahogany products using strong bicycle 'D' locks, have sat down on the floor or have begun putting up banners or leafleting the somewhat bemused customers. The store's security staff and management converge on the huddle of people but realize too late that this has all been a decoy disturbance, and that the overdressed customers have 'shoplifted' various mahogany items and taken them to a nearby police station, reporting them as 'stolen property'. Only two young men are apprehended, halfway across the enormous car park carrying a rather heavy mahogany table! The police are called in and confront the in-store demonstrators who appear to be used to dealing with the law in this manner. Two newspaper journalists photograph the event and one or two questions are asked of the activists. A deal is struck between the protesters, the management and the police that if the demonstrators leave the store the manager will meet two of the demonstrators and discuss the issue further. The police sergeant says that she will look into the claims about 'stolen property', and the demonstration moves outside and resumes leafleting and talking to the public until the negotiators finish their business inside. Despite a few points of conflict about whether the demonstrators outside are on or off the company's property, there is no trouble, and the demonstration presently moves off to try the same tactics on another outlet of the store in the same city.

This is an example of a typical demonstration by the radical environmental group Earth First! (EF!) which took place during 1993, in this case in Manchester, although the same event might easily have occurred in any number of sizable urban locations throughout the UK. This article seeks to use the described events — an 'ethical shoplift' — as a touchstone for exploring idealism in the EF! movement, and the kind of future which many of its activists envisage. To do this it will take three areas: philosophy, organization and campaigning strategy, and will look at the premises which underpin them, and which consequently play a part in shaping the EF! view of the future. Before this, however, it is necessary to explore the background and context of Earth First!

Who are Earth First!?

EF! was formed in April 1991 by two eighteen year old students from the southeast of England who had previously worked with Greenpeace and Friends of the Earth (Anonymous, 1993, p.16). Their motivation to start a new group stemmed from the lack of opportunity for direct action in environmental campaigning within these organizations, which to many young activists were increasingly seen as inaccessible and at a local level often more linked to fund-raising than action (Townley, 1992). EF! took its inspiration from the

North American organization of the same name which had formed in 1980 in response to a series of compromises by mainstream conservation organizations over how much Forest Service land should remain road free (Scarce, 1990, p.58). Major cultural and philosophical differences exist between the movements, but there are identifiable influences on UKEF! from their North American counterparts, particularly around the use of theatre, slogans and the choice of specific environmental issues.[1] Several USEF! activists were central to a major recruitment and 'empowerment' drive in early 1992, which, under the self-satirizing headline 'EF! Roadshow', visited eighteen English and Scottish towns and cities. As a result, the small network which comprised of only nine or ten groups or contact addresses in December 1991 has grown to between sixty and seventy groups at the time of writing, with many other organizations linking up for specific direct action campaigns.

Common to both the North American and British EF! movements is the belief that individuals have the power to act for themselves to save the environment without resorting to official bureaucratic conservation or governmental organizations to do it for them. An introductory briefing sheet for potential activists states that 'the greatest force for change is when individuals stand up to be counted and are prepared to put themselves and their bodies in the way'.[2]

EF! are here utilizing the philosophy of 'civil disobedience' which advocates confronting allegedly oppressive behaviour at its source by breaking the law in a non-violent manner, usually with large numbers of people. In this context, civil disobedience is usually referred to as Non-Violent Direct Action (NVDA). Its basic premise is that if enough pressure is brought to bear on a company or a government ministry through the repeated breaking of laws, the actions will result in a change of policy or practice. It is a course of political action which has been advocated by such diverse figures as Henry Thoreau, Mahatma Ghandi and Martin Luther King, three people who can claim to have some influence on the campaigning philosophies of some of the so-called New Social Movements (NSMs) which have emerged since the 1960s.[3] In seeking to locate EF! within the NSMs it is important to note that the Environmental movement has never had a mass grassroots wing which uses civil disobedience tactics unlike, of course, the Peace Movement and the Animal Rights/Liberation movements during the 1980s. In all of these NSMs, where a strategy of civil disobedience exists, the justification for breaking the law is one of appealing to a higher moral law, such as a United Nations declaration or arms treaty. One of the EF! activists involved in the ethical shoplift described above commented on another occasion that 'personally I agree with breaking the law to uphold the law'.[4]

EF! is predominantly a young persons' movement, mostly white and well educated, but economically 'decommodified' (see Offe, 1985) in the sense that the generation of young people growing up in the 1980s can no longer expect security of employment, guaranteed access to welfare provision or accommodation as a result of major economic, social and political changes (see Mole, 1994). Consequently there are many young people from classically middle class backgrounds in their twenties who are staying in education and training for as long as they can, or who are spending long periods of time unemployed, or choosing to try to live alternative lifestyles. These people constitute what may be termed an 'educated underclass': they are resourceful and rich in 'cultural capital' (Bourdieu, 1984) but subsist on very low incomes.

These economic circumstances exist alongside more cultural and existential factors which shape the radical green political psyche (see Eckersley, 1989). For instance, during the late 1980s there was an increased interest in green politics in the UK brought about by the high profile Green presence in the Euro elections of 1989, and during the same period the media became increasingly willing to broadcast or print informative and topical features on issues such as pollution, global warming, destruction of the tropical rain forests, animal cruelty and vegetarianism. Some of these issues have enjoyed a long history of documentation (Carson, 1963; Schumacher, 1973; Singer, 1976) and can be seen to have shaped the visions of the first generation of post-War environmental activists. In some cases these may well be the parents of some of today's (second) generation.

In addition, there is evidence to show that this generation of young people are contemptuous of the ability of current political and economic structures to solve either individual or global problems (see Roberts, 1992, p.10). Consequently this realization then manifests itself politically in a call for new or different forms of theory and practice, something which will be discussed in the sections on philosophy and organization.

The philosophy of Earth First!

When discussing idealism in relation to the philosophy of EF! there are three different levels which help us to understand an event such as an 'ethical shoplift': firstly on the basis of the actual aims and objectives of EF!; secondly in terms of the patterns of consumption in the Western world; and thirdly in terms of the relationship between humans and non-human life.

(a) The aims and objectives of EF!

A useful starting point for situating the aims and objectives of EF! is through Alberto Melucci's notion that NSMs are frequently characterized by a desire to 'render power visible' (1989, p.76). Melucci is just one of many theorists of NSMs who, in trying to describe new and distinctive features of political protest in the post-war period, have identified the role of information as a crucial factor. In a world which is increasingly organized around new processes of communication (see Lash and Urry, 1994), and where previous conceptions of time and space are increasingly 'compressed' (Harvey, 1989), there are political sensibilities which are developing in accordance with life in the 'global village'. Ulrich Beck perhaps identifies this best: for him there is a 'long-distance morality' being employed in contemporary hi-tech societies by pressure groups and individuals, rather than by governments who are tied to the structures of nation states (1992, p.137).

Although it has become a bit of a sociological and political cliche to talk of 'the local and the global', it is more usual that this sentiment is used to describe new economic and social phenomena **in** the world rather than as part of a philosophy **about** the world. A brief examination of the apparently scant aims of EF! as an organization however shows that their actual philosophy is very dependent on an understanding of new economic and social processes. According to their own literature, the aims of EF! — as drawn up at their first national gathering in 1991 — are:

(i) 'To defend the environment'.

(ii) 'To confront and expose those destroying the environment'.

(iii) 'To realise a human lifestyle that exists in balance and harmony with the natural world that has respect for all life'.[5]

What is striking about these aims is the fact that, although EF! is predominantly a direct action group, point (iii) clearly throws down the gauntlet for activists to start to think about how they want to live, yet the aim remains sufficiently vague to be open to interpretation. This vagueness is pertinent in particular to the open-ended and anti-authoritarian structure of EF! — an area to which we will return in the organization section.

However, points (i) and (ii) do read very much as philosophical premises that are required in order for (iii) to begin to take place. To put these 'premises' into some sort of framework so that we can understand exactly where (iii) is located, it is useful to add a short inventory of EF! campaigns other than the 'ethical shoplift'. In this manner it is possible to appreciate the systematic critique which EF! employ when examining environmental destruction.

*Opposition to the building of new motorways or roads which would involve the destruction of either: sites of special scientific interest, areas of outstanding natural beauty, ancient monuments, urban communities or green belt land.

*Campaigning against the main four High Street banks for perpetuating and profiting from the Debt repayments owed by Third World Countries, many of whom are not able to feed their people, and must subsequently chop down forests or plunder their natural resource at the expense of their ecosystems to keep up with the interest rates on the loans.[6]

*Opposition to the building of large out of town shopping centres some of which involve 'trespassing' onto 'green belt' land, and almost inevitably mean the building of more roads and car parks to serve the new 'demand'.

*Other actions have included opposition to CFC (chlorofluorocarbons) manufacturing companies such as ICI, solidarity actions in support of indigenous peoples' struggles against oil multi-nationals (Shell in Nigeria) or super-dam development projects (Narmada in India), and disrupting international conferences such as the G7 which are seen to promote environmentally damaging economic policies.

In most of these cases, opposition to the particular project in question also extends to the targeting of subcontractors, supporting financial institutions, security companies, haulage firms, either through occupations or organized boycotts of the services in question. Sometimes protesters may have purchased a small amount of shares in a company, for the purposes of gaining access to shareholders meetings.

The systematic nature of EF! campaigning reflects a belief that in the global system power is all pervasive, and that in order to change a process which is destroying ecosystems, it has to be confronted wherever it manifests itself. The fact that EF! concentrates on information here can be related to a second feature of their philosophy; namely that the patterns of consumption in the rich Western countries have to be understood holistically.

(b) The patterns of consumption

One would infer from the nature of EF! actions that the kind of world which people in EF! would like to see would be characterized by a radical reorganization of trading systems, including a huge reduction in the flow of raw materials and consumer goods from the Southern Hemisphere to the Northern. It is therefore important to understand the actions of EF! in the context of the literature of overdevelopment, over consumption and the limitations of growth economics (see Lang and Hines, 1993; Durning, 1992). The premises of much of this literature — that all aspects of our trading systems require reassessment — are mirrored in the actions of EF!, particularly in terms of responsibility. So, to use the ethical shoplift as an example, not only are the company (Texas Homecare) responsible for the mahogany trade, but so are transportation firms, logging companies, investors, the Brazilian and UK governments, with consumers equally culpable, too.[7] This kind of systematic analysis has become a common feature of alternative consumption practices since the late 80s, often involving very sophisticated boycotting procedures (ECRA, 1993). Whilst EF! as a group may concentrate on the most obviously 'criminal' companies, in their literature they may well also identify other 'suspicious' organizations and in their everyday lives activists usually monitor their own consumption patterns using ecological and other criteria.[8] Consequently we can see a politicization of everyday life and the emergence of a ecological notion of the 'personal as political'.[9] So, even though the actions of the 'ethical' type of consumer may not be more than the logical extension of 'consumer rights' in contemporary western democracies, when this new sensibility is linked to direct action, it is possible to see a dual type of resistance — both symbolic and economic — to the prevailing economic and political culture, on a local and a global basis. Furthermore, as Miller (1995, p.47) notes — 'the green movement is commonly considered an anti-consumption movement, but in many respects it is more realistically viewed as the vanguard of new forms of consumption', and this is also the case in terms of the manner in which EF! activists choose to live and work.

Given their rejection of many aspects of the Western consumer lifestyle, it is hardly surprising that there are some EF! activists who have been inspired to follow the example of very 'nature' oriented groups such as the Donga Tribe, and opted to live in 'benders' in the countryside on a more minimalist subsistence basis.[10] Such a choice could be construed as a very idealistic lifestyle option, but in the main, EF! activists are in fact city dwellers. This research reveals an awareness within EF! that the needs of the environment are seen to be tied to the needs of local communities, tenants and claimants groups and the provision of local services. As a result, EF! activists are often strongly motivated to become integrated and influential in the transformation of urban cultures and communities through methods such as food and housing co-operatives, participation in alternative economic networks,[11] reducing or sharing expensive consumer goods and aspiring to self-sufficiency. Here we see the strong socio-cultural dimension which typifies many of the groups within NSMs (Crook, 1992, p.151) and this again raises the issue of 'cultural capital', particularly with regard to work.

If EF! envisage a world without the trading systems which transport mahogany from Brazil and all of its associated bureaucracies, then, they also envisage a world where work becomes radically redefined. If, as one EF! activist remarked '95% of the jobs people do are a waste of space'[12] then the alternative is seen to be to promote work that doesn't contribute to any of the bad practices targeted by EF! and is fulfilling and creative rather than just for the purpose of earning money to survive on. It is debatable whether, despite the lack of opportunities for young people generally, EF! activists would be interested in taking on 'straight' jobs given the long list of ethical objections which they would have to most business. Instead, several of the participants in this research, when they have taken jobs, have secured work in non-governmental organizations, local co-operatives or the voluntary sector. As Kennedy (1995, this volume) argues, there is a green cultural *milieux* within which protest groups are 'embedded'. Also, as a social formation its members are more committed to the 'reskilling of everyday life' (Giddens, 1991) — through self and community development — than in demanding full employment. Sociologically this process might well be explained in terms of the need for EF! activists to exert control over many of the objects and systems around them — to try and claim back some of the territory which international capital and the technological state has been seen to increasingly 'colonize' (Habermas, 1981).

So, if EF! are predominantly urban in terms of how they live and the changes they want to see happen are community based, then, there is something paradoxical about their tendency to hold a central philosophy of nature in conjunction with this.

(c) Philosophy of nature

The cultural transformation which is envisaged by EF! is in fact best understood in terms of the philosophy of Social Ecology. This is an eco-anarchist perspective which is based on 'a comprehensive holistic conception of the self, society and nature' (Clark, 1992, p.85). It argues for a transformation of existing society into an ecological one based on 'non-hierarchical relationships, decentralized democratic communities, and eco-technologies like solar power, organic agriculture, and humanly scaled industries' (Bookchin, 1990, p.155). Social Ecology starts from the premise that the domination of nature stems from the domination of each other — emerging with the development of hierarchical power systems. It has been a philosophy, particularly with the emergence of the Social Ecology Network during 1992, that EF! activists have gravitated towards both as a movement and as individuals.[13]

As has been argued more extensively elsewhere (Purkis, 1995), there are many reasons why UK EF! might appear to be subscribers to the Deep Ecology tradition — which places the human species on an equal footing with all non-human life and seeks to celebrate that relationship (see Tokar, 1988; Devall and Sessions, 1985, for a more comprehensive treatment). However, despite the prominence in EF!

iconography of 'wilderness' themes, this impression can be misleading. Although EF! activists often draw inspiration from the beauty of natural places to energize their campaigning, the UK does not have large tracts of wilderness like those in the USA or Canada, and only small areas of 'unspoilt' or uncultivated land. This context produces a different discourse of 'nature' altogether so, despite being influenced by their North American counterparts, it is important to recognize that EF! groups in the UK are using certain icons within their own specific discourse of nature.

Consequently, many actions such as the 'ethical shoplift' try to integrate a sense of the theatrical in order to create an 'affinity' with the indigenous peoples of the rain forests, and to bring home to the general public and media that the mahogany trade effects real people. This is yet another link between local actions and global events within EF!, and can be seen as part of a trend within contemporary British 'alternative' culture to sympathetically appropriate 'ethnic' identities from around the world (Hetherington, 1992 p.94). Often these sensibilities do involve some of the more spiritual dimensions of Deep Ecology, such as those practiced by groups like the Donga Tribe, but EF! as a group — though not necessarily as individuals — tend not to refer to the Earth as 'Mother', they rarely speak of spirits in nature nor do they take note of the Solstices to any great extent. Similarly, there seems little evidence to suggest that UK EF! activists favour saving nature solely for its own sake, as has been espoused by some US EF! activists (Tokar, 1988, p.19). The EF! conception of nature leans much closer to that offered by Social Ecology: to quote one activist 'I'm not into politics to make nature look nice ... its more human based'.[14] In effect then, EF! are employing certain strategies which — consciously or not — appear to gravitate between the discourses of Social and Deep Ecology, largely depending on whether or not there is a theoretical or practical need for doing so.

The organizational structure of EF!

In terms of its organizational structure, EF! is unlike any of the major environmental groups, in that it has no membership lists, no paid workers, no central office, 'only individuals united by the practice of putting the earth first'.[15] Each group is responsible for its own finances and agendas, and the local autonomy of groups is strongly emphasized in the 'Principles' — agreed during 1991 at the same time as the 'Aims' mentioned above — thus giving them the right to draw up the ground rules for any action which other groups might support. National gatherings occur two or three times a year, where EF! 'policy' is discussed and formulated.

The decentralized and anti-hierarchical structure of EF! is, judging from interviews, one of the major appeals for potential 'recruits', and one activist described being in EF! 'like bloodletting' compared to the restrictions experienced when working within Friends of the Earth and the Green Party.[16] Equally relevant to participation is the 'underlying principle ... that how far people go is entirely a matter for their personal choice, commitment and responsibility'.[17] Similarly there is an appeal in contributing to a movement which practices consensus decision-making, a process whereby prospective policies are formulated and then reformulated until a decision everyone agrees on has been arrived at.

In pursuing this ideal, EF! inevitably encounter one of the classic dilemmas of 'structureless' organizations — that of informal hierarchies based on charisma, experience or belligerence (see Freeman, 1984; Levine, 1984). As a result, there is a strong commitment to processes of self and group monitoring, qualities which are generally recognized as being a characteristic of NSMs, particularly when related to identity and lifestyle. Beck (1992) for instance has argued that identities based around class, locality and gender have been eroding for several decades, and that culturally and politically 'new sociations' are emerging, sometimes forming 'neo-tribes' or 'bunds' (Hetherington, 1990; Hetherington, 1992). People in these 'new sociations' are characterized by the ability to think **reflexively**; that is to confront the self in a society dominated by 'risk'[18] (Beck, 1992; Beck, et al 1994), and are said to be active in the flexible construction of 'biographical projects' (see Giddens, 1991). Although many of the writers prefer to concentrate more on the search for new identities within the groups and their 'symbolicness' rather than on the motivating forces which brought them together in the first place, important points are being made. Clearly EF! is a 'new sociation' of some sort, and the open structure of the movement useful for the 'search for identity', but the need for 'involvement' (to paraphrase Hetherington, 1990, p.33) is not necessarily greater than the need for 'organization'. The evidence seems to suggest that EF! are as reflexive about themselves as a group as they are as individuals, and they take very seriously their commitment to working non-violently and non-hierarchically.

Serious or not, this commitment to alternative structures returns us to the point raised earlier concerning the 'vagueness' of part (iii) of the EF! aims.

The kind of society envisaged by EF! — read through Social Ecology — requires a radical reorganization of our relationships with each other, and for this to take place, power has to be seen to be completely devolved, and everyone accountable for their actions. However, though networked to a variety of other groupings EF! are relatively small and their influence is likely to be minimal, particularly as they are predominantly concerned with action.[19] Similarly, with a very full calendar of actions, and apart from the groups 'gatherings', there is little scope for encouraging movement analysis or for discussing EF!'s possible role in the community. More importantly, there is a certain reluctance to draw up comprehensive blueprints of a future society, either to work with themselves or to use in debate with the public or media.

It is possible to see here — as with the rediscovery of classic problems of 'structureless' in organizations (see above) — the common preoccupation that anti-hierarchical movements have with imposing authority or acting prescriptively, particularly with a view to future visions. Although most commonly associated with the Anarchist movement — with whom EF! show something of an affinity — at times their inability at a micro level to fully realize a political culture based on equal responsibility could be construed as a weakness.[20] Yet even to aim for something of this nature is very idealistic considering how most political organizations work with a fixed hierarchy of responsibility based around the length of time individuals have 'served', and prohibit spontaneous volunteering for particular posts.

The campaigning strategy of Earth First!

One of the most distinctive features of EF! campaigning is the use of the slogan 'No Compromise in the Defence of the Earth'. Apart from the fact that it has its origins in the North American canon of eco-slogans, the implication is that EF! are not prepared to follow other environmental groups down the path of a more 'reformist' politics.[21] Similarly we might expect that their campaigning strategies would also be very different. In this final section, this particular area will be explored and related to the issue of idealism and the kind of future EF! envisage. If there exists a focal point for this, it lies in the question 'how do you change the world?'.

Here, the question of 'compromise' is crucial. For groups such as Friends of the Earth or Greenpeace, activism has to be carefully sanctioned by their head offices, it is often planned months in advance with all of the legal permutations anticipated, and it is rare indeed for a member of these organizations to be arrested, with the exception of an 'elite' few Greenpeace activists. In contrast, EF! actively flaunt the law, believing that they are obeying a 'higher law' by doing so (see Background section) and the structure of EF! makes it impossible for companies to sue it as an organization. Since in Western Democracies change is usually seen to be negotiated through rational debate and compromise — with 'rational' read as reasonable, logical and ordered — this is a problem for EF! who regard the destruction of the planet as irrational (see Lange, 1990, p.457) Consequently whilst EF! appear not to be playing-the-game, they are in fact engaging in a complicated process of maximizing their political options. A non-negotiable slogan such as 'No Compromise in the Defence of the Earth' is both a way of indicating the type of society which they want, and also as a position from which to argue and negotiate, depending on whether they are dealing with the companies or the public (see North, 1994).

The 'ethical shoplift' illustrates the complexity of the issue of compromise: on the one hand they compromised by agreeing to talk to the management and leave the store, yet in another sense their preparedness to repeat the actions suggests otherwise. In effect EF! can be seen to be maximizing their options trying to keep in the public eye.

This very public nature of EF! actions marks their tactics out as different from other environmental groups in the following way. Most political activism of any kind takes place in streets, parks, forecourts and at factory gates. What is significant about many of the EF! actions is that they are taking the 'problem' to the people involved in creating it, and 'colonizing' private or capitalist space for short lengths of time. This is significant for two reasons:

(a) EF! are reaching the public in the very places which are normatively conceived of as safe from political agitation, and transforming them into sites for struggle.

(b) The location offers an unusual space for political debate, as activists mingle with the public, staff, the media and the police, sometimes for many hours at a time.

However, these unique situations do sometimes produce heated exchanges between EF! and other parties present, usually revolving around the argument that EF! are being too 'idealistic'. For instance, a fairly typical question which is often asked of EF! activists in such a situations is: 'but what about jobs?' It is important to see this as a pivotal issue for EF! campaigning strategy, since without a comprehensive answer to this question, EF! are not going to going to win over large sections of the population. Although there is now an extensive literature on 'green economics' (e.g. Elkins, 1986), the process of getting some of the more 'idealistic' visions across — many of which propose radical reorganizations of everyday living — can be quite difficult. These difficulties often result in a sense of pragmatism: thus an end to the mahogany trade is called for rather than the end of long distance trading *per se*; Third World Debt must be stopped, not the whole of international capitalism; road building is debated in conjunction with more public and co-operative transport systems, rather than demanding an end to car use as such. The information which is handed out on actions such as 'ethical shoplifts' is consistent with this, and is designed to provide the public with practical ideas to help end the practice in question, without using alarmist language or utopian projections.

The discussion in this section has so far concentrated on some of the conditions which 'frame' EF! strategies. I turn now to the wider issue of how EF! respond more directly to the question 'how do you change the world?'

As has been pointed out by several writers on contemporary society, it is not easy to locate 'green politics' in terms of left/right or reformist/revolutionary schematas (Dobson 1990; Ferris 1995). Whilst there are certainly sections of the Green movement who are active within these traditional parameters, many commentators overlook the fact that green politics is a **culturally** based phenomenon. Indeed, although there are many philosophical ancestors to green politics it is important to see what is happening in the 1990s as a new configuration, a new historical moment. When we try to understand the sensibilities of a movement such as EF! in terms of ideology, it is possible to see more than just a philosophy about the politics of distributing the earth's resources, but rather a way of 'being'. The matter of changing the world is best understood as something that is done in a variety of public and private contexts through a new ethical cultural process or 'aesthetic'. But new ways of 'being' and 'aesthetics' are not conditions which are necessarily appreciated by the wider population of Britain, and how they might come to entertain these notions is a question of how influential EF! are on political culture generally.

In terms of the themes of EF!'s campaigning in it's first few years there was a tendency towards exclusiveness, particularly on rain forest issues, but it's appeal has broadened in recent years mainly because of being in the vanguard of the anti-roads movement. The context for this has been the building of motorway extensions or link roads through or near to established communities — such as Leytonstone in East London and Pollock near Glasgow.[22] Consequently these campaigns have never really been the exclusive preserve of EF! or other young environmental protesters, and more a cross section of local communities — most publicly school children and pensioners.[23] As the momentum of the direct action against the roads has increased, so the focus of the new environmentalism has broadened to take on related issues such as local democracy, the destruction of communities and the right to protest (see Vidal, 1994, p.7). This has been the case also in Manchester, where most of this research has been conducted, as EF! have forged alliances on a number of issues such as inner city green spaces, air pollution, toxic waste incinerators and high profile reclaiming the streets for bicycles. It is possible then, that the more EF! become involved with community resistance, the more influence they will also have on issues such as lifestyle, trading systems, local self-determination and employment.

Conclusions

An action such as an 'ethical shoplift' can be understood as a manifestation of a particular political sensibility: one which focuses serious global concerns into a series of local practices governed by matters of responsibility and choice of lifestyle. Based on a 'holistic' analysis of Western consumption patterns, EF! as an radical direct action group believe that by contesting every conceivable situation in which ecological 'crimes' are deemed to take place, they can create a change both in company policy and in the public's attitude to the world in which they live. EF!'s organizational structure makes it completely unique within environmental politics due to its completely decentralized and anti-authoritarian nature. Indeed, when seem in the context of the explosion of 'green cultures' onto the political scene in recent years, particularly the anti-roads movement and the anti-Criminal Justice Act campaigns, it is possible to see EF! not just a movement with new agendas in alternative politics, but as part of culture adopting increasingly different structural forms.

However, although EF! are being idealistic in their long term vision of a society adhering to some of the principles of Social Ecology, in their day to day activism they show a pragmatism and a reflexivity of purpose as to what is feasible. The urban base to EF! also gives them access to a cross section of society, which other idealistic groups or tribes such as the Dongas or the New Age Travellers — living more 'wild' existence's — might not have, and this could have repercussions for how they are seen.

Ultimately, in terms of their position in the history of environmental protest, it is possible to see them as the first grassroots globally conscious environmental group in the West. Thus, as Luke has argued, EF! demonstrate an 'aesthetics of action' and a capacity to act swiftly, fuelled by a particular nature-philosophy, that illustrates 'all of the organizational possibilities of resistance in post-modern informational societies in one large but loose associational web' (1994 p.17).

Acknowledgement and notes

This chapter owes most to the wonderful and courageous people within the EF! movement — particularly those based in Manchester. I also wish to thank the following for their comments, support and stress management methods during the writing of the various draftings of this paper: Chayley Collis, James Bowen, Phil Mole, Paul Kennedy and those people who gave me words of encouragement or advice at the Alternative Futures and Popular Protest Conference during April 1995 in Manchester.

1. In North America, EF! origins lie in the radical wing of conservation organizitions such as the Sierra Club and Wilderness Society, whereas in the UK activists' histories are usually rooted in the Peace Movement, the Women's Movement, Anarchist Groups and organizations such as Friends of the Earth or Greenpeace.
2. *What is Earth First!?*, (1993), Manchester EF! p.1.
3. A vast literature exists on the organizational structure of these movements, their reasons for mobilizing, their continuity with or departure from 'older' social protest movements, and how the NSMs sustain their activities over time. These debates aside, I am referring here to the Peace, Environmental, Women's, Civil Rights, Animal Rights/Liberation, Lesbian/Gay Movements.
4. Christine, interview 26/11/92.
5. *EF! Action Update*, No.3, Spring 1992.
6. These so called 'bank actions' are done in conjunction with the group LAMB (The Lloyds and Midland Boycott Campaign).
7. Texas Homecare officially stopped stocking mahogany in early 1994. *EF! Action Update*, No. 9, March 1994, p.3.
8. A useful indication is the kind of criteria employed by *The Ethical Consumer* magazine: assessments of a company's ethicality is made on the grounds of whether they support the arms trade, experiment on animals, support oppressive regimes, and so forth.
9. The phrase was initially coined by the Women's Movement in the late 1960s, and emphasized the importance of consistency between public beliefs and private actions.

10. The Donga Tribe sprang out of the protest against the extension of the M3 motorway through Twyford Down in Hampshire during late 1992 and most of 1993. Abandoning most of the trappings of modern city living, the Dongas — named after the 3000 year old Celtic pathways — became the last line of defence to prevent the road being built. By living in makeshift tents or 'benders' made out of branches and tarpaulin, the thirty or so protesters have had considerable influence on the environmental movement in general and the anti-roads movement in particular. See for instance Plows (1995).

11. Here I am thinking of the Local Exchange Trading Systems (or LETS), where individuals 'buy' and 'sell' services using locally determined 'prices' or value, through a 'bank', thus by-passing the formal taxation system. Originating on Vancouver Island in 1982 as a means of helping communities survive a bitter recession, the LETS took root in the UK in the early 1990s, and in 1994 there were more than 200 such schemes in operation.

12. Alison, interview, 10/11/92.

13. The Social Ecology Network sprang out of a visit to the UK in 1992 by Murray Bookchin, and there has been something of an overlap between EF! activists and those in the Network.

14. Tamara, interview, 17/11/92.

15. What is Earth First!? , (op cit) p.1.

16. Louis, interview, 6/1/93.

17. *What is Earth First!?* (op cit p.1).

18. Beck's 'Risk thesis' is based around the notion that modern society has become one increasingly governed by economic and industrial transformations of an almost uncontrollable nature, and the repercussions of this socially, politically and even sexually, have moved us into an era where 'risk' permeates everything.

19. Without a membership list, and given a high turnover of in particular student activists, it is difficult to estimate numbers. If 70 groups exist, then since large cities like Leeds, Manchester, London and Birmingham are able to muster 20-30 people for an action, there must be at least 500 people.

20. There is a very strong overlap between what is written in *Green Anarchist* magazine and the ideas and action of EF!

21. The exception being that in the UK there has been a tendency to drop the word 'Mother' from the slogan
22. The M11 and M77 respectively.
23. At Pollock school children demanded time off from lessons to go and protest against the M77, arguing that their health was already suffering from traffic pollution (Counter Information, No. 42, 1995).

References

Anonymous, (1993), 'Earth First! — As much a way of life?', *The Ethical Consumer*, Issue 26, October/November.

Beck, U. (1992), *Risk Society* , Sage, London.

Beck, U. and Giddens, A. and Lash, S. (1994), *Reflexive Modernization*, Polity, Cambridge.

Bookchin, M. (1990), *Remaking Society*, South End Press, Boston.

Bourdieu, P. (1984), *Distinction*, Routledge, London.

Carson, R. (1963), *Silent Spring*, Hamish Hamilton, London.

Clark, J. (1992), 'What is Social Ecology?', *Society and Nature*, Vol.1 No.1.

Crook, S. et al (1992), *Postmodernization*, Sage, London.

Counter Information, (1995), No. 42.

Devall, B. and Sessions, G. (1985), *Deep Ecology*; Peregrine Smith,Layton.

Dobson, A. (1990), *Green Political Thought*, Harper Collins, London.

Earth First! (1991), *Action Update*, No. 2.

Earth First! (1992), *Action Update*, No. 3.

Earth First! (1993), *What is Earth First!?*

Eckersley, R. (1989), 'Green Politics and the New Class: Selfishness or Virtue, *Political Studies*, June, Vol. xxxvii No.2.

Ethical Consumer Research Association, (1993) *The Ethical Consumer Guide To Everyday Shopping*, ECRA Publishing, Manchester.

Elkins, P. (1986), *The Living Economy*, Routledge, London.

Ferris, J. (1995), 'Ecological versus Social Rationality: Can there be Green Social Policies?' in Dobson, A. and Lucardie, P., *The Politics of Nature*, Routledge, London.

Freeman, J. (1984), 'The Tyranny of Structurelessness', reprinted in *Untying the Knot*, Dark Star/Rebel Press, London.

Giddens, A. (1991), *Modernity and Self Identity*, Polity Press, Cambridge.

Habermas, J. (1981), 'New Social Movements', *Telos*, 49, Fall.

Harvey, D. (1989), *The Condition of Postmodernity*, Basil Blackwell, Oxford.

Hetherington, K. (1990), 'On the Homecoming of the Stranger: New Social Movements or New Sociations?', *Lancaster Regionalism Group Working Paper 39*.

Hetherington, K. (1992), 'Stonehenge and its Festival', in Shields R, (ed.) *Lifestyle Shopping*, Routledge, London.

Lang, T. and Hines, C. (1993), *The New Protectionism* , Earthscan, London.

Lange, J. (1990), 'Refusal to Compromise: The Case of Earth First!', *Western Journal of Speech Communication*, 54.

Lash, S. and Urry, J. (1994), *Economies of Signs and Spaces*, Sage, London.

Levine, C. (1984), 'The Tyranny of Tyranny', reprinted in *Untying the Knot*, Dark Star/Rebel Press, London.

Luke, T. (1994), 'Ecological Politics and Local Struggles: Earth First! as an Environmental Resistance Movement', *Current Perspectives in Social Theory*, 14.

Melucci, A. (1989), *Nomads of the Present*, Hutchinson/Radius, London.

Miller, D. ed. (1995), *Acknowledging Consumption*, Routledge, London.

Mole, P. (1994), *Manchester: Postmodern City?*, Unpublished paper, Department of Sociology, Manchester Metropolitan University.

North, P. (1994), *Save our Solsbury: the View from the Hill*, paper presented to Politics of Cultural Change Conference, July, University of Lancaster.

Offe, C. (1985), 'New Social Movements; challenging the boundaries of institutional politics',*Social Research*, 52 p.4.

Plows, A. (1995), 'Eco-Philosophy and Popular Protest: The Significance & Implications of the Ideology and Actions of the Donga Tribe', *Alternative Futures and Popular Protest Conference Papers*, Volume II, Manchester Metropolitan University.

Purkis, J. (1995), 'If Not You, Who? If Not Now, When? — Rhetoric and Reality in the Vision of Earth First!', *Alternative Futures and Popular Protest Conference Papers*, Volume II, Manchester Metropolitan University.

Roberts, K. (1992), *Young Adults in Europe,* Mimeograph, Department of Sociology, Liverpool.

Scarce, R. (1990), *Eco-Warriors.*, Noble Press, Chicago.

Schumacher, E. F. (1973), *Small is Beautiful,* Harper & Row, New York.

Singer, P. (1976), *Animal Liberation* , Jonathan Cape, London.

Tokar, B. (1988), 'Social Ecology, Deep Ecology and the Future of Green Political Thought', *The Ecologist,* 18.

Townley, A. (1992), 'Earth First!' (news feature), *Green Magazine,* July.

Vidal, J. (1994), 'The Real Earth Movers', *The Guardian* , (7 December).

11 The other side of the barricades: policing protest

P.A.J. Waddington

Contrary to the fears expressed during the passage of the Public Order Act 1986, the policing of most protest remains low key: the law is rarely enforced and force is even more rarely threatened or used. Yet, the police achieve extensive control over the conduct of protesters. They do so not by confronting them, but by using various stratagems to 'win them over' and subtlely control their actions. What the police seek is the avoidance of confrontation, minimization of traffic disruption and, most of all, the absence of any serious threat to established political institutions.

However, such low-key control of demonstrations by the police is both predicated upon, and in turn reinforces, the institutional order. As those institutions become increasingly irrelevant, there is the danger that the police of political protest will become increasingly coercive.

Introduction

Contemporary expressions of concern at the public order provisions of the Criminal Justice and Public Order Act are reminiscent of the anxieties that were expressed just as forcefully about the Public Order Act, 1986. Then, as now, the Act was thought to threaten democratic freedoms and usher in an era of police repression (Greater, 1985; Staunton, 1985; Thornton, 1985; Greater London Council, 1986; Hillyard & Percy-Smith, 1988; Robertson, 1989). However, the most feared provisions of the 1986 Act — those allowing the police to ban marches, and impose conditions on marches and assemblies — remain largely unused. The Metropolitan Police, in whose jurisdiction the vast majority of protest activities — certainly high-profile demonstrations — take place, has used the Act to impose conditions on no more than a handful of occasions and has imposed no bans. A survey of police forces throughout England and Wales indicated that few of them had ever used the powers the Act granted them (Waddington, 1994b).

The failure (or is it the refusal?) of the police to use the 1986 Act to restrain protest activity requires explanation. That explanation may enable us to make an educated guess about how alternative protest is likely to be policed in future. It is to these issues that this chapter is addressed.

Public order policing in a capital city

The research on which this paper rests was conducted between February 1990 and the early hours of New Year's Day 1993. It consisted of a participant observation of public order policing in the Metropolitan Police District (that is the area within the circumference of the M25 minus the City of London). Throughout this period I was advised by the police whenever they first knew of demonstrations due to take place within the MPD. Thereafter, I attended negotiations between the police and protest organizers, observed planning for the operations, and accompanied the senior forward commander responsible for the operation during the event itself.

The period of these observations was politically tumultuous: one of the first operations I attended turned into the poll tax riot of March 1990 and I observed two following anti-poll tax marches, one of which culminated in disorder. From September 1990 until March 1991 there was intense protest activity directed against British involvement in the Gulf War. Towards the end of the period the NUM and TUC organized huge marches to protest at the closure of coal mines. Throughout the period there were marches by the NUS against student grants, gay rights campaigners, opponents of British involvement in Northern Ireland, trade unions, sundry emigre groups protesting about conditions in their homelands, and often violent confrontations between neo-fascist and anti-fascist groups. In all 61 political protests were observed. In addition, I observed two

Notting Hill Carnivals with their overtones of 'resistance through ritual' (Gutzmore, 1978, 1982; Cohen, 1980, 1982; Pryce, 1985).

The 'trouble' with public order policing

Why, then, did the police not use their legal powers more assertively to control protest activity? The simple answer was that to do so was not worth the 'trouble'. To understand why not involves analysis of what constitutes 'trouble' for the police.

Chatterton (Chatterton, 1979; Norris, 1989) has convincingly argued that routine police work by low ranking officers is motivated by the desire to avoid trouble. He distinguishes between two types of trouble: 'on the job' and 'in the job trouble'. 'On the job trouble' refers to the problems which officers routinely confront in the course of their duty on the street. It includes pacifying rancorous disputes, asserting police authority against those who might challenge it, dealing with worthless items of 'lost' property handed to the police, and temporarily abandoned vehicles blocking the traffic. In other words, the myriad incidents that police are called upon to deal with. In dealing with them, police habitually rely upon expedient and informal solutions — the 'Ways and Means Act'. Rarely is the law enforced, but it is sometimes used to achieve other purposes. Thus, non-compliant parties to a dispute might be arrested in order to facilitate the pacification of the dispute, but the offence with which they are charged is likely to be a 'resource charge' bearing only an arbitrary relationship to the reasons for making the arrest (Chatterton, 1976, 1983).

'In the job trouble' refers to managing the officer's relationship with the police bureaucracy and criminal justice system. For example, having made an arrest on a 'resource charge', the officer will need to ensure that the paperwork conveys the impression that the arrest conformed scrupulously to correct procedures. What officers seek to avoid is any 'comeback' either from their superiors or from others within the criminal justice system.

Chatterton's analysis applies remarkably well to the policing of public order. Despite the fact that such operations are commanded by officers of senior rank and occur often in the glare of publicity, rather than the obscurity of encounters on the street, those involved seem to be motivated by the same desire to avoid these two sources of 'trouble'.

Confrontation - a recipe for trouble

On the job trouble

Contrary to what might be imagined, banning a march or imposing conditions is perceived by senior commanders not as a means of asserting control, but as a recipe for 'trouble'. The issue arose most acutely with respect to the two anti-poll tax demonstrations that followed in the wake of the poll tax riot (this is considered at greater length in Waddington, 1994a). There was no doubt that the police would have preferred neither march to have been held, but given that the protests were going to take place officers saw little purpose in needlessly confronting marchers with a ban. They anticipated that if the march was banned protesters would seek to frustrate the ban. This they might do in two ways: on the one hand, by exploiting the law which does not allow police to ban assemblies. Thus, protesters might be invited to attend an assembly to be held where the banned march would have departed from, and then be invited to walk en masse to another assembly at the place where the march had been intended to terminate. Such a 'walk' would undoubtedly constitute a 'march' in contravention of the ban, but to enforce the ban would require a huge police operation and probably spark disorder. Alternatively, protesters might express their frustration at the ban by engaging in disorder at locations remote from the site of the original march. Either way, an organized march that assembles at a known location and proceeds to a predetermined terminus is far easier to police than some form of disorganized and indeterminate action.

In both these cases conditions were imposed on the route of the marches. Even this was done with some trepidation and accompanied by attempts to placate the organizers of the demonstration. Thus, in the case of the second anti-poll tax march in south London, the police assisted the protest organizers to find an assembly place that was not prohibitively expensive and prevailed on the local authority to allow the use of a local park in which to hold a rally. On the occasion of the last anti-poll tax march the route stipulated by the police was identical to that proposed by the organizers. Its purpose was to demonstrate to powerful political interests opposed to the march that the police were 'doing something' without antagonizing the protesters.

However, these two cases were quite exceptional. Normally, not only did the police avoid recourse to their powers to ban and impose conditions on marches, they were reluctant even to make arrests for straightforward breaches of the law. There was no shortage of occasions when the police would have been entitled to arrest protesters, but they abstained from doing so. During briefings subordinates were instructed not to make arrests unless authorized to do so by senior officers. Again, the concern was to avoid confrontation that might rapidly escalate into serious disorder.

Why this aversion to possible escalation? First, and probably foremost, senior officers were aware that disorder entails the threat of injuries to officers and members of the public alike, and damage to property. If they needed a reminder, the anti-poll tax riot provided it. The action of trying forcibly to remove a small disorderly and violent group from the entrance to Downing Street escalated into the most serious riot in central London for a hundred years. Secondly, senior officers are also aware that once disorder erupts it is extremely difficult for them to control, a difficulty that even extends to controlling the actions of their officers. Again, the poll tax riot provides ample illustration: co-ordination of police actions broke down, particularly since the radio system was unable to cope with the demands placed upon it. Officers under the influence of 'red mist' (that potent cocktail of frustration, anger, aggression and exhilaration that is experienced in such circumstances) failed or refused to comply with the orders of their superiors. For example, despite repeated requests not to use two-tone sirens (thereby 'advertising' the occurrence and location of disorder), drivers of personnel carriers continued to use them late into the night. Thirdly, officers were also aware that in the 'heat of battle' officers are prone to act in ways that discredit them and the Metropolitan Police.

In the job trouble

There was, however, another source of trouble that arose from confrontation and disorder — 'in the job trouble'. At the termination of a public order operation involving any disorder officers are required immediately to complete a detailed report to the Assistant

Commissioner responsible for 'Territorial Operations' at Scotland Yard. Serious disorder would almost invariably be followed by an inquiry which, officers fear, would second-guess their decisions with the benefit of hindsight. Thus, following the poll tax riot a team of eight officers under the command of a Deputy Assistant Commissioner spent over a year compiling a debrief report that was savagely critical of the planning for and command of the operation and made over 150 recommendations (Metcalfe, 1991). Officers also confidently anticipate that their actions and those of their subordinates will be subjected to criticism in parliament and the mass media. Apart from being intrinsically uncomfortable, such retrospective scrutiny is thought to pose a threat to careers. Throughout the planning of major operations close attention is paid to how decisions might appear to any subsequent inquiry.

In addition, officers were anxious to avoid legal challenges to their actions. Legal commentators may confidently assert that the courts would be unlikely to interfere with the professional judgment of responsible police officers (Smith, 1987), but the police themselves were not so sanguine. The law might give them the power to impose bans and conditions, but that law had yet to be tested before a court and if they lost a precedent-setting case, the consequences might be felt throughout the police for years to come.

Confrontation threatened not only 'on the job', but also 'in the job trouble'. Enforcing the law might be regarded as unduly provocative and, therefore, it was regarded as better that alternative means be employed to exert control over protest demonstrations.

'Winning over'

The police could not afford to allow protesters to do as they wished. Indeed, they sought a measure of control far beyond that which the law allows. The 1986 Act merely requires the organizer of a march to notify police of the day and date of the march, its route and his or her name and address. Although these requirements were justified by the government as initiating a process of negotiation, strictly speaking the organizer is only obliged to furnish this minimal information. The police want to know much more in order to plan their operation and they also want to influence the conduct of the demonstration. Their aim is not just a peaceful demonstration, but a minimally disruptive one.

Like low ranking officers on the streets, officers engaged in the planning of public order operations achieve their aims through informal expediency. What the police exploit are not their legal powers, but their much more formidable social position. First, they rely upon organizers approaching them, which they almost invariably do long before the demonstration is due to be held. There is a simple and compelling reason why protest organizers approach the police — to seek assistance. The law no more requires that the police provide assistance to protesters than it demands that protesters furnish the police with all the information required to plan the policing operation. However, without police assistance most marches would find it difficult, if not impossible, to negotiate the traffic congested streets of central London. Therefore, the police are able to offer a service to protesters in return for the latter's willingness to negotiate. Those who negotiate in 'good faith' find that there is much more that the police can offer them. First, they find that the police are personally friendly and helpful. Negotiations are habitually conducted in an amicable atmosphere: protest organizers are greeted with handshakes and sometimes the offer of refreshment, jokes are exchanged and offers of assistance made — it is anything but confrontational. Perhaps the most dramatic example of this was the organization of the NUM march in protest at the closure of the coal mines in October 1992. Despite the fact that the union was unable to give the statutory six days notice, no mention was made of that requirement. Instead, the police virtually organized the demonstration on behalf of the NUM. They arranged the parking of coaches; they negotiated with the authorities responsible for Hyde Park to close the roads that traverse it during the march; they arranged to facilitate the transfer of leaders from Hyde Park to Central Hall where the lobby of Parliament would take place and when the park became so congested that marchers were unable to exit easily, they arranged for alternative exits to be opened. Indeed, as the negotiations were concluded at Scotland Yard on the Saturday prior to the march, the senior forward commander joked to the NUM representative that if the march was a disaster he expected the NUM to offer him a job!

Secondly, the police have many resources that they can exploit to convince protest organizers to comply with their wishes. Negotiations almost invariably take place in police premises, in which the organizer is the 'guest' and implicitly expected to act as such — this, the police call, the 'home ground advantage'. The organizers find themselves dealing with a large bureaucracy which selectively facilitates certain courses of action. For example, the police obtain all the information they feel they need by the simple expedient of supplying an official notification form which blurs the distinction between information that is legally required and that which is simply requested. The police issue a receipt confirming that notification has been given which acts as an incentive to complete the form. Organizers are also amateurs amongst professionals. Police officers know the detailed topography of an area, how long it will take to march from one point to another, the precise time at which darkness will fall, and whether roadworks are planned that will interfere with the march. The possession of so much expertise is a powerful instrument with which to convince organizers that they should comply with police wishes. A sharp intake of breath and the phrase, 'I wouldn't do that if I was you' can have a remarkable impact in such circumstances.

Finally, police officers employ certain negotiating tactics to object to organizer's plans without antagonizing them. The principle tactic is to appeal to safety. This is neatly illustrated by a well-rehearsed objection to the presence of vehicles at the head of any march. The reason why protest organizers seek to head marches with vehicles such as flat-back lorries is obvious: it provides an elevated platform on which to display and from which to broadcast slogans. The reason police object is equally obvious — the protesters own vehicle would not be under police command. Wittingly or not, the vehicle might take the wrong route leading the marchers astray, and it may be used as barricade and a ready supply of petrol bombs. However, it is not these arguments that police use to persuade protesters.They oppose such vehicles on the grounds of safety and convenience. Organizers are warned that vehicles tend to attract marchers who may try and climb aboard with the danger that they will fall beneath the wheels. They are also told that vehicles are ill-suited to being driven at walking pace for an extended period. This has two consequences: first, the vehicle is likely to breakdown thus obstructing the march and obliging marchers to pass by the obstruction in the face of oncoming traffic. Secondly, the exhaust will quickly disgorge thick oily smoke that will envelope the marchers. Having persuaded the organizer not to head the march with a vehicle, the police then head the march with their own vehicle. During these observations, the 'control vans' that were used were aged and tended, in their dotage, to breakdown, necessitating police (and often marchers) pushing them aside. However, these were police vehicles under police command.

'Neat and tidy'

Police continue to use non-confrontational methods of controlling marchers on the day of the march. The public image of public order policing is dominated by the presence of officers in riot-gear. However, whilst 'mobile reserves' (frequently equipped with protective clothing and shields) were often deployed, the police went to considerable lengths to ensure that they were not seen by protesters and not deployed in riot-gear unless disorder had already broken out. Even sensitive high-profile demonstrations, such as the anti-poll tax demonstrations and Gulf War marches were policed predominantly by officers in ordinary uniform, in order to avoid accusations of 'provocation'.

How, then do the police exert control over the conduct of marchers? The principal agents of control are traffic officers who accompany the march and guide it through the streets. Traffic officers precede the marchers, closing intersections and diverting traffic whilst the march passes. Seeking to minimize traffic disruption, they usually allow oncoming traffic to pass on the off-side of a march and where the road is wide enough they will allow traffic to overtake. What they actually, and knowingly, achieve is to contain the march within a small, mobile traffic-free zone, surrounded on all sides by a 'moving wall of steel'. Not only does this contain marchers within this zone, but the police are seen as protecting the march, keeping passing traffic at a safe distance and preventing motorists performing dangerous manoeuvres in the immediate vicinity of the march.

In sum, by these various expedients the police contrive to achieve their goals of staging a peaceful and minimally disruptive protest march. Not only is the law an irrelevance, it is a positive threat. Only inept and inexperienced officers make any mention of the law at all. The Public Order Act is mentioned only in private, it is the 'Ways and Means Act' that prevails.

'Troublemakers'

Does this mean that whatever legislators might do, democracy is safe in the hands of the police? No, it does mean that safeguards and threats to democratic structures not only reside in formal constitutional arrangements, but in the actual practices of those who participate in protest and its control. The principal threat to democratic protest is not simply (or even principally) the Criminal Justice and Public Order Act, but rather the capacity of some external actors to make trouble for senior police officers. That is, they can create 'in the job trouble'.

Whilst the 1986 Public Order Act is largely redundant, other legislation is rigorously enforced during public order operations. The most notable example is the Sessional Order, whose enforcement relies on charging offenders with petty offences that the police confess are difficult successfully to prosecute. What is the Sessional Order? At the beginning of each parliamentary session both Houses of Parliament pass an order instructing the Commissioner of the Metropolitan Police to keep the highways in the vicinity of the Palace of Westminster free from obstruction and disorderly gatherings. It is enforced by sections 52 and 54 of the Metropolitan Police Act 1839, under which the Commissioner issues directions. By convention, an area of approximately a mile radius stretching from the Palace of Westminster to the north of the river Thames is designated as the Sessional Area. Whilst parliament is sitting, all processions and assemblies are strictly forbidden in this area. Indeed, the enforcement of the Sessional Order is so rigorous that it exceeds the strict parameters of the law, for even the display of placards in the immediate vicinity of the Palace of Westminster is effectively forbidden.

Why do the police, who are prepared to be so tolerant of so much protest, refuse to tolerate even the mildest displays of dissent within the Sessional Area? It is because they fear the 'trouble' that parliamentarians can, and occasionally do, cause if any violation of parliamentary privilege occurs. Protests staged within the Sessional Area, especially if they become in the slightest degree disorderly, are expected to occasion questions being asked on the floor of the House of Commons, complaints by parliamentarians to the Home Secretary, and thence to the Commissioner, who in turn will pass them to his subordinates. There will be, in short, a considerable amount of 'paper' to be written: explanations will need to be proffered, senior officers will be held to account and careers threatened.

The Sessional Order is not alone: protest is allowed in only one royal park — Hyde Park. No law (apart from the park bye-laws) forbids it, but the royal parks are notionally the private property of the sovereign and their purpose is not for holding protest demonstrations. Thus, when the militant (but entirely non-violent) gay rights campaign group, 'OutRage!', attempted to hold a rally at the Queen Victoria Memorial (the 'wedding cake' that stands immediately in front of the public face of Buckingham Palace), the police hurriedly mobilized a small army to prevent them. The capacity of the royal household to create 'in the job trouble' is legendary.

A similar view is taken towards the dignity of foreign embassies. Britain is treaty-bound to maintain the dignity of all diplomatic premises, but the legislative underpinning for this is insecure. However, this does not deter the police from taking vigorous steps to protect embassies. For example, throughout the Gulf War the police routinely mounted a large operation to protect the US Embassy, even though it was never threatened. When, during a small march by Iraqi sympathizers, one protester tried to burn an American flag, it was snatched from his grasp and quickly extinguished in an uncharacteristically confrontational manner. This action was justified on the grounds that staff in the embassy would complain if they saw their flag being burned. Although I did not witness it, I was told by several independent sources that the long-running picket of the South African Embassy by opponents of apartheid had caused the police in central London tremendous problems. On the one hand, they were being pressed by the Foreign Office to 'do something' about the picket but, on the other hand, were unable to secure convictions in the Bow Street Magistrate's Court when they did make arrests.

In other words, whether or not the police confront political protesters is strongly influenced by political pressure. For the police, the Sessional Area and locations like royal palaces and embassies offer no room for manoeuvre. They are where officers feel obliged to 'die in a ditch' (Waddington, 1993).

Institutions and protest

The dual forms that 'trouble' takes are but two sides of the same coin. 'Trouble' is the manifestation of institutionalized power as it affects the police. 'Trouble' arises when social and political institutions are threatened. However, institutions not only suppress dissent, they also protect it — provided, of course, it remains within the 'rules of the game'.

The lengths to which the police go to avoid confrontation indicates the extent of institutional restraints over police action. Police are the custodians of the state's ultimate monopoly of legitimate force, but the use of force — indeed, any form of coercion — is precarious for the police. The legitimacy of police authority in a liberal democracy relies on the claim that they protect citizens, not threaten them (Waddington, 1991). Protest activity is an expression of citizenship par excellence and any police interference with it exposes officers to the de-legitimating accusation that they are suppressing democratic dissent. Although the police rarely articulate respect for the democratic rights of protesters, their practice is suffused with such respect. Protesters routinely violate the law with effective immunity, for whilst their actions may be illegal they remain within the institutional 'rules of the game'. It is these rules that police both utilize and reproduce in the course of steering protesters towards peaceful and non-disruptive expressions of dissent. They are utilized when police appeal to the need for protesters to act responsibly, for example by paying due heed to the safety of marchers and not inconveniencing other road users. Such institutional expectations are reproduced by the repeated occurrence of peaceful protest. At the same time, of course, if protesters breach those institutional parameters then they will find themselves confronted by the police who fear the 'trouble' that such a violation will arouse.

Thus, unwittingly, the police routinely reproduce the boundaries of legitimate protest. Those who do not threaten 'trouble' find that the police facilitate their protests, possibly even lend it a measure of legitimacy as they escort it through the streets, stopping traffic that might impede its progress. Those who threaten trouble find their actions frustrated and possibly confronted. In doing so, the police act as a conduit for institutional pressures to be felt.

The politics of policing 'alternative' protest

This analysis has direct and important implications for the future policing of protest. It is not only to the provisions of the Criminal Justice and Public Order Act that we should turn our attention, but to changing institutional structures within which that Act may be used.

The police do not view all protesters with hostility, on the contrary, they have considerable affection for the trade unions, the Campaign for Nuclear Disarmament, the National Union of Students, Anti-Apartheid and other 'professional protesters'. This is more than a expression of opinion: at one Gulf War march the forward commander expressed apparently genuine relief that the chief steward was a national organizer of a large trade union; he was reassured that the stewarding of the march would be competently done and trouble was unlikely. These are organizations that play within the 'rules of the game'.

The 'opposition' are extreme left-wing and anarchist groups who show scant respect for the 'rules of the game' and, thereby, threaten trouble. Even anarchist groups who agree to 'play the game' can find that the police facilitate their democratic rights. Thus, an anarchist group who sought to protest against the holding of the 1992 general election, found that the police allowed them to do so despite the refusal by the Department of the Environment of permission to assemble and hold a rally on Trafalgar Square. Not only did the police protest strongly to the Department about their refusal, they refused to enforce the Trafalgar Square Regulations, deciding instead merely to report the organizers to the DoE and leave it to them to prosecute.

Why do 'professional protesters' abide by the 'rules of the game'? In doing so, they reflect the historical settlement between labour and capital that incorporated the working class into established institutions. As Geary has documented (Geary, 1985), during the early years of this century the Labour Movement and the authorities tacitly conspired to 'cool' picket-line confrontation because it was in their mutual interest. Thus, conflict was deflected from the streets into institutionalized channels of parliamentary politics and 'collective bargaining'. Protest was transformed from 'stoning and shooting' to 'pushing and shoving' because its role was merely symbolic. Trade unions could rely upon the parliamentary arm of the Labour Movement to apply political pressure and solidarity of labour to enforce strikes, and, therefore, had little need of forcibly closing strike-bound premises.

This settlement did not, at least initially, embrace the unemployed. The Unemployed Workers Association did not benefit from low-key policing. Early 'hunger marches' were subjected to close police surveillance, not infrequent harassment and occasional violent suppression. It was not until the TUC recognised the UWA, thus bringing it within the framework of institutional politics, that policing shifted from suppression to accommodation.

However, institutionalized class conflict is now beginning to crumble with the result that strikers are once again feeling the coercive power of the state to an extent that had previously been restricted to those outside institutional structures, such as the unemployed. Since the 1960s strikes have been increasingly regarded as a major cause of Britain's relative industrial decline (Department of Employment, 1969). The collapse of traditional 'smoke stack' industries has undermined trade union power and their virtual exclusion from a position of influence over government during the Thatcher administration marginalized them even further. Increasingly unable to succeed by appealing to labour solidarity and exerting parliamentary pressure, unions finding themselves with little to lose have reverted to picketing methods designed forcibly to close premises. This, of course, has brought them into increasingly overt confrontation with the police (Bunyan, 1985; Scraton, 1985; Wiles, 1985). Thus, the confrontations between striking miners and the police during the miners' strike of 1984-85 was utterly predictable. To have negotiated 'peaceful' picketing would have been to embrace ineffectual means of prosecuting the strike. For their part, in the absence of alternative ways of containing the disorder associated with attempts to forcibly close coal pits the police made recourse to their ultimately coercive role.

Disadvantaged and deprived sections of the population find themselves excluded from institutionalized channels for the expression of grievances and resolution of conflict as the principle divisions in the social structure have become racialized. Racial and ethnic minorities find that institutions rooted in class relations are ill-suited to their needs and unresponsive to their problems (Lea & Young, 1982). However, as disturbances in Oxford, Cardiff and on Tyneside also testify, the alienation of young people who have little stake in the existing social order is not restricted to ethnic minorities alone.

New issues — feminism, environmentalism, animal rights — find little expression within these established institutional structures. Accordingly, excluded groups and those pursuing issues unrelated to employment relations have little incentive to 'play by the rules'. Equally, many of the more militant exponents of these 'new social movements' ideological eschew any accommodation with established social institutions, preferring to challenge public policies and vested interests through direct action that is calculated to bring them into confrontation with the police.

Furthermore, as the recent protests against live animal exports illustrate, institutional power is also shifting in ways that make incorporation into the institutions of the nation state increasingly irrelevant. Animal rights protesters seem successfully to have convinced even government ministers and the National Farmers Union of the rectitude of their cause, but this is of no avail if power rests in the European Union. Environmentalists who persuade their own government to eliminate 'acid rain' win a pyrrhic victory if sulphurous clouds originate from beyond national boundaries. In an increasingly global economy, national political institutions are inevitably marginalized.

This suggests that protest is unlikely to remain within the 'rules' of a 'game' that is increasingly ill-suited to the needs of participants. Therefore, police strategies based upon the existence and maintenance of those rules will become increasingly redundant. However, this does not mean that the police will be free from 'trouble', for there will continue to be powerful institutional interests capable of making trouble for the police if protest is not contained. Private corporations can effectively commandeer police resources by pointing to the illegality of their opponents' actions. New technologies that disrupt or destroy established patterns of work can be introduced in pursuit of profit, secure in the knowledge that any forceful opposition to such change will be contained by a legally empowered and riot-trained police force. The confrontations at the Warrington Messenger and at the News International plant at Wapping, and even more so during the 1984-85 miners' strike, may be portents of what is to come.

Nor should it be assumed that confrontation will necessarily be between the public police and new generations of protesters. The police itself is not immune to institutional change and may be marginalized as the state pulls back from its involvement in society and the economy. The private security industry may increasingly recognize a 'market opportunity' in protecting vested interests from the activities of protesters. Increasingly cash-strapped police forces find it difficult to maintain large and costly public order operations. In 1972 the Chief Constable of Birmingham ordered the closure of Saltley coke works rather than risk continued confrontation and possible escalation. Thus, mass picketing succeeded and the miners won a crucial victory. In the 1990s his successors might decide that they too must allow protesters to succeed because the police lack sufficient resources to prevent it. However, it would be naively optimistic to assume that private interests will comply as meekly as did the National Coal Board at Saltley. Under the commercial pressure of global competition, companies may very well conclude that if the public police are unable to protect them, they must protect themselves. Private detective agencies played a long and ignoble role in labour conflicts in the United States (Weiss, 1986, 1987) and there is no reason, in principle, to suppose that they could not fulfil an equivalent role in Britain.

Conclusion

The successful maintenance of order more by guile than by force may be just one aspect of an order that is fast disappearing. If it does, then the provisions of the Criminal Justice and Public Order Act may well be used to suppress dissent, along with other legislation and the common law. The police in Britain have never wanted for adequate public order powers, but they have been consistently disinclined to use them. As the institutional structures that supported such restraint atrophy, so may restraint itself.

References

Bunyan, T. (1985), 'From Saltley to Orgreave via Brixton', *Journal of Law and Society*, Vol.12, pp.293-303.

Chatterton, M. R. (1976), Police arrest powers as resources in peace-keeping, *Social Work Today*, Vol.7, pp.234-37.

Chatterton, M. R. (1979), 'The supervision of patrol work under the fixed points system' in Holdaway, S. (ed), *The British Police*, Edward Arnold, London.

Chatterton, M. R. (1983), Police work and assault charges in Punch, M. (ed.), *Control in the Police Organization*, M.I.T. Press, Cambridge, Mass.

Cohen, A. (1980), 'Drama and politics in the development of a London carnival', *Man*, Vol.15, pp. 65-87.

Cohen, A. (1982), 'A polyethnic London carnival as a contested cultural performance', *Ethnic and Racial Studies*, Vol.5, pp. 23-41.

Department of Employment (1969), *In Place of Strife*, H.M.S.O., London.

Geary, R. (1985), *Policing Industrial Disputes: 1893 to 1985*, Cambridge University Press, Cambridge.

Greater, L. (1985), *Public Order Plans — The Threat to Democratic Rights*, Greater London Council, London.

Greater London Council (1986), *The Control of Protest*, Greater London Council, London.

Gutzmore, C. (1978), 'Carnival, the state and the Black masses in the United Kingdom', *Black Liberator*, Vol.1, pp.8-27.

Gutzmore, C. (1982), 'The Notting Hill Carnival', *Marxism Today*, pp.31-33.

Hillyard, P. & Percy-Smith, J. (1988), *The Coercive State*, Fontana, London.

Lea, J. & Young, J. (1982), 'The riots in Britain 1981: urban violence and political marginalisation', in Cowell, D., Jones, T. & Young, J. (eds.), *Policing the Riots*, Junction Books, London.

Metcalfe, J. (1991), *Public order debriefing: Trafalgar Square riot*, unpublished, Metropolitan Police, London.

Norris, C. (1989), 'Avoiding trouble: the patrol officer's perception of encounters with the public', in Weatheritt, M. (ed.) *Police Research: Some Future Prospects*, Avebury, Aldershot.

Pryce, E. (1985), 'The Notting Hill Gate carnival — Black politics, resistance and leadership 1976-1978', *Caribbean Quarterly*, Vol.31, pp.35-52.

Robertson, G. (1989), *Freedom, The Individual and the Law*. Penguin, London.

Scraton, P. (1985), 'From Saltley gates to Orgreave: a history of the policing of recent industrial disputes', in Fine, B. & Millar, R. (eds.), *Policing the Miners' Strike*, Lawrence and Wishart, London.

Smith, A. T. H. (1987), *Offences Against Public Order*, Sweet and Maxwell, London.

Staunton, M. (1985), *Free to Walk Together?* National Council for Civil Liberties, London.

Thornton, P. (1985), *We Protest*, National Council of Civil Liberties, London.

Waddington, P.A.J. (1991), *The Strong Arm of the Law*, Clarendon, Oxford.

Waddington, P.A.J. (1993), 'Dying in a ditch: the use of police powers in public order', *International Journal of the Sociology of Law*, Vol.21, pp.335-53.

Waddington, P.A.J. (1994a), 'Coercion and accommodation: policing public order after the Public Order Act', *British Journal of Sociology* Vol.45, pp.367-85.

Waddington, P.A.J. (1994b), *Liberty and Order: Policing Public Order in a Capital City*, UCL Press, London.

Weiss, R. P. (1986), 'Private Detective Agencies and Labour Discipline in the United States, 1855-1946', *Historical Journal*, Vol.29, pp.87-107.

Weiss, R. P. (1987), 'From 'slugging detective' to 'labor relations': policing labour at Ford, 1930-1947', in Shearing, C. D. & Stenning, P. C. (eds.) *Private Policing*, Newbury Park, California: Sage.

Wiles, P. (1985), 'Policing industrial disputes' in Fosh, P. & Little, C. R. (eds.), *Industrial Relations and the Law in the 1980s: issues and future trends*, Gower, Farnborough.